Trafficking

DUKE UNIVERSITY PRESS *DURHAM AND LONDON* 2020

Narcoculture in Mexico

Trafficking

and the United States   HECTOR AMAYA

Library of Congress Cataloging-
in-Publication Data
Names: Amaya, Hector, author.
Title: Trafficking : narcoculture
in Mexico and the United
States / Hector Amaya.

Description: Durham : Duke
University Press, 2020. | Includes
bibliographical references and
index.
Identifiers: LCCN 2019035439
(print)
LCCN 2019035440 (ebook)
ISBN 9781478007647
(hardcover)
ISBN 9781478008040
(paperback)
ISBN 9781478009030 (ebook)
Subjects: LCSH: Drug
traffic—Prevention—Mexico. |
Violence—Prevention—Mexico.

Classification: LCC HV5840.
M6 A43 2020 (print) | LCC
HV5840.M6 (ebook) | DDC
364.1/33650972—dc23
LC record available at https://
lccn.loc.gov/2019035439
LC ebook record available at
https://lccn.loc.gov/2019035440

Cover art: Spent bullet casings
litter a road after authorities reported a gun battle with armed
men near the beach resort of
Mazatlan, Mexico, July 1, 2017. AP
Photo/Mario Rivera Alvarado.

Contents

Prologue

I began writing this book a long time ago out of desperation and impotence, out of the terrible pain and obfuscation that appears when great tragedy strikes the ones you love. I could not help the feelings, nor could I help my people with anything other than my thinking and writing. The resulting work is my attempt at using my thinking and writing to engage the bloody violence tearing Mexico apart, particularly the country's North, where I come from.

The reader will notice that the book is a stubborn retrenchment into historiography and publicity theory, at times an excursion into the past, at others into abstraction. Given the gravity of the events the book tackles, this stubbornness may seem irresponsible to some. Shouldn't my intellectual efforts concentrate on solving actual problems, alleviating the material suffering of those who live with the violence or who attempt to document it and expose those responsible? Shouldn't I propose actionable ideas, things that Mexicans and US Americans can do to reduce the violence, and the culture it inspires, which envelops us all?

Although I perhaps cannot convince all readers that theory and history are more practical than, let's say, policy prescriptions, I can at least share how I believe theory and history will be useful. I don't mean useful in a narrowly conceived sense that defines usefulness only in terms of practicality, and practicality only in terms of a solution to a problem narrowly conceived. Usefulness in this sense may describe something that can be used to reduce violence, such as normative proposals that Mexico improve its legal system broadly speaking and cultural and media policies in particular. I don't believe this is the only way of conceiving usefulness. Understanding usefulness always depends on our ability to answer the question "Useful to whom?" and thus on understanding context and, in my case, potential readers and publics.

For good or for bad, the context of my work is the academy, and within the academy my work is meant to be useful to those thinking and writing about violence, about cultures of violence, about contemporary Mexico, about Latinos in the USA, and about the cultures surrounding the drug wars in the Americas. Importantly, my work is a response to the gaps in our knowledge of these subjects. I have found plenty of excellent work that archives and analyzes particular events in Mexico and that recommend astute policy and legal prescriptions that may indeed ameliorate the violence. By comparison, I have found little work on issues that historicize and deeply theorize these events. I hope *Trafficking* strengthens this reading list and helps the community of thinkers develop frameworks that can better explain what is happening in Mexico, through attention not only to the moment but also to the longer, broader genealogy that has created the conditions of possibility and meaning for these current events. I also hope the findings and insights in this book can be generalized beyond Mexico and beyond the West. This is the value of theory. Last, my analyses are meant to help us see deeper into our shared past with other Western nations and intellectual traditions as well as with other nations in the so-called Global South. This is the value of history.

This book is indebted to many people and institutions. I am thankful to the University of Virginia, particularly to the College of Arts and Sciences, current dean Ian Baucom, and former dean Meredith Woo, now the president of Sweet Briar College. Associate Dean Leonard Schoppa was particularly instrumental by giving me intellectual support and by granting me time and resources when needed to write and research. I am thankful also to the faculty of the Department of Media Studies, in particular Bruce Williams, Andrea Press, Siva Vaidhyanathan, Aniko Bodroghkozy, Christopher Ali, and Andre Cavalcante. They all read parts of this book and provided wonderful feedback. Moreover, this community of scholars, together with Jennifer Petersen, my wife and the only person who has advised me on the whole manuscript, has provided the intellectual landscape that nurtured every page. I would be remiss if I didn't also thank Barbara Gibbons, the administrator of the Department of Media Studies at the University of Virginia, who, in addition to helping with the daily activities of processing stipends, grants, and other financial manners, gave me also her wisdom and support when it was most needed.

Others were also key to this project. Marwan Kraidy, at the Annenberg School for Communication at the University of Pennsylvania, provided different intellectual spaces to present and discuss my work and gave wonderful feedback on specific chapters and ideas. I need also to thank the Center for Advanced Study in the Behavioral Sciences (CASBS) at Stanford University, which provided me a year of intellectual camaraderie and nurtured the interdisciplinary ambitions of this work. In particular, I am thankful to Margaret Levi, CASBS's director, and Professors Daniela Bleichmar, Caitlin Zaloom, Eric Klinenberg, Mark Greif, Gabrielle Jackson, Deborah Lawrence, Allison Pugh, Jesse Ribot, and Andrew Lakoff, whose ideas and friendships fueled my steady pace throughout the year.

Last, I need to thank Jennifer, my wife and my intellectual partner of almost two decades. Although I am certain that whatever I write will fail to capture the deep and broad scope of her influence and impact in this and all my work, I must at least try. Jennifer has taught me about history and theory; she has debated with me my sometimes-dubious ideas and pushed back against my bad intellectual habits, helping me see my limitations. She has also shown me the potential in my work and has kept my faith in intellectual inquiry and my ambition. At times when the writing was painful—and, believe me, pain was unavoidable—she held my hand.

I began this book years ago, and it took longer to write than I expected. Sometimes I thought that the book would be ready at a time when the violence in Mexico had dwindled and readers would be less interested. But sadly, that is not the case. The violence is plentiful and, it seems, neverending. In fact, 2019 is likely to be the most violent year so far. Perhaps the new presidency of Andrés Manuel López Obrador will succeed where others failed. Perhaps.

Introduction

Salieron de San Isidro
Procedentes de Tijuana,
Traían las llantas del carro
Repletas de yerba mala.
Eran Emilio Varela
Y Camelia la Tejana.
—Los Tigres del Norte, first stanza of "Contrabando y traición"

The first megahit by Los Tigres del Norte, the norteño band that made narcocorridos famous, was the 1972 song "Contrabando y traición" ("Contraband and Betrayal"). Also known as "Camelia la Tejana," "Contrabando y traición" tells the story of a couple of smugglers, Emilio Varela and Camelia, who travel from San Isidro through Tijuana, cross the border into the United States in San Clemente, fool the customs officials, and make it to Los Angeles, where they deliver the marijuana that was hiding in their car's tires. Emilio then stupidly tries to leave Camelia, who up to that point has been his lover. In response, she empties her revolver into him. I begin this book with a reference to "Contrabando y traición" because this song is emblematic of the type of public culture inspired by drug violence in Mexico and the United States. This song clues us in to the complex imaginary landscapes and types of narratives that drug violence inspires.

"Contrabando y traición" is a story about trafficking and displacement: the illicit or unwanted or forced movement of people, goods, and desires. In this song, as in much public culture that connects to drug violence, movement does not have the utopian connotations of expansion, freedom, and growth that we may find, for instance, in the road-trip movie.[1] In this song, movement is transgressive, a difficult process of overcoming the challenges brought about by seemingly static giant obstacles, such as the custom officers, the US-Mexico border, and the impractical reality of having to transport an illicit product thousands of miles to consumers. It is a story of border crossings, of displaced people who are here and there, who see the Mexican North and the US Southwest as one and the same territory, even if fences and walls divide it up. It is a story peopled by individuals with complex identities, who are at once fundamentally Mexican and who are also Latina and Latino or, to be more precise, Mexican American. It is a story of money, crime, and violence, the things that move them to trafficking and the essential items of the impassioned, imagined biographies of Emilio and Camelia.[2] The next chapter details the historical context from which the current drug violence in Mexico emanates and the culture that gave meaning to this popular song.

Here I use the song to illustrate some important theoretical and critical concerns that the book develops chapter by chapter. In particular, "Contrabando y traición" illustrates three central ideas shaping this book. (1) The huge popularity of the song reveals that criminal drug violence is quite *visible* and *audible* in public culture. That is, criminal drug violence is an object of inspiration and public fascination, a topic of public engagement, conversation, opinion, and expression. (2) The song's narrative is an example of public culture that captures the sense of *placelessness* experienced by those wrapped up in, or affected by, the drug trade. This is a common feature in criminal drug narratives, and as I show throughout the book, place and displacement are key elements in the structuring of publicity pertaining to criminal drug violence. (3) The visibility of the violence and the feeling of displacement common in these narratives are partly furnished by *media technologies* that increasingly defy space and time constraints, including national boundaries. For instance, songs like "Contrabando y traición" were widely distributed with media technologies available in 1972, which included the cassette tape, a common recording and distribution technology among Mexican Americans and Mexicans from the 1970s to the early 2000s. Current digital media technologies and the World Wide Web (www) only exacerbated what the cassette tape began.

This book is an inquiry into the way Mexico's criminal drug violence and media technologies structure publicity, or *publicness*. Although publicness has a theoretically rich and at times contentious history, here I am referring to the communicative processes of criticism that bring together differ-ent social groups to attend to, influence, and/or shape the social collective (Petersen 2017: 153). In Enlightenment and post-Enlightenment democratic theory, publicness is a foundational concept and the wellspring from which other important ideas have flowed, such as the public sphere, public cul-ture, and public opinion. As a concept, publicness is as old as democratic theory itself and has deeply influenced disciplines attentive to expressive culture and communication practices.

Although the term *publicness* is used differently in different intellectual strands, here I am interested in the most common one among communi-cation and media scholars, a Kantian usage in which publicness resolves conflicts between politics and morality and is essential to the process of reasoning needed to create shared meanings, shared ethics, and just laws.[3] Publicity legitimates the state, for it is only in the public realm and through reasoned debate that a government may have the right to rule.[4] Kant thus places the concept of publicness at the heart of the Enlightenment, and though Kant is not the only great thinker of democracy to have engaged with the notion—for instance, Jeremy Bentham's take on publicity is in-fluential and almost purely utilitarian—Kant's normative engagement with the issue inspired many later scholars, including Hannah Arendt and Jürgen Habermas, two thinkers referenced later in this book.

In communication and media studies, this Kantian approach to public-ness is often associated with media and visibility. Scholars use the phrase *the politics of visibility* to highlight the role of publicity in constituting politi-cal objects, subjects, and themes. It is typically a Kantian take on the con-cept, one that instructs us that justice cannot happen without something or someone becoming public—or, in other words, part of public discourse, debate, or opinion. Visibility does not guarantee justice, but it is a prereq-uisite to it.

Although terms like *public sphere, public culture, public opinion,* and *publics* are different from each other, in this book I am not interested in drawing lines that separate them. Instead, herein I presume the shared origin of the terms and examine the original concept, the Kantian take on publicness. This approach has important consequences for the rest of the book, as I will try to swim against the current and explore what is in and around the wellspring of publicness. I must note one more thing: even though the drug violence cases at hand can be gripping and painful, I try to abstain from nor-mative thinking, as normativity is part of the downstream force that I am trying to avoid. Below I expand on the three central ideas fueling this book as well as on my concern with defying normativity. I also finish outlining the influence of mobility studies on publicity theory, which I will develop throughout these chapters.

THE VISIBILITY AND THEMATIC POWER OF VIOLENCE

The visibility of drug criminal violence was significant in 1972, the year of the release of "Contrabando y traición," and this visibility is even greater today. The reasons are obvious. Mexico's contemporary violence due to criminal drug organizations is massive, with more than 230,000 people killed from 2007 to 2018. Predictably, Mexico's public sphere has been focused on the violence all this time; images of the drug war's horrors have also been quite visible in the United States and the rest of the world.

I began by referencing Los Tigres del Norte's song to illustrate the connection between violence and publicness. "Contrabando y traición" is public culture that happens in the public sphere and that shapes public opinion and brings together immigrants as a public who, thanks to the song, can recognize their shared struggles, the danger they have faced, and the temptations that may ruin them. Criminal drug violence most visibly connects to publicity in this way, as a preferred theme for narratives that circulate as public culture.

This theme has proliferated in fictional and nonfictional forms, shaping political debates in Mexico and the United States and generating aesthetic forms like music, television, film, literature, and other artistic genres in both nations. The drug-inspired film genre of "cine narco"—with films like *Los chacales de Sinaloa*, *Tierra de sangre*, and *Narcos y perros*—has gained viewers on both sides of the US-Mexico border. Narcocorridos, or songs that lionize the lives and deeds of drug criminals, have risen meteorically to prominence in Mexico and the United States, overtaking other popular music genres on the *Billboard* charts. Popular television shows like the US-Mexican-Spanish telenovela *La reina del sur* (Telemundo) have succeeded in both countries.

The theme of criminal drug violence is not only common among Spanish-speaking Latinas/os in the United States. It has huge crossover appeal. Television shows like *Breaking Bad* (AMC), *The Bridge* (FX), *Graceland* (USA Network), and *Ozarks* (Netflix) circulate these narratives among English-speaking audiences seeking "quality" television.[5] Serious filmmakers like Oliver Stone, Gerardo Naranjo, Steven Soderbergh, Natalia Almada, Luis Estrada, and Michael Cuesta have directed compelling films about the violence.

If a structure is understood as the frame that configures an edifice, the proliferation of popular narratives dealing with criminal drug violence suggests that one of the structural elements of the edifice of publicness is economic gain. There is profit to be had in stories about drug violence, which I explore in chapter 4 in the context of narcocorridos in the United States. But the theme of criminal drug violence is not important only to entertainment media. The theme of criminal drug violence has also been important to news organizations, which routinely cover it on both sides of the border. How this theme is covered and discussed and what types of public debate criminal drug violence has generated are important indicators of the discursive connection between violence, publicness, and democracy, as I show in chapter 2. The connection between publicness and criminal drug violence does not end there. Criminal drug violence is also a structural force because it transforms the rules of cultural distribution, shaping cultural policy and law, which I explore in the context of Mexico's changes to censorship laws due to violence in chapter 3. Criminal drug violence alters the rules of public participation and thus structures presence and social membership, as I explore in chapters 5 and 6 in the context of the rise and proliferation of the anonymous blogosphere. In short, this book shows that criminal drug violence structures what we talk about, how we share ideas with each other, and the conditions for participating in public conversations.

The book is not meant to be a catalog of the myriad instances of publicness about violence in these two nations, nor a repository of the many examples of cultural and aesthetic creativity and innovation inspired by the violence. It is an argument about the most salient ways in which criminal drug violence is shaping publicity and a query into the consistencies that animate the structural power of violence. Less interested in description than in reflection, I ask a fundamental question: Why does criminal drug violence have the power to structure publicity in the first place? To answer this question, I use evidence from television, popular music, top newspapers and their websites, and highly trafficked blogs.

The public culture analyzed in the following chapters expresses diverse ideas and feelings about drug violence, revealing common views, fears, and anxieties about violence, illegality, and criminality. Although diversity of views is the norm, the topic of violence has a way of reducing the range of voices, bringing a sort of uneasy harmony across national borders, media, and people. Violence seems to be the thing that most people simply want to stop, and we talk about it in that way. In public, at least, nobody wants violence.[6]

This use of the public sphere fits its normative potential. At least from a normative standpoint, it would appear that one of the goals of being in public, of publicity, is the elimination of violence. This insight has strong supporters. In its broadest sense, publicity emerges as a way of constituting social arrangements free of violence. Arendt embraces this broad position and argues that publicity appears any time people "act together in concert," for this is possible only through the coming together enabled by language and human communication (1958: 26). Publicity thus refers to a very particular way of being in a very specific kind of space. It follows that publicness has at the very least two essential elements: a performance of self and a stage or, if you prefer, an agora-like space. Arendt's emphasis on these two elements is the reason hers is called a dramaturgical approach to publicity.[7]

In her analysis of Greek life, Arendt reminds us of the premodern roots of publicity, publicity's relationship to violence, and the inextricable connection between publicity and politics: "To be political, to live in a *polis*, meant that everything was decided through words and persuasion and not through force and violence. In Greek self-understanding, to force people by violence, to command rather than persuade, were prepolitical ways to deal with people characteristic of life outside the *polis*" (1958: 26). From these powerful sentences one can quickly infer that the Greeks, like our contemporaries, were concerned with avoiding violence and with finding methods of social interaction that would eliminate it. Violence existed, but not in the sphere of politics that was ruled by talk, rhetoric, and the ideal of shared understanding. These two sentences yield one more important lesson. Arendt does more than argue that violence is the boundary of and the reason for publicity. At least in her Aristotelian and Kantian understanding of publicity, violence, too, is a boundary of politics.

From Athens to today, the conditions for publicity have changed dramatically. Liberal and democratic arrangements in the West, including Mexico, have made normal the peaceful, even if fiery and constant, debate of political ideas. More people and communities are able to participate in the public sphere, and though the conditions of participation are imperfect, the fact remains that more people than ever in history can be part of public debates. Media technologies have revolutionized the way in which ideas are shared and debated, even if at the same time they have constituted a more dispersed and porous public sphere. In general, violence seems a distant specter, an ancient devil that shaped, but no longer substantially influences, today's conditions for publicity. In today's North America, violence is the thing of video games and blockbusters; criminal violence in the United States—and, until recently, in Mexico—has been declining.

Then it all changed.

Almost overnight, the conditions in Mexico transformed. This also meant a shift in the United States, the nation with more to lose by the increase in power and bravado of the Mexican drug criminal organizations (DCOs). Mexico's homicide rate, which had trended downward for a decade, from 14.3 per 100,000 in 1997 to 8.4 per 100,000 in 2006, quickly reached 18.4 in 2009, according to Mexico's National Institute of Statistics and Geography (Gutierrez 2011: 29). In the border states, violence skyrocketed. The murder rates in Chihuahua rose to a scandalous 93 per 100,000 in 2009, and Baja California reached 41 per 100,000. Mexico's interior did not go unscathed. Durango saw homicide rates of 47 per 100,000; Guerrero's rate swelled to 45 per 100,000, and Sinaloa's to 42 per 100,000. By comparison, the murder rate in the United States has remained between 4 and 5 per 100,000. Canada's hovers around 1. In Mexico, DCOs took control of huge swaths of rural territory, particularly in Guerrero, Durango, Michoacán, and Sinaloa, and in cities like Juárez, Tijuana, Monterrey, and Culiacán.

Publicity in the Mexican and US public spheres, the right to free speech, the desire to create expressive public culture, all seemed to be captured by the swirling rise to power of the DCOs and the catastrophic effects of widespread violence in Mexican society. Today Mexicans are again painfully reminded of the structural role violence plays in publicity.

DISPLACEMENT AND PUBLICNESS

As diverse as public views and narratives about criminal drug violence in Mexico are, quite often they narrativize violence in relation to space and to displacement.[8] In some cases, as in "Contrabando y traición," publicity captures the sense of placelessness felt by those exposed to violence. It is as if one of the characteristics of publicity is to explain violence as a by-product of displacement and, thus, in spatial terms.[9]

This finding is the most striking when viewed against the diversity of the structural locations analyzed. In this book, I locate displacement at the core of the way we talk about criminal violence and the state (chapters 1 and 2). I identify displacement as one of the core issues addressed through the censorship of violent narratives in Mexico (chapter 3). Displacement has to be addressed in order for a narcocorrido singer to commercially succeed in the

United States (chapter 4), and displacement is a rule for safely participating in the Mexican blogosphere (chapters 5 and 6).

Why is displacement so prominent in the public sphere's engagement with criminal drug violence? I hypothesize that displacement is so prominent because contemporary mainstream uses of violence are often anchored in the political category of order, and we often talk about order in spatial terms. This was true in Kant's take on publicness, which is framed in terms of peace and the orderly constitution and legitimization of government. In most cases documented here, order is imagined as the result of either spatial fixity or disciplined movement through space. These discourses have social counterparts. For instance, Wendy Vogt argues that "everyday physical acts of violence must be understood as arising at the intersection between local and global economies that profit from human mobility. The spatial liminality of transit migration exacerbates processes of exclusion and violence" (2013: 764–65). Others, like Vogt, connect this process of profit extraction from human mobility to "historically deep" and "geographically broad" systems of structural violence (Farmer 2004: 309). They are, in other words, common through time, maybe even traditional, and they happen in particular places.

The connection between publicity and drug violence is important not simply because it clues us in to the way social realities are represented, but also because it sets the terms of public debate in both nations. Take, for instance, the way we imagine solutions to the social problem of violence. Because violence like that which Mexico experiences due to drug criminal organizations is so painful, bloody, and spectacular, in most contemporary political speeches and debates, news reporting, blogging, and in the words of public intellectuals, violence, defined as bloodshed, is the thing that we all simply want to stop as quickly as possible. While this desire to stop the violence is understandable, debating the violence in its bloody dimension can reduce the scope of solutions to the problem of violence. In 2006, contrary to wisdom suggesting that President Felipe Calderón should concentrate on going after the money-laundering operations that financed drug cartels, President Calderón went after the heads of the cartels, the quick fix. This tactic fostered the militarization of the conflict, further disarticulating whatever system cartels had to remain in relative peace with one another. This police strategy, which included turning the Mexican Armed Forces against its own people, fueled the flames, and the violence skyrocketed (Anguiano 2012: 16; Flannery 2013: 182; Ravelo 2011).[10] From December 2006 to September 2013, Mexico's National Human Rights Commission, the

Comisión Nacional de Derechos Humanos (CNDH), received more than 8,000 complaints against the army and 116 cases in which the army committed serious human rights violations. The CNDH is also investigating the disappearance of almost 3,000 people by state agents and hundreds of cases of torture and other forms of state abuse (Human Rights Watch 2014). The "solution" to criminal violence has created its own set of terrible problems, but the police approach continues being legitimized by hegemonic voices in Mexico and the United States, including then US president Barack Obama, then US secretary of state Hillary Clinton, and then Mexican presidents Calderón and Enrique Peña Nieto.

There are other important reasons that the connection between publicity and criminal drug violence matters. The normative impulse underlying common ways of speaking about violence can be a significant limitation. It is typically articulated by placing the nation-state as the centerpiece to both the problem of and solutions to violence. After all, the nation-state can provide the *order* needed to end the violence (see, for instance, Strydom 2000: 20). Yet the violence in Mexico is clearly due to factors beyond the nation and beyond politics, factors that are transnational, highly dynamic, and, as suggested by Vogt (2013), as much embedded in global capitalism and culture as in state politics. Drug trafficking relies on *structures of disorder* and *cultures of displacement* that obey the logic of neoliberal exploitation (Bauman 2000; Escobar 2004; Kun 2005b; Ong 2006).[11]

VISIBILITY, DISPLACEMENT, AND NEW MEDIA TECHNOLOGIES

A culture of displacement is a social and expressive framework for lived experience without the warm promise of the home or the homeland. This culture of displacement is dramatically manifested in the way digital culture inspired by drug violence is organized at the levels of practice, technology, and text. Two things support this hypothesis. First, like "Contrabando y traición," which today thrives in digital form, mediated culture engaging the violence is quite often transnational, inspired by movement, migration, and crime, and is concerned, like the fictional Camelia, with the dehumanizing and uprooting realities of economic exploitation (Herlinghaus 2009). Second, this mediated culture relies on structural tensions engendered by new technologies, often digital, that undermine state institutions and national realities. This goes to the heart of Kantian publicness, which frames the problem of democracy and justice in terms of the sharing of ideas and ethics. New media technologies are quickly changing the conditions for "sharing" and, predictably, forcing us to alter our understandings of publicness. Thanks to these technologies, Los Tigres del Norte have been able to constitute multinational publics and, from California, become Mexican stars. Their displacement, their migration, and their expressive practices were partly defined by the technologies at their disposal (Kun 2007). Hence, contemporary digital cultures, new media technologies, and media texts that engage with criminal drug violence provide partial, if sometimes contradictory, answers to the need to engage with the excesses of global capitalism at the root of drug violence. Digital cultures are therefore better theorized using what James Hay calls "spatial materialism," a notion that complicates matters of media, culture, and ritual by recognizing that they are always already embedded in space and structured by political economy (Hay 2004; Hay and Andrejevic 2006). Thanks to the fluid nature of new media technologies, cultures of displacement embodied by those who take part in, or are inspired by, the drug trade take up "residence," if you will, in the ether—in the blogs, websites, and music downloaded globally. It is here that "displaced culture" finds its place.

Drug trafficking does not happen in a technological or cultural vacuum, as the foot soldiers, warmongers, and money launderers rely on high-tech specialists, chemists, engineers, and transportation specialists to efficiently carry out their illicit tasks. Beyond depending on increasingly sophisticated technologies for production and distribution of illicit drugs, those who join these complex criminal organizations have cultural incentives (i.e., music, film, video, video games, television, and the internet, or what some call "narcoculture") that are shaped by technological innovation.[12] As this book shows, the trafficking of narcoculture in Mexico and the United States and between the two nations is shaped by the media technologies that allow for its quicker and cheaper production and faster and boundless distribution. This narcoculture has given cartels a rich and sympathetic presence in the daily lives of immigrants to and from Mexico, and Latino and Mexican youths who, some fear, may then model their lifestyles and aspirations to match the fantastic images of wealth and success surrounding "el narco," Emilio Varela's end notwithstanding.

Narcoculture and new media technologies are particularly important to disturbing social relationships set in motion by drug trafficking because they connect two nations, Mexico and the United States, in which, under neoliberalism, the principles of economic and political egalitarianism are thinning. Neoliberalism, an economic system and economic culture that naturalizes the increasing divide between the wealthy and the poor as long as a nation's GDP is growing, has gained a solid foothold in Mexico through the North American Free Trade Agreement (NAFTA), which has engendered a steady northward flow of consumer goods. A shared culture of neoliberalism has eased the travel northward of drug money; in the United States the money finds a financial system all too happy to launder the blood out of each billion. Mainstream US culture trades in images of drug consumption that portray it as an acceptable form of social transgression, a common way of escaping the realities of social and economic inequality, or a chemical tool helpful in the search for more and more personal productivity. For large swaths of the population, consuming drugs is seen as okay, even if the systematic consumption and trafficking of drugs has ravaged US populations, including African American and Latino youth who make up the bulk of the more than 2 million incarcerated due to drug violations.

Two cultures of growing economic inequality set the stage for displacement, disorder, and violence, and on this stage, new media technologies record and share the lives, dramas, dreams, and nightmares of the millions caught in the crossfire. In our public spheres, the trafficking of images of violence, torture, dismemberment, and beheadings have become normal. More than two hundred thousand have been killed in Mexico in the name of trafficking, and millions of lives have been devastated on both sides of the border. Two nations, Mexico and the United States, are joined by the pain caused by this traffic and are immersed in a sea of recriminations and historical amnesias. Meanwhile, the world watches, marveling at how the power of organized crime in the era of globalization, neoliberalism, new media, and war technologies can so swiftly erode the peacemaking capacity of Mexico, which has the eleventh-largest economy in terms of purchasing power parity in the world. Illicit, criminal, and cultural, the shockwaves of trafficking and displaced populations are transforming the North American continent, altering some of the foundational ways of being public, the way we share ideas and views, and, thus, the way we perform publicness. At stake is more than expression. If publicness is, of necessity, defined in spatial ways, how is publicity altered in the conditions of spatial instability that characterize displacement and trafficking?

THE PROBLEM OF NORMATIVITY

The first edition of Abraham Kaplan's classic *The Conduct of Inquiry: Methodology for Behavioral Science* includes one of the earliest published uses of the saying "If all you have is a hammer, everything looks like a nail" (1964: 28).

Kaplan, a remarkable philosopher of science, was responding in this book to the increasing hegemony of positivism in the behavioral sciences and the need to reintroduce pragmatism. He used the hammer vignette ("Give a small boy a hammer . . .") in a section criticizing the way behavioral scientists used the notion of the scientific method to formally and institutionally marginalize nonpositivist styles of inquiry. His goal was not to criticize the way scientists defined problems depending on the methods they knew, which seemed unavoidable, but to warn us against marginalizing some methods simply because others are in fashion.

It is currently fashionable to use a law-and-order framework to talk about the drug violence in Mexico and to define it as a crisis of law and order in state institutions (Astorga 1999; Beittel 2013; Grillo 2012; and many others). This normative perspective on the problem can be synthetized as follows: Mexico's inefficient, insufficient, and/or corrupt police, juridical, and legislative institutions cannot properly investigate, detain, prosecute, and jail drug cartel members. Their actions, however violent, go unpunished. Many remark on the fact that more than 90 percent of homicides are never solved. Impunity is the norm. The state is at fault for not having the proper institutions in place. This is the normative hegemonic frame for thinking about Mexican drug violence, and the reason for its hegemony is perhaps because the majority of those commenting on violence are interested and even trained in politics. Thus, politics, the science of state institutions, provides the theoretical context that defines the problem of violence, and it is thus from the political science imaginary that we determine its solutions. Politics is the hammer that most choose.

I find value in the typical solutions of fixing law-and-order state institutions like, for instance, the Mexican court system and police academies, but I also find limitations in the way violence is defined by this current and most influential approach. The problem Kaplan refers to as "the law of the instrument" does more than marginalize methods: it makes it hard to see beyond the nail. These inquiries, which reduce the causes of drug violence to institutional shortcomings, frame the violence in a narrative of conflict that is both predictable and traditional: criminal violence is a law-and-order problem that would be solved if all criminals died or went to jail. Even if this view is partly true, it assigns blame to traditional culprits and imagines quick answers and solutions. Criminals are an easy target. So is the Mexican state (most states are), and corruption is such a slippery problem that at once we can blame a culprit and rationalize the continuation of violence.

Corruption is slippery; impunity is terrible; and Mexican institutions must improve. Yet I want to see beyond and around the nail, beyond and around the law-and-order framework. Underpinning this exploration is a deep belief in cultural inquiry and in the capacity of expressive culture to give us unique insights into criminal violence and into the cultural roots of our current normative framework. Popular songs like "Contrabando y traición" can help us see the violence in its human dimension, not simply as a state crisis but as a human crisis, one affecting hundreds of millions of people in the Americas.

There are many potential lessons in "Contrabando y traición," but here I want to start with one: the violence of the drug trade has to be understood against the backdrop of immigration, border crossings, and transnational cultural practices. In a study of migration patterns from Mexico, Viridiana Rios Contreras (2014) argues that 264,692 Mexicans migrated to the United States due to fear of organized crime from 2006 to 2010 alone. Violence breeds migration. For this reason, drug-trade violence has to be set in the context of globalized displacement. I define "globalization" here as the most complex of structural transformations occurring in the world due to the increasing rate and speed of mobility of people, goods, information, and culture. This mobility makes possible immediacy where it did not exist, restructuring systems of power and generating new potentialities that are hard to regulate, for they are hard to account for. Globalization produces disorder and conflict. Movement joins two points, but, paradoxically, transnational movement also disjoints, producing friction and energy that may be violently released. This is evident in the histories of immigration, border crossings, and transnational culture. Arjun Appadurai (1996) uses the term *disjuncture* to describe the particular tensions and points of friction brought about by globalization and mobility. These disjunctures are unstable and hard to perceive, and they easily become blind spots. Moreover, as Appadurai notes and this book corroborates, these disjunctural spaces are fertile ground for culture. Just as mediated culture sets in and thrives between these global disjunctures, so do crime, trafficking, and violence, three interrelated types of social practice that benefit from the cracks in institutions found in nation-states *and* the disjunctures between global systems of power and culture.

"Contrabando y traición" itself is an example of the culture of displacement thriving in the disjunctures caused by transnational mediation and immigration. The members of Los Tigres del Norte are all immigrants from northern Mexico who found their sound and fame in California but who use Mexican musical styles. As importantly, Los Tigres rely on Mexican audiences habituated to norteño music, and on Mexican American audiences who hear in their music the nostalgic call of the homeland. The song itself, a story of crime, trafficking, betrayal, and violence, explores, makes public, in a narrative form, the global disjunctures that give rise to drug trafficking. Culture flourishes in the crevices, between the blind spots, in the cracks of reality.

This song is also a powerful reminder of the political fantasies at the heart of normative law-and-order approaches to violence and culture. State-centric, politics-first, and institutional explanations of violence imply that healthy policy processes, laws, and politics will yield docile and law-abiding populations. For the most part, they are correct if we consider the docility of the majority of Colombians, Mexicans, Brazilians, and US Americans, who carry on their lives in almost perfect legality. But the perspective from the underbelly of society is different: sizable portions of these populations are simply unruly, restless, and seemingly unstoppable. Tracking confrontations of what Erving Goffman (1971) would have termed worlds of front stage and back stage, "Contrabando y traición" reminds us of the unpredictable dynamism of social life; the cunning that so many commit to bypassing institutions, breaking laws, and cheating policies; and the profound political effects of the ghostly, always disappearing, dark practices that nonetheless produce a lasting and powerful criminal world. The network of conceits that gives life to criminal organizations is also found in mediated culture and energized by media technologies. These two networks are evidence that the strength and power of the criminal world have media and technological counterparts that normalize, even if briefly, in evanescent form, the symbols, values, behaviors, and modes of expression within organized crime.

Recognizing the importance of global disjunctures between different planes of reality (what Appadurai terms ethnoscapes, mediascapes, financescapes, ideoscapes, and technoscapes) carries its own methodological and theoretical complications. Let me quickly illustrate these complications by returning to Goffman, whose theories of society have been called, like Arendt's theories of publicity, dramaturgic. He (1971) believed that people behaved very differently when performing their actions in private, backstage, in front of their kin, as opposed to the way people behaved in front of others, in public. This performative theory of society has been useful in helping us understand how behavior is symbolic of an individual's understanding of the situation in which the behavior takes place, the social landscape, if you will. It gives us clues as to what we think is public and to the particular meanings of public spaces. A man stops us on a dark street past midnight to ask for the time. Is he young? Is he dressed well? Does he have tattoos or scars? Is he wearing clothing that could hide a gun? This mental checklist exists because we know to interpret behavior based on location, nonverbal cues, and on the manner in which the behavior is carried through. If some of this does not check out, we may have to run. But if the dark street happens to be our street, and the man asking us for the time happens to be Freddie, and we recognize his voice from elementary school, and we understand the question because we borrowed a watch from him two weeks prior, we may have to smile. We behave differently, Goffman notes, based on the meaning we give to the space in which a social interaction is taking place.

Dramaturgical approaches to social interactions have their limitations. Separating back stages from front stages is as difficult as understanding the divisions of what is private and public. To put it simply, things are not so neat in life, not with the type of symbolic behaviors that flourish in disjunctural spaces. In the song, Emilio perhaps thought that romancing Camelia was a way of making business more pleasant. Camelia disagreed. As noted from the beginning of this chapter, drug violence and the culture it inspires often are symbolic of transgressions, border crossings, transnationalism, and the disjunctures between social, economic, legal, and cultural structures. All of these issues complicate symbolic space, whether it is public or private, thus making behavior, including criminal violence, political action, and cultural production difficult to assess, particularly with theoretical and methodological tools that were not built with these issues in mind. What would Goffman, Arendt, or Habermas say about political corruption due to organized crime in Mexico, for instance? This is behavior connecting two discrete back stages, that of a criminal organization and that of politics. When a practice happens in the disjunctural space between two back stages, how is symbolic behavior to be interpreted? The publicity this book analyzes, like the example of the fictional Camelia la Tejana, shows evidence of spatial complications due to mobility that impede quick evaluations based on dramaturgy. Publicity, which should always be articulated in relation to space, is quite diverse, and it invites different sets of rules and structural forces. These complications and their ensuing ambiguities necessitate the use of conceptual tools built specifically for the type of spatial transgressions analyzed here and the type of publicity these transgressions call for. It is in this spirit that I use trafficking and displacement as conceptual tools.

The critique of violence is the philosophy of its history—the "philosophy" of this history, because only the idea of its development makes possible a critical, discriminating, and decisive approach to its temporal data. A gaze directed only at what is close at hand can at most perceive a dialectical rising and falling in the lawmaking and law-preserving forms of violence.
—Walter Benjamin, "Critique of Violence"

In the epigraph, Benjamin reminds us that the law-and-order approach is a "gaze directed only at what is close at hand." A critique of violence must engage the philosophy of its history: it must query the way violence has collected meaning through time, thanks to historically contingent ways of understanding it as a law-and-order issue. It is not simply an effort to give historical grounding to contemporary phenomena. As Reinhart Koselleck ambivalently notes, the philosophy of history is essentially critical as it positions the object of historical inquiry under critical judgment (1988: 9–10). *This book's first theoretical and methodological goal is to amplify the historical and philosophical range regarding violence, displacement, and publicity so that we can critique violence against the historicity of the law-and-order framework.*[13] I carry on this amplification not at random. In this book I am inspired by mobility studies, which allow me to engage publicity theory at its primordial level.

Mobility studies provide useful ideas for the study of mediated culture, violence, and publicity. John Urry (2000), for instance, uses mobility as a dissenting motif that has the capacity to disarticulate the typical conceptual systems of the social sciences, including, I argue, publicness. Contrary to most sociological approaches, which start with the central metaphor of society to investigate the real, Urry proposes that the central metaphors characterizing contemporary social phenomena are network, flow, and travel and that these metaphors should guide research. He also proposes that the concept of society at the base of most sociological inquiries is both outmoded and narrow. Concept(s) of society have dominated the social sciences particularly in the West, in Europe and North America, and these concepts have often implied or explicitly stated that societies are composed of citizens whose legal rights define them as members of the social body.[14] If society's members are citizens, society thus has political and geographical boundaries, and these coincide with the borders of the nation-state. Perhaps predictably, the mental image that first comes to mind with the word *society* is not a human collective that expands across several nation-states or that is composed of residents of all kinds, including undocumented immigrants, but a human collective that, at its most expansive, is as large as a nation-state.

Theorizing movement requires theorizing space and time, which are two of the analytical categories central to global theory, as in the work of Anthony Giddens, Henry Lefebvre, and David Harvey. Because of this connection, mobility studies is concerned not simply with documenting movement but also with recognizing that the increasing changes in the rate of speed, as in our ability to transverse geographical space in faster trains or planes, is transforming human experience.

The transformations to human experience and societies engendered by mobilities and globalization are useful for reimagining modernity, which has profound implications for publicity theory. Instead of linking the rise of modernity to the development of a particular set of political ideas (e.g., the protoliberalism of the Magna Carta or the rise of Enlightenment thought in the seventeenth century) or ways of producing knowledge (e.g., René Descartes's *Discourse on Method* [1637]), modernity could be documented in relation to social, technological, and phenomenological transformations. Geographer Tim Cresswell (2006) goes so far as to argue that the history of mobility is tied to the history of modernity, which he understands as a period of acceleration of movement. Sociologist Piet Strydom similarly locates the rise of sociological thought in the transition between feudal and modern times, which he also links to communication and the new social possibilities of new communication technologies (2000: 9). In feudal times, Cresswell notes, workers were literally attached to the land. It is only through the process of detaching people from the land that we see the rise of protocapitalism, the beginnings of free labor, and the internal and external migrations that made possible urbanization and, eventually, the Industrial Revolution. In the last two centuries, mobility becomes more than the epiphenomenon that allows us to analyze modernity. Mobility becomes the cultural marker of the modern. During the last two centuries, being modern has meant being mobile, in movement—being able to travel, to live your life by the promise of social mobility, to acquire and master technologies of movement, and to break with tradition, the sedentary and static imaginary location of the past (see also Bauman 2000).

Although mobility may better describe the historical and phenomenological experiences of modernity, the history of modern political and communicative ideas, which include publicness, is mostly a history of the orderly. Publicness, as it is historicized and theorized by Kant, Habermas, and others, is a communicative practice that reinscribes order in conditions of mobility and instability in postfeudal Europe. I am referring here to the rise of religious pluralism in the fifteenth century aided by the printing press; the transformative emergence of mercantilism and colonialism as the two pillars of European power; the massive migrations from rural to urban settings that followed the modernization of agriculture and the beginning of industrialization; the multiplication of the mercantile, professional, and bureaucratic classes; the rise of absolutism that followed and the birth of social criticism during absolutism that Koselleck and Habermas historicize; and the emergence of the political theories of the Enlightenment, which normalized democratic arrangement that relied on the formation and control of public opinion. Publicness is an answer to the question of political and economic disorder that Europe experienced from the sixteenth century onward, and it is not surprising to find Kant's first flirtation with the idea of publicness in *What Is Enlightenment?* (1784), in which public reasoning is a guarantor of public peace, nor is it surprising to find a greater elaboration of the idea of publicity in the appendices to *Perpetual Peace: A Philosophical Essay* (1795), where publicity legitimates government. As I show throughout this book, publicity theory fits within the normative law-and-order mindset that emerges during these troubling centuries in the West.

James Scott's work (1998) is helpful at explaining the theoretical harmony between publicity theory and the law-and-order framework. He argues that modern nation-states are organized to bring fixity to the mobile and to organize space and time. According to Scott, the modern nation-state is a project of order. In what follows, I argue that the power and appeal of publicity theory is in its promise to constitute the orderly process of communicative interaction between citizens and the state and to potentially fuel orderly processes of government in pluralistic and mobile societies.

For this reason there is a significant tension between the experience of being modern, and normative theories like publicness, which become encrusted in our political culture even if the conditions of politics and power cannot sustain the type of orderly promise fueling publicity theory. This book locates this tension in different structural elements of publicness and invites a deep engagement with publicity theory to salvage those parts and ideas that can exist both in the real realm and in the normative realm.

This book puts into practice Benjamin's advice cited above. The book is a critique of violence because it is an inquiry into the "philosophy of its history," examining the manner in which this history connects to publicity theory. It is not an argument about criminal violence as such but, rather, an argument about the way the violence becomes historicized and made public; how it becomes talk, symbols, and meaning; how it becomes memorialized in expressive culture; and how it is embedded in narratives of institutions and practices, which give violence philosophical power, temporality, and specificity. Because histories that win over other histories are those that are repeated and mediated, this critique of criminal violence's publicity is attentive to mediation and to the mediating institutions, as these are not neutral channels or blank canvases on which symbols simply appear. Mediation is a social, economic, and technological practice, the product of choices, biases, affordances, limitations, and power, and it is shaped by its own specific histories.

Each chapter examines one or more structural elements of publicity that are saliently shaped by or affected by criminal drug violence. It is important to make distinctions here. In some cases, criminal drug violence is an agent of change, as when DCOs attack or threaten journalists or news institutions. These threats and attacks have led to changes in publishing policy and a reduction in reporting about violence (see chapter 5). In other cases, an existing structure reacts to criminal drug violence in such a way that it redirects resources or focus to violence, changing its shape in the process. When criminal drug violence first skyrocketed in 2007, news institutions in Mexico reported endlessly on the violence, and even news institutions in the US refocused their attention on Mexico and regularly published on the violence. In both cases, criminal violence is part of the restructuring of news practices, but in the first case the violence spurs the change while in the second the structure adapts to the changing context of news produced by the violence.

By structural elements of publicity I am referring here to social, political, economic, cultural, material, and technological elements central to, paraphrasing Habermas, the "traffic" of news, ideas, experiences, and values that become public opinion, that are subject to public diffusion, public debate, and that need public visibility (1989: 15). The book is not meant to explore every structural element of publicity, only those that are clearly affected by criminal drug violence. My research investigates three broad structural categories by focusing on cases that yield particular but generalizable findings:

1 Public discourse and debate: The massiveness of criminal drug violence in Mexico incites a very particular type of public discourse and debate. Instead of debates about individual deviance, criminal drug violence in Mexico incites debates that are social and political.

2 Mediation: Criminal drug violence transforms the rules of cultural distribution, and it thus structures mediation.

3 Participation and membership: Criminal drug violence alters the rules of public participation, and it thus structures public presence and membership.

Criminal drug violence, of the type that Mexico has endured since the end of 2006, structures discourse, mediation, and participation, and it shapes publicity both in Mexico and in the United States. Besides tracking down these structural changes, this book is attentive to the disrupting and generative concepts of trafficking and/or displacement, to the particular ways in which place, displacement, and mobility become identifiably important notions in the restructuring.

Chapter 1 lays out a basic historical context to the recent violence in Mexico and the manner in which the spike in violence was treated in the public sphere at the level of both broad state publicity and what I call micropublicity. The first section narrates the rise of the powerful contemporary DCOs, the manner in which the violence is being addressed by the government of Mexico, and the arguments that influential public intellectuals in Mexico have made regarding the limitations to these approaches. It starts with a historiography of illicit drugs in Mexico, continues with the development of drug-trafficking organizations in the twentieth century, and ends with the rise of the contemporary forces, which, fueled by cocaine wealth, have taken over drug production and distribution in Mexico and the United States. The chapter also provides a background to the type of solutions the Mexican government has implemented in the last decade regarding the increasing problem of drug crime and violence, the law-and-order side of the equation. This is the chapter in which I provisionally accept the presuppositions and premises of the law-and-order approach and start testing their limits. I locate these limits in the contradiction inherent in imposing state solutions in Mexico to a problem that, at the very least, involves multiple nation-states, including the United States, Colombia, Bolivia, Cuba, and, increasingly, Panama, Venezuela, Peru, and Ecuador. This contradiction is masked by a law-and-order approach that reduces the scope of public debate to, in the Mexican context, issues of corruption and legal and political underdevelopment, rather than issues of economics and neoliberalism.

The massive character of the drug violence in Mexico has permitted very particular types of discourse. Since violence spiked in 2007, there has been a public debate on whether Mexico is at risk of becoming a failed state. With an emphasis on the connection between violence and the nation-state, chapter 2 examines print and digital sources in the United States and Mexico that participate in the failed-state debate. This particular debate does not exist in a discursive or historical vacuum. The chapter locates the terms of the debate in political theories that, since Thomas Hobbes, have claimed that nation-states are primarily violence-deterrent social organizations. Critical of this position, the chapter notes that since Hobbes, the discourse of state violence has always depended on the spatialization of violence. Violence is, in Hobbes and onward, invasion, a spatial transgression that legitimates the use of force. This legitimization cannot happen without a legal discourse of space, which the chapter locates in the history of property and its connection to the rise of the modern nation-state. The rise of the "property regime," as Carol Rose (1994) calls it, is set against the backdrop of colonialism, the rise of capitalism, and the liberal legal state. Joshua Lund (2012) further reminds us of the particular way in which the Mexican national project in the nineteenth century was articulated as a process of internal colonization that integrated the vast territory that was Mexico into a single, orderly, and productive space. He writes: "If liberalism, whether neo- or classical, relates to space, it does so through its tenacious drive to make space productive, enlisting the state (the government and its armed forces) in this task" (Lund 2012: 3). These histories show how the particular Western fantasies of peace and stability have often been articulated within and against the reality of Western colonialism, trafficking, movement, and technologies of war. This reality is present in the way conservative and nativist voices in the United States continue using the image that Mexico is a failing state to justify the increasing involvement of the United States in Mexico, the militarization of the US-Mexico border, and the social and political marginalization of Latinos in the United States.

The centrality of law and order to modern nation-states does more than structure discourse. It positions nonstate violence as the other of the social: we even use the term *antisocial* to describe behavior that engenders violence. Law and order also structures the way culture and ideas are disseminated in their physical manifestations. By controlling and policing media technologies, media systems, and commerce, the modern state becomes the architect of cultural environments. The goal is not to shape culture, but to craft cultural environments that can become ecosystems for the shaping of good and useful citizens. In this sense, law and order are constitutive of modern citizenship. They are central to the state's authorial function, which involves producing governable citizens. This authorial function is partly accomplished through culture and the state's capacity to censor, which is most active in cases in which cultural expressions embrace violence that threatens the state, such as criminal violence. This authorial function is at its weakest when culture, even violent culture, is transnational and new media technologies subvert the censorial power of the state.

Chapter 3 investigates the musical genre of narcocorridos to illustrate fundamental contradictions within the modernist goal of authoring citizens and the disarticulation of the property regime due to new technologies and global capitalism. Narcocorridos, a type of folkloric music born in northern Mexico that narrates the lives and exploits of drug traffickers, has gained increasing popularity since the violence began to increase on both sides of the border. Different Mexican states have prohibited the broadcast and sale of narcocorridos, but the music has continued to be popular. The chapter shows how new ways of using the internet and digital recording to distribute music have all but thwarted state efforts for censorship. Today a large portion of this recording and distribution starts in California and ends in Mexican homes. Casting the censorship of narcocorridos within the history of a modernity shaped by nation-states, the chapter shows how new media technologies have subverted the ability of the Mexican state to censor by constructing cheap and efficient transnational ways of recording and distributing music and other cultural forms dangerous to the state.

The constitution of governable citizens relies on culture attentive to place and locality. When (violent) culture is deterritorialized, culture stops being tasked with an authorial function and can freely become a vehicle for other social, political, and economic tasks. In the United States, narcocorridos have become hugely successful, fueling the new corporate arrangements that have made Spanish-language radio one of the most dynamic and successful sectors of the US music business. Chapter 4 shows how in the United States, narcocorridos, aided by the systemic marginalization of Spanish-language media in mainstream society, go under the radar of legal cultures, all while the narco-imaginary continues gaining strength among Mexican Americans. Censorship is out of the question. The corporate centrality of narcocorridos in the United States contrasts with its censorship in Mexico. This suggests the conclusion that new digital technologies, when transnational, are powerful systems of ambiguity, for they disarticulate modernist notions of citizenry. Although censorship is not yet a factor in structuring the US public sphere in terms of the distribution of narratives about Mexican criminal drug violence, the violence does play a role in the structuring of US music distribution. The chapter also shows the types of narratives musicians have to present in order to properly embody the symbolic power of narcos.

In violent times, not all remedies to criminal violence are enacted by the state. Contemporary citizen subjectivities include heroic modalities that task them with getting involved in efforts to try to stop the violence. Yet citizens wishing to involve themselves in the fight against violence in Mexico must carefully weigh personal risks. Chapter 5 examines one salient way in which criminal drug violence has changed the rules of participating in the public sphere. It analyzes the citizen journalism blogosphere in Mexico in relation to the uses and misuses of anonymity by and around two popular blogs, *El Blog del Narco* and *Valor por Tamaulipas*, and the connections between opacity, displacement, and technology. Opacity, especially anonymity, allows for participation in the Mexican public sphere, and it is particularly necessary in situations in which coercion and violence go unpunished. However, the chapter shows that a public sphere based on opacity is fraught and often disintegrating.

The need for opacity is closely connected to the lack of "spaces of trust," public communicational spaces that allow for self-disclosure. Chapter 6 analyzes the famous Mexican website *El Blog del Narco* as symptomatic of the type of publicity common in contemporary Mexico and the way violence has structured the citizen journalism sector of the Mexican blogosphere. The article interrogates how the blog's mode of production and its reliance on anonymity has propelled the bloggers—in particular, an anonymous blogger who calls herself "Lucy"—to the level of civic heroes and how a global community of sympathizers made sense of her actions. In this violent context, Lucy has used anonymity as a necessary mechanism to construct a place of trust and safety. In the process, Lucy has embodied the contradictory figure of the anonymous hero. The analysis is indebted to Seyla Benhabib's classic interrogation of Hannah Arendt's notions of publicity—in particular, Arendt's ideas of heroicness and self-disclosure.

My concluding chapter returns to the theoretical issues animating the cases: the relationship of violence and publicness. It links the history of publicity theory to the history of the law-and-order framework that most people use to define criminal drug violence today. But the history of the law-and-order framework, which is partly shared with publicity theory, is a troubling history that depends on society being blind to the possibility that the political economy of publicness is dependent on violence and coercion. The conclusion makes a case for at least considering this possibility and reimagining publicness as an European answer to the question of violence that could be implemented only in nations profiting from colonialism and mercantilism. Theories of violence and publicness, both of which present themselves as law-and-order discourses in contemporary times, are grounded in ideas about the state and violence reverting back to the origins of the modern nation-state, the emergence of the international order, the beginnings of capitalism, the rise of the property regime, and colonialism in the sixteenth and seventeenth centuries.

1

Prelude to Two Wars

We must remember that those who commit the crimes are, indeed, the
criminals; that those who do violence are the violent ones; that those
who do the killing are the murderers, not the authorities, who are required
to subject those criminals, and face those murderers.
—Felipe Calderón, "Dialogues on Security"

Most Mexicans, myself included, wished that President Calderón, as quoted
in the epigraph, had been simply correct. Even if you begin by looking at
the violence in state-centric terms, even if you begin with the assumption
of clear distinctions and oppositions between state authorities and the bad
guys, history quickly shows how insufficient the state-centered narrative is.
There is a deep history where the production, consumption, and regulation
(criminalization) of drugs are intertwined with governmentality, Mexican
state formation, and the social and cultural construction, negotiation, and
disciplining of race and class. These dynamics are simultaneously national,
transnational, and local. We wish that the boundary between state authorities and the criminals, between the violent ones and the security forces, was
strong and clearly defined.

Instead, the boundary is ambiguous except in one way significant to this
chapter: Calderón speaks on behalf of the state; the criminals do not. This
distinction makes no claim on whether Calderón is or is not a criminal,
whether the state is or is not corrupt, or whether the state, that gigantic
bureaucratic machinery, can be represented by one single voice. This distinction is political, traditional, and dramaturgic. Calderón *performs* the

role of head of the state, so his speech is imagined as an expression and personification of the otherwise abstract network of institutions that we call "the state." Calderón exercised this role by declaring an all-out war against the drug criminal organizations (DCOs) in December 2006, a war that he immediately militarized and one that many Mexicans supported.

By way of understanding this institutional power of performance, this chapter investigates how Calderón's policy goals and opinions shaped news coverage in Mexico at the onset of the rise in violence in late 2006 and 2007. It is not an analysis of his presidency, but only of how his voice and early decisions constructed the "drug war" that Mexico is still experiencing. Any war needs an enemy, and any decision to go to war will depend on how successfully a leader is able to symbolically construct the enemy and the antagonistic relationship that defines both parties, one that Calderón so clearly depicts in the epigraph. Violence in these contexts is not simply utilitarian; it is also symbolic, and in the strictest sense, violence is an act of publicness. It is partly this characteristic of violence that accounts for how violence is carried out and what violence communicates. In the case of the conflict in Mexico, the symbolic construction of the enemy—drug cartels— did not happen in a vacuum, nor did the meanings of violence between cartels and the government. The conflict escalated to the level of war in 2006, but the terms of the antagonistic relationship between the Mexican state and the DCOs were set through time. By examining particular policies and ways of speaking about drug trafficking and consumption, this chapter demonstrates how drug trafficking became an object of political scrutiny in Mexico.

This chapter thus historicizes and contextualizes the rise of the DCOs, the enemy, laying out the immediate issues and factors in the current spike in violence and providing the background to some of the police and legal efforts to manage and clamp down on the violence implemented by the Mexican government. This chapter is not designed to be a comprehensive analysis of all of these issues, but one that provides a useful, even if brief, historical description to the political stage Calderón entered on December 1, 2006, the day his presidency began. It is an analysis particularly attentive to place. In much the same way that Jürgen Habermas (1989) showed how the precedent to the public sphere was the constitution of routes of trade in the sixteenth century, this chapter makes the history of drug trafficking legible through place and highlights how criminal drug violence is connected to and acquired political and legal meaning from the places in which it happened. The last goal of the chapter is to show the limits of the solutions embraced by Mexico's state-centered approach against the DCOs. As I show in the last section, President Calderón embraced these solutions to shape public debate, to retake control of political narratives about the democratic transition in Mexico.

Let us first trust Calderón's surprise and indignation that anyone may confuse who the good guys are. Let us then imagine that state authorities and the bad guys are different people who indeed are antagonistic to each other in the drama that is Mexico today. Let us start with the fiction of Mexico, of the nation-state, of politics and democracy, and phrase the central questions: How did Mexico get to this point? How did Mexican DCOs gain so much power? And, last, why did Mexico's drug war begin?

THE DISPLACEMENT OF THE DISPLACED

Marijuana has long been part of Mexico's culture. It came with the Spanish colonization of Mexico in the sixteenth century, brought originally as hemp to be cultivated in the auspicious climates of the Mexican central plateau, particularly in the area of Chalco, near Mexico City. The plant did not remain a source of fiber for very long, as growers quickly noted marijuana's additional properties. Over the centuries, marijuana became increasingly common in the pharmacopeia of indigenous peoples who were attentive to the drug's medicinal purposes and mind-altering characteristics. As a result, marijuana's cultivation morphed. As hemp, it remained part of the agricultural goals set by Spain in the Americas, but it also became important to the daily lives of indigenous communities and other marginalized peoples who adopted it as part of their traditions. Banned by the Mexican Inquisition for the herb's psychic effects (referred at the time as *pipiltzintzintlis*; see Campos 2012: 57), marijuana became symbolic of the worst tendencies of indigenous people, including their propensity toward idolatry, divination, and devil worship. The Inquisition's concerns transformed with modernity, and by the nineteenth century they had moved from concerns about the spiritual life of the consumers to worries about their psychic health. In 1842, for the first time in Mexico, the drug was reported to have psychoactive, not magical, effects, and throughout the century the drug remained part of a culture of fear created by newspaper reports about users who committed horrible crimes. Given that readers of newspapers were mostly the educated criollo or mestizo upper classes, reports of drug consumption, which often involved crimes of the darker-skinned lower classes, were evidence of class and racial anxieties of the time. States and localities began intervening in the drug's distribution, curtailing its sale as medicine and eventually prohibiting it altogether. However, it was not until 1920, with the arrival of the new postrevolutionary government, that a nationwide ban on the sale and distribution of the drug was imposed. Isaac Campos (2012) argues that the surge of policies and laws prohibiting the drug in the nineteenth and twentieth centuries must be seen as part of Mexican elites' efforts to discipline marginalized groups. The state deemed marijuana illegal, and the political and social elites favored propagandistic uses of culture that characterized the drug's consumers as people to be feared. Marijuana, like alcohol, was seen as part of the culture of violence that characterized Mexico's male indigenous, rural, and laborer populations. It is thus clear that the production, consumption, and regulation (criminalization) of drugs is linked to the social and cultural construction, negotiation, and disciplining (policing/regulation) of race and class in Mexico. These dynamics were and are simultaneously regional, transnational, and local.

The transnational roots of marijuana cultivation, consumption, and trafficking in Mexico are also at the origins of Mexico's heroin growth and trade. Nineteenth-century Chinese immigrants moving to Mexico to work on the construction of the railroad and to do dangerous mining work, particularly in the states of Sonora, Baja California, and Sinaloa, brought with them the agricultural and chemical knowledge to cultivate poppies and to process them into opium and heroin (Astorga 1996: 18; Grillo 2012: 25–26).

This wave of immigration began toward the end of the nineteenth century at a disjuncture between Mexican and US economic goals and racial policies and cultures. The dictatorship of Porfirio Díaz, which ran from 1876 to 1911, was intermittently concerned that Mexico could not reach its economic potential without increasing its workforce, and in response it created immigration policies to attract Chinese laborers, who mostly settled in the northwestern states of Sonora, Chihuahua, and Sinaloa that today we associate with the drug trade (Velázquez Morales 2005: 467). Due to the Chinese Exclusion Act of 1882, which restricted migration directly to the United States, many who wished to migrate away from a China in crisis went to Mexico. This diverse immigrant population, which never exceeded thirty thousand, enjoyed some periods of social and economic success, but also suffered through periods of persecution and systematic marginalization in Mexico. The legal and policy systems that emerged treated the Chinese unfairly through laws that prohibited the intermarriage of Mexicans and Chinese, persecutory tax policies, and, eventually, massive deportations.

Just as the Spaniards used marijuana to mark populations as undesirable and constitute racial and ethnic categories as polluted, the Mexican state used heroin with Chinese immigrants.

Poppies grew well in the states where these new immigrants had arrived, particularly in the Sierra Madre Occidental, the ragged mountain range that extends from the border with Arizona all the way to the central Mexican plateau, around Guanajuato, and that has served as the preferred location over the decades for the growth of marijuana, poppies, and DCOs. Reports of opium dens began to appear in Mazatlán and Culiacán by the end of the nineteenth century, and Chinese communities were increasingly blamed for the social and health problems caused by the drugs. George Grayson (2010: 20) reminds us that these events in Mexico echoed what was happening in the United States, where President Theodore Roosevelt, seeking Chinese markets for US goods, began supporting Chinese efforts to curtail opium consumption and smuggling by launching a national and international war against opiates. Scapegoating the Chinese for health issues in Mexico simply followed the US trend. Health and other economic and cultural recriminations constituted the basis for the later massive, unjust deportation of, and violence against, Chinese immigrants in Mexico. In Sonora, the state that had at one point welcomed the largest number of Chinese immigrants, the Chinese community went from having 4,486 members in 1910, the first year of the Mexican Revolution, to 92 in 1940, a dramatic decline that can only be explained by the violence and systematic aggression against the Chinese Mexican community, or, if you prefer, the displacement of the displaced.

Luis Astorga (1996: 15–28), a sociologist who has written some of the most important works on the history of the drug trade in Mexico, reminds us that these early tendencies to use the discourse of health and criminality to define those who consume and deal illicit drugs were always meshed in a web of international politics, particularly international efforts to control and criminalize opiates, as well as border negotiations between the Mexican and the United States governments aimed at eliminating or at least controlling drug trafficking. With the Harrison Narcotics Tax Act of 1914, a ban on marijuana beginning in 1925, and, in 1920, the Volstead Act (Prohibition), the United States asserted itself as a leader in these efforts. With growing opium and heroin production systems, an established marijuana trade, and, later, an illegal alcohol trade, the illicit movement of drugs from Mexico to the United States became an issue that allowed for the reconstitution of neocolonial relations between these two neighboring nations, roughly sixty years after the United States had colonized half of Mexican territory. In addition to pressing the Mexican government to carry out its policy goals throughout the twentieth century and today, the United States has carried out legal and illegal police work in Mexico with the goal of fighting drug organizations.

For centuries, marijuana cultivation and use were sustained among indigenous and rural populations, taking root in many areas including the central plateau, Michoacán, Oaxaca, Veracruz, and Sinaloa. Later, opium and heroin became common narcotics to consume and trade in the states of Sonora, Sinaloa, Durango, and Chihuahua. But the drugs' illegality in Mexico and the United States is what brought the most significant changes to the practices of growing, selling, and consuming them. These changes, in turn, reflected the drugs' new status and higher prices. Growing marijuana and poppy remained important, but trafficking became essential. Moving the illicit and increasingly expensive drugs from the rural and relatively remote areas where they grew or were produced to consumers within Mexico and the United States stopped being a casual practice and became an increasingly specialized, organized, and well-rewarded activity.

Some of the early traffickers were Chinese Mexicans who were able move opium and heroin through Tijuana up the coast of California, where they connected with Chinese Americans running opium houses. This did not last long, as Chinese Mexicans were early victims of the North American drug wars both in Mexico and the United States. Anti-Chinese sentiment in Mexico was an ideal cover for violence against these early immigrant narcos in Sinaloa and Chihuahua. In Sinaloa, the expulsion of Chinese Mexicans left open poppy fields, trade areas, and trafficking routes to Nogales and Tijuana. In Chihuahua, mestizo mobsters were able to exercise violence, including homicide, with impunity during the early 1930s against Chinese Mexican narcos and take over their trafficking advantages (Grillo 2012: 33). Soon the rough, resourceful mestizos that lived in the hills of the Sierra Madre replaced the early Chinese Mexican traffickers, and it is these *serranos*, the residents of the Sierra, who began some of the most successful drug organizations from the mid-twentieth century to today. They clearly were not alone: they relied on the complicity of state institutions and their racial policies in articulating the role of the state in the organization of the modern drug trade. In particular, the articulation of the rough, resourceful serrano as an identity was itself informed and legitimated by the encounter with the Chinese and the role that the state took in oppressing and expelling this racial group.

The ability to grow marijuana and poppy is irrelevant without trafficking routes. For instance, Sinaloa is a long, skinny state with the Gulf of California and the Pacific Ocean on its west side and the Sierra Madre Occidental to its east. It borders four other states: Sonora to its north, Chihuahua and Durango to its east, and Nayarit to its south. Since the 1930s, thanks to the Pan-American Highway, the state has been an essential connector between the industrial centers of Mexico City and the western United States. Though the US border with Nogales, Sonora, is closer to Sinaloa, what connects Sinaloa to California, the huge economic engine to the north, is the border city of Tijuana. Traveling rapidly east from Sinaloa is also possible thanks to Highway 87. On a beautiful drive that begins at the Pacific, runs through mountainous pine forests, and arrives at a dramatic desert, one can drive 87 from Mazatlán to the city of Durango. Once in Durango, one can quickly reach the US border either by traveling north toward Ciudad Juárez, or northeast toward Nuevo Laredo. All of the states and border cities adjacent to Sinaloa are today associated with a major DCO. The Sinaloa Cartel, the largest and most successful DCO in the world, controls Sinaloa and parts of the other territories just mentioned. The Juárez Cartel is located in the border city of Ciudad Juárez; the Tijuana Cartel spans the area toward California, while the Gulf Cartel and, recently, Los Zetas, fight over Nuevo Laredo.

Roughly half the size of Connecticut, Badiraguato is the second-largest municipality in Sinaloa and also one of Mexico's poorest. With hundreds of tiny towns in the Sierras, the municipality seems perfect for hiding, for secrecy. Badiraguato, the head of the municipality, is nearly five hundred years old and has less than four thousand inhabitants; it lies twenty-seven miles away from the Pan-American Highway and roughly two hundred miles from Highway 87. Surrounded by rough terrain that becomes more difficult as it travels east, this poor municipality is often described as the origination site of many of today's cartels. Whether or not this designation is fair, the municipality is certainly the birthplace of Pedro Avilés Pérez, a DCO leader from the 1940s to the 1960s; Ismael "El Mayo" Zambada García, a leader in the Sinaloa Cartel; Ernesto Fonseca Carrillo (the Guadalajara Cartel); Rafael Caro Quintero, the convicted killer of Drug Enforcement Administration (DEA) agent Enrique Camarena Salazar; Joaquín "El Chapo" Guzmán Loera, the head of the Sinaloa Cartel; and the brothers Arturo, Alfredo, Carlos, and Héctor Beltrán Leyva, who headed their own powerful cartel. Badiraguato, then, is a place, or a network of places, where the traditions of marijuana- and poppy-growing have linked up with a defiant attitude toward law, a strong code of honor, old-fashioned machismo, and an entrepreneurial spirit that help define the meaning of life. Violence is at the center, as is evinced in the local saying: "Better to live like a *rey* [king] for six years than as a *guey* [ox, or fool] for sixty" (Luhnow and de Cordoba 2009).

Starting in the 1960s, the Mexican illicit drug trade gained steam as hordes of new consumers north of the border constituted new and aggressive cultures of drug consumption. More consumers meant more wealth, and the Mexican-based DCOs reaped the benefits of these new markets. Marijuana and heroin flowed through the Mexican highway system, often from the hills of Badiraguato to remote places beyond the border. Small-scale criminal practices became large-scale but still relied on the organizing principles of honor, secrecy, and machismo borrowed from the serranos. Isolated from other economic systems and marginalized in the national imagination, which had crafted a national identity around the ethnic, social, economic, and cultural realities of central Mexico, pockets of rural people and some serranos became the growers, horticulturalists, drivers, and muscle behind these growing and unstable illicit activities. Perhaps the biggest reason was poverty, but this poverty was experienced at a moment of rising opportunity and in a context in which Mexico was ruled by one single party, the PRI (Partido Revolucionario Institucional), which remained in power for seventy-four years partly as a result of its ability to coexist with and grease the wheels for all sorts of licit and illicit economic activities and powers.

Poverty redefines the local. Instead of producing simplistic attachments of love and devotion, poverty causes the local to be experienced and understood in ambivalent ways. We learn to hate a place, even if we grew up loving it. Poverty pushes people away, invites them to move on, even if it simultaneously produces a melancholic attachment to that very place. In the century of mobility, the highways and railroads that were meant simply to power Mexico's export economy also became lifelines for those from rural communities who wanted to try their luck in the big cities. After 1940, Mexico's cities had grown at a rate faster than the overall population (Kemper and Royce 1979; see also Alejandro Porter 1998 on negative social capital). Mexico City swelled from 1.5 million people in 1940 to 15 million in 1980. Today a third of Mexico's population lives in the metro areas of Mexico City, Guadalajara, and Monterrey.

But many had other dreams. Throughout the 1960s, roughly 200,000 Mexicans migrated to the United States, and this trend has grown in each decade since. In the 1970s, almost 1.5 million migrated north. More than 2 million immigrated during the 1980s. The 1990s—the decade of NAFTA and neoliberal entrenchment in the Mexican state, and the period when Mexican cartels consolidated their power and structural advantage in the cocaine trade previously dominated by Colombians—had the largest migration period yet, with almost 5 million Mexicans crossing the border (Stoney and Batalova 2013). Although the population flow has slowed down, more than 2.5 million Mexican migrants have crossed the border since 2000, making the US-Mexico border the busiest in the world. For those who stayed, poverty meant different things. In the Golden Triangle—the states of Sinaloa, Durango, and Chihuahua—poverty often forced people to join the rising DCOs, even if that further complicated their relationship with the nation and, certainly, with the state of Sinaloa.

Since the 1960s, as urbanization and emigration have gathered steam, the DCOs have experienced steady growth. The explosion of drug consumption in the wealthy Western nations redefined for many in rural Mexico, as in rural Turkey, Afghanistan, and Colombia, what it meant to be poor. For some, there was at least one option other than leaving the beloved parcel and town behind, even if this meant breaking, or at least bending, the law. Marijuana production, distribution, and consumption had been, at least in Mexico, somewhat socially accepted, even if its sale was considered illegal. During the 1960s, more poor farmers were invited to participate in the network of growers that dotted the Mexican countryside from Oaxaca to Sonora, as US and Mexican traffickers took advantage of a cultural moment that made it fashionable to smoke Acapulco Gold in the growing and restless US American university system and, increasingly, in US suburbia. From Cambridge to Berkeley, from Austin to Madison, consumption exploded (Grillo 2012: 38–54). A movement of gringos to Mexico in the 1960s and 1970s also cued rural Mexicans to the profitability of feeding US drug consumption. Truckloads moved across the border even as illegal airports began to appear in Mexico and the United States that would allow rapidly accelerated movement of illicit Mexican drugs to every corner of the United States. From the 1960s until the mid-1970s, Mexico supplied three-quarters of the marijuana consumed in the United States and around 15 percent of the heroin, a share that grew to 25 percent by 1980 (Nathan 2002: 761). Although many traffickers moving illicit Mexican drugs during the 1960s were American, the Mexican DCOs steadily increased their control over the products, becoming more violent, wealthy, and organized. Steadily, too, the border between Mexico and the United States became more securitized, as federal initiatives from Nixon onward tried to curb trafficking by increasing the number of border patrol agents and their technological tools (Marcy 2010: 10).

Internal and external pressure on Mexican state authorities to clamp down on the growing DCOs reached a head, and in 1976, the Mexican federal government launched Operation Condor, a huge army and police offensive against growers and DCOs in the Golden Triangle. Hundreds of thousands of acres were sprayed with 2,4-D acid and paraquat, and hundreds of serranos were killed or detained, tortured, and imprisoned. The Mexican police work also targeted leftist groups, something that the CIA approved of and that President Jimmy Carter's administration condoned. The offensive worked to some extent: Mexican marijuana became less common in the United States; by 1979 it constituted only 11 percent of US consumption. However, overall US marijuana consumption did not decrease, and the pushback against the Mexican DCOs simply meant opening the door to the Colombian cartels, which, by the end of the 1970s, would come to take 42 percent of the marijuana trade in the United States. As is common with drug-related police efforts, Operation Condor's crackdown on marijuana and heroin failed to reduce the US drug problem and indirectly created the structural conditions for the arrival and structural success of cocaine distribution and consumption. In a different but related twist, US pressure on Turkey during the 1970s to crack down on poppy growth and heroin production also succeeded in reducing Turkey's heroin in the United States, but prompted the Mexican cartels to shift from marijuana to heroin, and by 1980 they had captured a quarter of the US heroin market. Heroin, more profitable than marijuana, maintained the growth and power of the Mexican DCOs. In yet another structural twist, the increased border security forced more sophisticated trafficking practices, which would later benefit the Mexican cartels: in the late 1980s, the Colombian DCOs began hiring Mexican DCOs to move South American cocaine across the Mexico-US border. Inevitably there are cracks in the social fabric and disjunctures between levels of reality, and the Mexican DCOs have exploited them in a tireless way. The rewards were evident: in 1966, the Federal Bureau of Narcotics estimated that $600 million of heroin—roughly $4.5 billion in today's dollars, the most profitable of the illicit drugs at the time—were sold on the US black market (Grillo 2012: 43). According to the United Nations Office of Drugs and Crime, by the end of the 1980s the value of the US illicit drug market, including marijuana, heroin, and cocaine, had risen to $107 billion in today's dollars (UN Office on Drugs and Crime 2005: 123). From the 1960s to the present—and particularly since they entered the cocaine business—the Mexican DCOs have captured a growing share of this rich bounty.

Mexican DCOs and the Cocaine Trade

Different drugs connect to different consumers and moments in history. Opiates like heroin and opium—like morphine and, to some degree, codeine—give users a very particular high. These natural alkaloids work on the brain by attaching themselves to neurotransmitters in charge of movement, mood, and physiology and causing them to fire up at a faster rate, as if the body were in extreme stress. Opiates are chemicals similar to endorphins, and like endorphins they function to help the body deal with stress by, for instance, reducing pain, producing euphoria, and making us feel good. Opiates can help people function during times of extreme pain, which is why morphine has been such a medical hit for more than two hundred years, but overall, opiates produce psychic states that are antithetical to physical and intellectual work. This is why even codeine, one of the weakest forms of medical opiate, carries warnings against driving after its ingestion. Opiates slow you down. So does marijuana, another endorphinlike chemical. Cocaine, though, is another story.

Cocaine is a drug for movement. Just as coca leaves have been used for millennia in the Andes by workers needing to suppress hunger and get some extra energy to tolerate brutal labor conditions, cocaine, coca's purified alkaloid, allows users to stay up and to experience seemingly boundless energy. At lower dosages, cocaine has been responsible for enhanced alertness; at high dosages, cocaine makes users euphoric (NHTSA 2005).

Cocaine was thus perfectly suited to supply the energy and euphoric demands of the disco craze in the late 1970s, and the energy and time demands of Wall Street junkies. Cocaine is, in a sense, like coca, a productivity drug that allows users to remain awake, in movement, and it is perhaps fitting that it took off as the illicit drug of the time during the Reagan era, the period in American economic and social history that strengthened neoliberalism and eroded the notion that the professional class should work less than sixty hours per week.

Capturing the zeitgeist of the 1980s, this new affection for hyperproductivity at whatever cost is perhaps best captured by the film *Wall Street* (1987, dir. Oliver Stone) in the character of Gordon Gecko (Michael Douglas), a ruthless Wall Street financier and a monument to Reaganism who reminds his protégé, "Lunch is for wimps." A drug that arrived in the 1970s, cocaine took hold of the US imagination during the 1980s as a drug for professionals and, as crack, a cheaper version of the same drug, as a drug for the racial and ethnic underclass. Films like *Wall Street*, with scenes showing Bud Fox (Charlie Sheen), Gecko's protégé, and a prostitute shooting a line of cocaine in a limousine, and films like *Boyz n the Hood* (1991, dir. John Singleton), where African American characters discuss the negative effects of crack in their neighborhoods, depict the impact of coca-based drugs at opposite ends of the socioeconomic spectrum. Just as the 1980s came to be associated with the reimagining of the US racialized capitalism that today we call neoliberalism, cocaine came to be associated with Miami, as memorialized by Brian De Palma's *Scarface* (1983).

In the 1980s, up to 90 percent of the cocaine that entered the United States was pushed through Miami–Dade County. In go-fast boats and planes, using some Caribbean islands and Central American nations, including Jamaica, Bahamas, and Belize, as transshipment stations, Colombians found that the roughly 1,500 miles separating Medellín from Miami were a small obstacle for traffickers with access to the best mobility technologies and strategies that money could buy (Decker and Chapman 2008: 63; Haughton 2011: 67). This emphasis on mobile technologies reached perhaps its most colorful extreme in the introduction of increasingly sophisticated submarines that could deliver the cocaine in many places along the roughly twelve thousand miles of US coast.

This sophisticated trafficking came from humble beginnings. In the 1970s, cocaine was a relatively scarce drug in the United States; throughout the 1960s, marijuana was still the drug of choice. Marijuana-trafficking Colombian organizations, which were given a boost in the aftermath of Operation Condor, also began moving small quantities of cocaine in pieces of luggage during the 1970s. Carlos Lehder, a very successful marijuana smuggler, convinced the Colombian organizations that they could use small planes to fly the drug directly to the United States (Bunck and Fowler 2012: 94). So they did. Soon the Medellín Cartel grew in power, wealth, and violence. The Cali Cartel followed, and the cocaine empires of South America were established.

Throughout the 1980s, US police and security agencies improved their techniques to stop cocaine trafficking through Miami. The Coast Guard and the DEA went after the traffickers and practically closed Miami out for the smugglers. Forced to cope with this new situation, Colombian DCOs sought out other ways of smuggling and, throughout the 1980s, as things got harder in Miami, the Colombians increased their reliance on Mexican DCOs to move their cocaine into the US. Mexican DCOs achieved the expertise to smuggle almost anything across the US-Mexico border. In the beginning, the Mexicans would charge as little as $1,000 per kilo of cocaine smuggled, but the price kept going up, ending up with prices up to 50 percent of the street cost of cocaine.

A turning point came in the 1990s when the Mexican DCOs forced the Colombians to pay them with cocaine, in effect taking control of more of the profits and more of the actual cocaine (Beittel 2013: 8; Grillo 2012: 83). This gave the Mexican DCOs the opportunity to control distribution of cocaine in the United States, which dramatically increased their profits. Instead of being simply the traffickers, in the 1990s the Mexican DCOs took control of many of the US distribution points, except for those on the East Coast, which remained under Colombian control. With an increasing share of cocaine profits and distribution networks, control of almost 50 percent of the marijuana trade, and an increasing share of heroin production, trafficking, and distribution, the Mexican DCOs were on the fast track to becoming the wealthiest and most powerful DCOs in the world.

From the end of the 1980s, the time when a large portion of cocaine profits shifted from Colombia to Mexico, to the beginning of the 2000s, Mexican DCOs rapidly grew. El Chapo Guzmán, the leader of the Sinaloa Cartel, accumulated his first billion dollars. Things were relatively stable, although this was not totally true for those who, like me, grew up in a region neighboring the drug empires. Sinaloa, Chihuahua, and Baja California were violent states, and this violence expanded as the century grew old. However, the violence then was far from the excesses of the last few years, so it is easy to claim, from today's perspective, particularly if you did not live in the northern areas in the 1990s, that the Mexican DCOs operated in relative stability at the time. That stability, many argue, was possible for the Mexico DCOs because they operated in a nation-state with a deep-seated tradition of corruption, backroom deal-making, and structural violence, three factors that allowed the DCOs to place themselves as hidden allies of politicians, media owners, and corporate magnates, as I show below. The decade of NAFTA, a free-trade treaty opposed by the left in Mexico, who saw the treaty as pushing their country's political and economic culture toward neoliberalism, was also the decade of consolidation for the DCOs. These organizations took advantage of the economic restructuring and crisis that followed NAFTA, a period that saw, alongside the structure of corruption and clientelism common in circles of power, the rise of other criminal activity such as kidnappings and robberies that were documented and painfully experienced by Mexicans. Towns like Badiraguato and regions like the Golden Triangle (Sinaloa, Chihuahua, and Durango) do not exist in a social, political, economic, or cultural vacuum. In the views of many, the increasing size and power of the DCOs, the chief reason behind the current violence, happened because Mexico presented particular characteristics that made it a good place for cartel growth.

DEMOCRACY COMES KNOCKING

The rise of the Mexican DCOs has always been a transnational affair connected to colonialism and Mexico's relationship with the United States. As Colombia has experienced since the 1980s, the success of DCOs in Mexico translated into a radical increase in profits and violence. This did not happen immediately, though. From 1990 until 2006, the very years that Mexican DCOs were gaining the most power, the murder rate in Mexico actually decreased or remained flat. In 1990, there were 19 homicides per 100,000 inhabitants. This figure continued to decrease every year until its lowest point in 2007, when it was at only 8 homicides per 100,000, which made Mexico one of the safest nations in the developing world. For comparative purposes, the United States homicide rate seems to hover around 4 to 5 murders per 100,000 inhabitants. Canada's was 1.6 per 100,000 inhabitants in 2011. Colombia's has remained around 31 murders per 100,000 inhabitants. After its lowest statistic in 2007, Mexico's homicide rate in 2011 was the highest in its history, at 23.4 murders per 100,000 inhabitants (UN Office on Drugs and Crime 2012: 22–24). The Golden Triangle and the border states are the worst off. In Chihuahua, for instance, the state that contains Ciudad Juárez, between 2006 and 2010 the homicide rate jumped from 14 per 100,000 inhabitants to 185 (Aguilar Camín 2012: 49). Overall, these rates have translated into between 10,000 and 15,000 homicides per year. By 2012, most estimates placed the number of killings due to drug-related activities at 60,000 since 2007, when the worst of the violence began. I use the metric of homicide not because it is the most important form of violence. It is simply the one category of violence that is tracked with the most precision. Others, like kidnappings, assaults, robberies, sexual violence, and intimidation, are ever present, but they are typically underreported. Even though homicides are, at the very least, reported, the numbers are always in dispute, particularly given that numbers released by state agencies tend to be lower than those from some journalistic institutions like *Reforma, El Universal,* and *Milenio,* all of which have tried to keep their own databases of drug-related fatalities.

Typical accounts of why the violence has increased start with the pronouncement that, until 2000, the year the Partido Acción Nacional (PAN) defeated the Partido Revolucionario Institucional (PRI), the cartels were able to coexist with the government because of informal and corrupt arrangements with politicians and corporate leaders at all levels, and with security forces ranging from local police all the way up to the Mexican Army. These accounts—advanced by renowned political author Jorge Fernández Menéndez, national security expert Ana Maria Salazar Slack, celebrated author and journalist Anabel Hernández, specialist in organized crime Carlos Resa Nestares, British journalist Ioan Grillo, and the award-winning journalist Marcela Turati—argue that the escalation of violence is the result of increasingly resolute government behaviors to eradicate the cartels and the structural destabilization of DCOs brought about by the arrival of the PAN.

Because of the complex ties between DCOs and government officials, it is hard to disentangle government actions against organized crime from convoluted types of corruption. Take the case of Ernesto Zedillo, whose presidency from 1994 to 2000 made him the last in the line of unbroken PRI presidents since 1929. On the one hand, he seemed interested in not getting in the way of democratic reform and actually championed some of the structural changes needed for free elections (Alatorre et al. 2009: 484; Carpenter 2009: 8), so in a sense he paved the way for the victory of PAN presidential candidate Vicente Fox over his own party. Zedillo also oversaw important anti-DCO operations. His biggest misstep, and later his biggest success, came when, in 1996, he selected General José de Jesús Gutiérrez Rebollo as his "drug czar," in charge of coordinating security, police, judicial, and armed forces efforts against the increasingly powerful DCOs. General Gutiérrez Rebollo, as head of the National Institute to Combat Drugs (INCD), also became the point man with the White House and thus a key player in joint US-Mexico antidrug efforts. All this came to a dramatic end in February 1997, when Mexican security forces arrested General Gutiérrez Rebollo on charges of protecting the Juárez Cartel, led by Amado Carrillo Fuentes, who, according to the DEA, was the most powerful drug trafficker of his era. This scandal, followed by the arrest of two other generals accused of protecting other cartels the following February, almost pushed the US Congress to decertify Mexico as an ally in the war on drugs (Fazio 1997).[1] President Bill Clinton, advocating on behalf of Zedillo, finally succeeded in gaining Mexico's recertification and in restoring Zedillo's credibility and the funds and assistance associated with certification (Fineman 1998; Storrs 1997).

Even if secrecy makes corruption difficult to historicize and evaluate, as with Zedillo's antidrug efforts, it is possible to assess what we know about actions taken. The mistake of appointing General Gutiérrez Rebollo as head of the INCD was not simply about franchising corruption; it was also about the increasing militarization of the national security apparatus. Senator Francisco Molina Ruiz, who had been the head of the INCD for roughly a year just before General Gutiérrez Rebollo, had already asserted in 1997, before the Rebollo scandal, that it was very difficult for civilians to work with and oversee the military, an institution that was accustomed to secrecy and reluctant to share information. The military, he argued, was set simply on crop eradication and, more troubling, existed in a state of legal exception (Astorga 2001: 434).

Molina was pointing to a trend. Military agencies were already in partial control of the Procuraduría General de la República (PGR), the investigative arm of the federal government, and in 1997 they controlled twenty-three of thirty-five national airports, central interdiction points in the fight against drug trafficking. If we consider that the Mexican Armed Forces have carried out a great number of police actions against DCOs for decades, we can safely state that by the end of the millennium the war on drugs was mostly fought, controlled, and managed by military personnel. The "muscle" of the Mexican state had become its "head" against the DCOs. The military, an organization in charge of safeguarding the territory, was asked to protect Mexican laws and the rights of its citizens. No good outcomes could come from those arrangements.

The democratic opening of 2000 signaled by the election of President Vicente Fox brought some institutional changes that improved the government's efforts against DCOs, but it also created conditions of instability, disjunctures between what government was and what it could become, which the DCOs were able to exploit. As Juan Lindau notes, "The PRI . . . used cooptation and coercion, along with a host of other practices, to construct governability. These practices . . . [created] a set of unwritten rules that partially regulated the conduct of [drug trafficking] organizations and their relationship (heavily tinged with corruption) with the Mexican State" (2011: 179). This relationship had the practical outcome of securing the mobility of some people and some illicit drugs, but also heavily restricted the mobility of others.

The control of a plaza, which in Mexico's drug lore refers to a specific territory for drug trade and traffic, is a control of movement, of traffic.

Figure 1.1. A soldier stands guard in Tijuana on October 20, 2010, as marijuana is incinerated. Source: Guillermo Arias, AP.

With the demise of the PRI, Sam Quinones argues, a political and structural vacuum "unleashed new opportunities for criminality, and Mexico's institutions were not up to the new threats that emerged" (2009: 76). The PAN's ascendancy to power alongside the weakening of the influence of the PRI fractured what otherwise was a "somewhat regulated system of production and distribution" of drugs (Lindau 2011: 179). Because of the fractures, new opportunities for DCOs were created, and because of new state players, there was a need for increasing anticorruption efforts. Relationships that existed and that allowed the DCOs' somewhat-peaceful coexistence with society and the government went away. DCOs responded by trying to establish new relationships with the state and reestablish conditions of mobility.

But things were more vexed than that. In the moment a new politician took power in a specific locale, and in the moment that the PAN positioned new state actors in security, judicial, and military posts, a cartel's traditional position of strength in a city, border town, or region was at its weakest. This created a momentous possibility for competing cartels to seek influence in a new plaza. Violence ensued, and with more violence, DCOs quickly understood the need for more and better weaponry, more and better-trained people. Although the violence skyrocketed under President Calderón from 2006 to 2012, the conditions that made this escalation possible originated in the democratic opening of the Zedillo and Fox administrations (Lindau 2011; Quinones 2009).

The cleanup of Mexican security, police, and military forces happens regularly, and, to be honest, it seems to never end. Each Mexican presidency since the 1980s, like Zedillo's, has done some type of anticorruption campaign, but the efforts of DCOs to buy these representatives of the Mexican state, members of the police, the armed forces, and the notorious *judiciales*, which until 2002 were Mexico's federal police, are relentless and, often enough, successful (Lindau 2011: 193). President Fox went beyond a purge of corrupt security forces. Continuing reforms initiated by Zedillo, Fox's administration led a reorganization of key judicial and security institutions, systematically increased their funding, and, reluctantly, accelerated both the militarization of nonmilitary security organizations and the overall militarization of the nation-state (Astorga 2001: 433).

The most visible reorganization of security organizations was the disbandment in 2001 of the federal police, the *judiciales*, which had been at the center of numerous corruption scandals throughout the years. This reorganization came with a purge of roughly 2,600 federal agents, many of whom, trained and connected as they were, quickly joined the ranks of the DCOs. The remaining agents became part of the newly created Agencia Federal de Investigación (AFI), which, modeled after the US Federal Bureau of Investigations (FBI), aimed to become an investigative agency, not simply a law enforcement agency. In 2009 the AFI was renamed Policía Federal Ministerial (PFM). Corruption quickly infiltrated this new federal police organization, and by 2005, PGR made it publicly known that 1,500 of the 7,000 AFI agents were under criminal investigation (Weinberg 2008: 26). Though Fox's administration succeeded at reimagining this key organization, forces outside his control had derailed the project.

Perhaps the most lasting and successful changes Fox's administration brought to Mexico were judicial reforms, some of which he initiated but could not finish. In 2004, David Shirk (2010) argues, the administration proposed changes to the fundamental ways that legal processes were carried out in Mexico. The proposal pressed for "a shift from Mexico's unique variation of the inquisitorial system toward a more adversarial mode" (Shirk 2010: 215). In an inquisitorial system, the court is actively involved in the investigation. In an adversarial system, the court is simply an arbiter of law. Although the proposal lost in Congress, it planted a seed that paved the way for reforms that President Calderón, Fox's successor, was able to pass in 2008. Shirk lists four key elements to the 2008 reforms connected to Fox's efforts: "1) changes to criminal procedure through the introduction of new oral, adversarial procedures, alternative sentencing, and alternative dispute resolution (ADR) mechanisms; 2) a greater emphasis on the rights of the accused (i.e., the presumption of innocence, due process, and an adequate legal defense); 3) modifications to police agencies and their role in criminal investigations; and 4) tougher measures for combating organized crime" (Shirk 2010: 216). Although the implementation of these reforms is ongoing, the first two reforms significantly shifted the legal paradigm, making typical trials similar to more judicially egalitarian processes found in the United States, the United Kingdom, Chile, and Germany.

Despite these and other positive gestures toward improving security and juridical institutions, DCOs continued to thrive during Fox's presidency. Violence was steady, even if it had not officially spiked. Mexican and US authorities carried out significant arrests and killings, but cocaine, heroin, marijuana, and, increasingly, methamphetamines were flowing north, while profits flowed south, and *sicarios* (hit men), accountants, chemists, tech specialists, and the corrupt network of involved politicians and security personnel were getting paid. North of the border, Mexican DCOs cemented control of cities, prisons, and street corners, establishing a feudalistic grip on territory, people, and resources that expanded from Mexico to the United States and, increasingly, to Central America— thanks to transnational gangs like the Mara Salvatrucha, or MS-13—and Colombia itself.

In the early twenty-first century, the biggest DCOs were the Sinaloa Cartel (previously the Pacific Cartel); the Gulf Cartel; the Juárez Cartel; and the Tijuana Cartel. The Sinaloa Cartel, based in Sinaloa and named the world's largest drug-trafficking organization by the DEA in 2011, controlled large sections of the Golden Triangle, Sonora, Nayarit, and Chihuahua, and had smaller claims in other states, including the State of Mexico, the Bajas, Guanajuato, and Querétaro. The Gulf Cartel controlled the transportation hub of Nuevo Laredo and access to I-35, a highway that connects the small Mexican city with the US Midwest and the Atlantic states. The Gulf Cartel had at least partial control of drug distribution in the US states of Texas, Oklahoma, Louisiana, Illinois, and Florida. The Juárez Cartel controlled Chihuahua and Ciudad Juárez, the second-most-important access point after Nuevo Laredo for commodities entering the United States from Mexico. The Juárez Cartel also partially controlled distribution in Texas, Oklahoma, Kansas, and New Mexico. The Tijuana Cartel controlled the port city and the border area around Tijuana, as well as distribution in California.

And then the wars began.

There are at least two wars going on in Mexico. One is a war of DCOs versus DCOs. The other is a war between state security forces and DCOs. Each involves multiple actors, reasons to go to war, and timetables. The war between the DCOs has involved at least a dozen cartels fighting over different territories. The battles are dispersed and specific, as they often center on who can use a particular plaza or access to routes and distribution points, and they typically involve two competing organizations. The war between state forces and DCOs is even more complicated, as it involves all of the DCOs plus several state agencies, including the armed forces, the *judiciales* before they were disbanded, the PFM, local police, and other drug enforcement and police agencies. Each war began at a different time, with the DCOs' war starting around 2003 and the warlike state efforts against DCOs beginning toward the end of 2006. Each war has a different connection to the concepts of publicity and mediation; this section explores how publicity connects to displacement and our understanding of each war.

The War between DCOs

In the war between DCOs, place and displacement are central, the very reasons for war. Violence is often essential to secure a territory or *plaza*, to expand into new plazas, to maintain the discipline within the organization, to protect cartel members and operations from unfriendly state organizations, and to discipline media and government officials interested in investigating or even prosecuting their members.

Because competition for plazas has increased significantly since 2003, and because changes in the political system have destabilized old arrangements between state actors and organized crime, violence has grown exponentially and now seems to have at least two complementary roles. One is purely "utilitarian," such as the violent harassment of a storeowner who is extorted monthly in exchange for protection. Violence may simply be a means to extortion. Utilitarian violence, which may or may not be visible, accounts for the majority of criminal violence in Mexico and is often not deadly. The second role of violence is communicative and "public"; such violence is carried out in spectacular forms, to send messages to rival organizations, media, citizens, and/or government officials. Unsurprisingly, it is precisely in these years of intense territorial competition and government reform that we have witnessed the greatest amount of "publicity violence." In both cases, violence is more than a means to the end of controlling a trading place. Violence is also performative, communicating and incarnating power, gendered identity, and the type of ethical world the perpetrator, victim, and bystander or witness inhabit. In many cases, as in the violent threats that are key to extortion schemes, violence has become routinized business behavior that undermines or challenges the power of the government. In the state of Michoacán, La Familia has normalized extortion of most businesses and politicians. Even teachers may be forced to pay a tax-like stipend to low-ranking members of La Familia for the privilege of work. The threat of violence is not a *means* to business. It *is* the business—the thing the cartel trades for.

Publicity violence, such as the dropping of bodies in the middle of a highway, the rolling of heads into a public place, the posting of an execution on the internet, or the frightening display of armaments in the middle of a city, is part of an organization's ongoing negotiation with competing (other cartels) and regulatory (government) forces. Because publicity violence relies on dissemination, one of its goals is mediation. Publicity violence is often mediated by the DCOs themselves, with photos, videos, or statements posted on the web; in other cases it is mediated because it is carried out in manners so horrific that news organizations cannot ignore it (see chapter 6). Publicity violence, thus, is calibrated by organized crime and is sometimes meant to be covered by news organizations in the least critical fashion, as a datum that has a simple message such as "Fear us," "Traitor," or "Trespasser."

In an ideal state, publicity is the enemy of impunity. The perfect crime, we are told in detective novels, depends on the criminal staying invisible. Everything must be planned; every element must be a means to an end. But Mexico is far from ideal, and more than one hundred thousand perfect crimes later, reality and fiction combine to tell us that publicity and impunity can happily coexist. Thanks to impunity, violence is freed from the constraining logic of means and ends. Violence can thus be staged out in the open or remain hidden; it can have tactical goals, become a commodity, or simply be the sick expression of a social pathology, or it can be all of them at once.

In the war between DCOs, violence with a publicity motive describes a rich array of communicative practices with violence at the center. Publicity violence, often in the form of executions, becomes more common in places in which two or more cartels operate simultaneously and increases even more when state authorities increase policing efforts (Coscia and Rios Contreras 2012: 152). This type of violence typically has very targeted public and communicative goals. Although some of the violence circulates in broader contexts and impacts the broad public sphere, this is only a small fraction of publicity violence. The majority is meant to catch the attention of a few hundred people: the enemy, one's own cartel members, and, perhaps, the authorities. In the context of advertising, one might call publicity violence "microtargeting," an advertising technique meant to address a small and highly differentiated segment of the public.

In the war between DCOs, most publicity violence microtargets, and for this reason we can call it "micropublicity" and define it as the use of highly localized publicity efforts that rely on barriers to access and to sharing. Micropublicity relies both on new technologies, computers, phones, and the videographic and photographic capabilities of these devices, as well as on very old-fashioned media technologies such as "*narco-mantas*," large signs made of cloth displayed prominently in places such as central plazas with statements meant to be read by a very selective public: the enemy, other members of one's own cartel, and the local community. Either because the digital posts are lost in the deluge of data that characterizes today's information age or because a narco-manta can be seen only by people passing by (unless it is photographed and broadcast), micropublicity is both open and closed. It can be found and used by those in the know, but it takes some effort to be found by those not privy to the particular conversation and the places in which this conversation happens, whether the places are digital or physical locations. Micropublicity is also useful to help us understand the beginning of the war between DCOs and the particular ways this beginning is related to space.

Micropublicity tactics are meant to mediate between competing cartels, and as incidences of micropublicity escalate so do competition and violence. Micropublicity can thus be used to understand highly disseminated conflicts, particularly in contexts where state authorities and nongovernmental organizations (NGOs) are incapable of providing reliable data. This was the working hypothesis of political scientist Viridiana Rios Contreras (2013), who has carried out the most sustained effort to understand Mexico's violence in relation to micropublicity and place. With Michele Coscia (2012), Rios developed the algorithm MOGO (Making Order Using Google as an Oracle) to track down the millions of mentions of DCO activity on Mexico's internet. Her methodology relied on the correct assumption that Mexican DCOs "are noisy. They discuss their actions in digital forums and blogs. They share messages and advertise their crimes on billboards" (Coscia and Rios Contreras 2012: 20). Coscia and Rios tracked down and found more than 1,800 narco-mantas from 2006 to 2016, dispersed in twenty-nine states in Mexico, and millions of instances of digital micropublicity (20).

This big-data methodology was meant to substitute for the lack of reliable information from authorities, Mexican or international. The Mexican government began tracking down drug-related homicides in December 2006, with the arrival of the Calderón administration. Before Calderón, all homicides were undifferentiated. Underreporting crime and lack of a coherent national effort to bring data together meant that nobody, including US and Mexican authorities, had a way of "seeing" the big picture and understanding local events as part of larger national or transnational trends. No one could answer the question of when the war between the DCOs began in earnest.

Coscia and Rios help us understand the war between DCOs as a war that began in 2003 with the territorial expansion of the Sinaloa Cartel, followed in 2005 by similar expansions of the Beltrán Leyva and La Familia cartels. They are able to track down these conflicts by tracking down the places in which the DCOs were operating. By 2007, all of the cartels were in conflict and trying to expand. Importantly, Coscia and Rios show that cartels were able to share plazas without violence and thus that violence, particularly deadly violence, was not the automatic result of competing for plazas. In many instances, the war between the DCOs was a "cold" war, not violent or deadly. The bloodiest of today's cartels, Los Zetas, separated from the Gulf Cartel in 2008. This splintering skyrocketed drug-related violence to its highest levels in 2010 and 2011.

Their research also helps to see the localized nature of drug-related violence. Only 30 percent of Mexico's municipalities have drug activity. Even in states like Sinaloa, cartels do not operate in every municipality. Rios argues that DCOs "only want to subjugate the areas necessary for their business. Although some like La Familia, which would later become The Knights Templar, have expanded into extortion and protection rackets that involve the occupation and control of space, the majority are entrepreneurs, not territorial conquerors" (2013: 22). That is, most cartels tactically move into plazas where drug trading is easy and profitable or into plazas that are tactically necessary for trafficking, such as border towns and cities alongside important highways and airports. Very importantly, the DCOs do not operate their businesses in the same way. Some, like the Sinaloa Cartel, the longest-operating DCO, tend not to be competitive, and expand slowly and cautiously. Others like the Barbie or the Sinaloa splinter Nueva Generación are also noncompetitive and operate in a few locations typically abandoned by other cartels. La Familia represents a third category of cartels that are competitive but not expansionist. Los Zetas and the Gulf Cartel are both expansionary and competitive, and use violence to invade territories. Highly mobile, they arrive in places faster and also abandon them faster (Rios 2013).

Because internet technologies are so new, most research on the mediated public sphere engages publicity from the perspective of mass media and broadcasting and thus assumes publicity is essential to the national or regional process of consensus building. Rios and Coscia help us see publicity at a micro level, one that often depends on the particular characteristics of new media to be micro and macro at the same time. Their research is also a reminder that some of the biggest transformations to publicity are due to new technologies, which force us to engage publicity in a more disseminated and spatially dispersed fashion, one that recognizes that micropublicity is both local and global, that it is often meant to communicate very localized events, and that states have little control over it.

The Mexican State War

The war between the Mexican State and DCOs, like most state wars, is a broad engagement that also utilizes micropublicity. However, it also heavily relies on broad consensus and thus instrumentally uses massified forms of publicity including broadcasting and mainstream media in print and digital forms. It fits the conceptual parameters of traditional discussions of the mediated public sphere even if today's world is also dependent on new media technologies. This war has been highly mediated and even narrativized, and I take these narratives as a continuation and an escalation of a colonial paradigm set on understanding drug users and smugglers as nonmembers of the nation, rightless and killable, deserving to be opposed not by police and the judicial system but by the bloody power of the military.

There are crime waves, and then there is Mexico's tsunami. At least in the way many learned about the rise of criminal drug violence, it would seem that this began almost overnight, sometime around December 2006, but definitely by spring 2007. Although researchers like Rios and Coscia have helped us see otherwise, the typical narrative of Mexico's state war against DCOs starts with the assumption that there was a particular spike in violence in 2006 or 2007. This is a sentiment connected to mediated publicity, to the manner in which narco-traffic gained prominence in public debates and media. This sentiment is not necessarily correlated with a sudden increase in drug-related crime, which, as Rios and Coscia help us see, had been rising steadily since 2003. This sentiment is instead a reflection of the unwise tactics by President Calderón, who engaged the problems of criminal drug violence with police and military strategies that hugely escalated the violence, indeed producing the greatest spike in violence in 2008. That is, the rise in the publicity of violence comes years after the rise of the violence itself. The increase in press coverage within Mexico that began in January 2007 is not the result of news organizations more closely paying attention to violence. Rather, it is the result of news organizations being attentive to political power and interested in covering what the presidency wanted it to cover.

Although news organizations have reported violence due to organized crime for a long time, the likelihood that they would print news related to organized crime hugely increased with the presidential election of Felipe Calderón. The Harvard-trained economist ran on an economic platform centered on job creation, conservative fiscal and monetary policy, foreign investment, and exports counterbalanced by a populist position of increasing state investment in higher education (Domínguez, Lawson, and Moreno 2009). Using chiefly economic policies, he would continue the process of democratization that began in the 1990s and had gained huge steam with the election of Vicente Fox in 2000, a candidate from Calderón's own party, the PAN. Though his electoral campaign was not centered on security issues, Calderón's most powerful opponent, Roberto Madrazo (PRI) had made security central to his.

In a startling turn of events, spurred on by the United States, Calderón took power on December 1, 2006, and almost immediately militarized an anti-DCO strategy. He appointed a former governor of Jalisco, Francisco Ramírez Acuña, famous for his harsh and oppressive style of ruling, as secretary of interior. Days after this appointment, Ramírez Acuña stated the central mission of his agency: "We are looking to take back the spaces that organized crime has seized." With Calderón's blessing, he quickly sent seven thousand troops and other security forces to Michoacán, Calderón's home state and one that had seen four hundred drug-related homicides that year alone (Rosen 2007: 12). At that point in December 2006, Mexico had enjoyed its safest year on record, with a homicide rate so low that, as I noted above, Mexico had to be considered one of the safest developing nations in the world. News coverage in 2006 reflected that level of safety even though criminal drug activity had steadily increased and, as Coscia and Rios show, cartels had been expanding. Coverage of DCOs was there, but it was steady or dropping. Using data from *El Universal*, one of Mexico's most respected newspapers, the one with the highest digital distribution, I was able to track

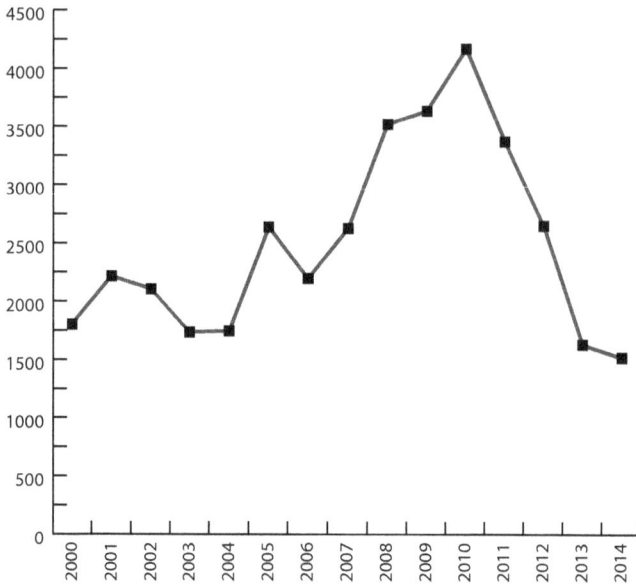

Figure I.2. A basic content analysis listing the number of times each year between 2000 and 2014 that a news piece in *El Universal* mentioned the word *narcotráfico*. Source: *El Universal*, Mexico, 2000–2014.

a 16 percent drop in coverage of narco-traffic-related news from 2005 to 2006.[2]

At that point, although DCOs were expanding, deadly violence was going down and so was coverage.[3] In November 2006, the word *narcotráfico* was mentioned in 182 articles.[4] By January 2007, only weeks after Calderón and Ramírez Acuña had declared a war on drugs, *narcotráfico* was mentioned 327 times, a huge increase of almost 80 percent that can only be attributed to the centrality of militarized anti-DCO policies implemented by the Calderón administration. Here coverage follows public debate by political elites and indicates a point of agreement for most researchers: Calderón caused the escalation in Mexico's drug-related violence, at least partly.

Figure I.2 presents a longer time frame, from 2000 to 2014. It is a basic content analysis listing the number of times a news piece in *El Universal* mentioned the word *narcotráfico* each year during that period. As the figure shows, narco-traffic has been part of the paper's coverage, but there are increases and decreases in coverage in 2006 and overall coverage peaks in 2010. The rate of change is substantial between 2004 and 2005, when cov-

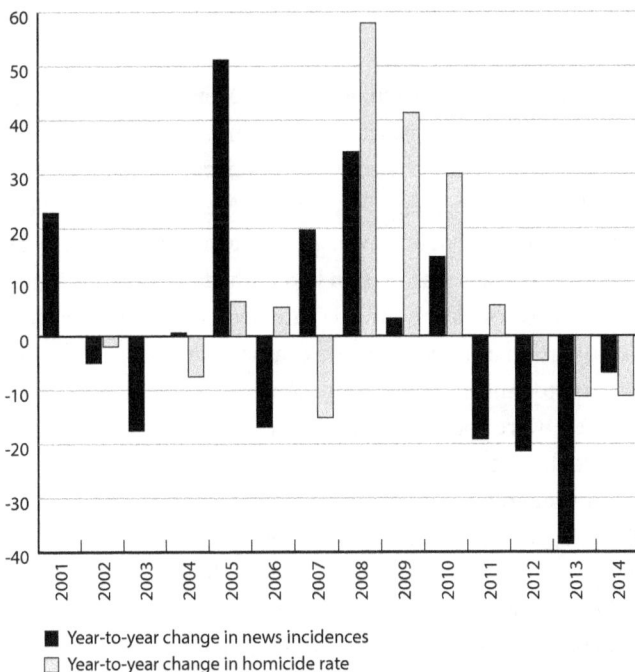

Figure 1.3. Year-to-year changes in both news coverage of narco-traffic and Mexico's homicide rate from 2001 to 2014.

erage increases 51 percent, and then again between 2007 and 2008, when coverage jumps another 34 percent. These numbers do not fully correlate with the increase in violence in Mexico, and this divergence is the most striking in 2007.

Meanwhile, figure 1.3 shows year-to-year changes in both news coverage of narco-traffic and Mexico's homicide rate from 2001 to 2014. If we assume news coverage follows or represents, at least roughly, social changes and social realities, one would then assume that increases in drug-related violence would be followed by changes in coverage. However, what figure 1.3 shows is that news coverage more closely follows state objectives so that increases or decreases in coverage reflect changes in state policies and focus. Although 2005 is striking for the difference in the size of the two columns, the most telling of the years is, again, 2007, a year in which news coverage escalates 20 percent from the previous year but actual criminal violence, as represented by homicides, decreases 15 percent from the previous year. The figure corroborates what I noted above. The tsunami Mexicans saw, as represented by the news they consumed, was a reaction to policy, not reality.

It is easy to miss this point, particularly as the Mexican state policies indeed were the chief cause for an escalation of violence, but this escalation was reflected the following year, 2008, in which Mexico saw its most dramatic spike in homicides at 57 percent. By then, the Mexican public sphere was primed by the escalation of news coverage. An agenda had been set. By the time 2011 arrived, four years of escalation had pushed the violence to terrific levels. From 2007 to 2011, the homicide rate had grown by more than 300 percent, with more than 27,000 violent deaths in 2011 alone. The decreases since then are promising, but the rate of violence is still at the level of war. In 2007, there were roughly 8,000 homicides in Mexico. In 2014, there were still more than 20,000 homicides.

It is unclear why Calderón decided to engage full force against the DCOs and use the military as the main instrument of securitization, but glimpses into why this happened began to be revealed toward the end of 2010 when WikiLeaks distributed thousands of secret records pertaining to US-Mexico relations that revealed the tone and shape of US involvement in Mexico's politics and affairs. These records show the very real influence that the United States government has had on Mexico's state affairs, including the way in which the Mexican drug war has been modeled on the failed Colombian model.

Pedro Miguel Arce, a senior journalist at the leftist Mexican newspaper *La Jornada*, got a call on November 29, 2010, in which he received instructions to fly to Britain, where Julian Assange would meet with him. Together they came to an agreement about the distribution and publication of materials pertaining to Mexico. On his return, Arce organized a team of reporters and editors to go through the materials to analyze the almost eight thousand pages of items related to Mexico. Blanche Petrich Moreno detailed this and other related matters in her reports in *La Jornada* (Mexico) and *The Nation* (USA).

These secret records show how the Bush administration was concerned that Calderón's victory, by the narrowest of margins, would weaken the presidency and would thus threaten US interests that needed Mexican strong leadership. These reports offer a rare glimpse into the private and even secret dealings between the two governments. A confidential cable written by US ambassador Antonio Garza shows that even in mid-2006, Calderón was already concerned about the growing power of the DCOs and considered the need to take stronger measures than Fox had done.[5] In

September 2006, Ambassador Garza commented on the relatively positive reception in Mexico of the US consul's announcement on Mexico's rising border violence.[6] This announcement, delivered by Garza himself, pointed to the rise of insecurity in border states and highlighted the threat this had to US citizens. Without denying the huge power that DCOs had accumulated in Mexico, it is important to note that 2006 was a year characterized by lower levels of violence. Garza's statement reflects chiefly US interests, not Mexican ones.

Calderón came to power on December 1, 2006, and within days had already restructured his security cabinet to reflect the new emphasis on antinarcotic securitization. Suggesting Washington's intentions and priorities in Mexico, a confidential cable by Minister Counselor Charles Barclay dated December 11, 2006, shows that the new security leaders— Secretary of Defense Guillermo Galván Galván, Secretary of the Navy Mariano Francisco Saynez Mendoza, Secretary of Public Security Genaro García Luna, and Attorney General Eduardo Medina-Mora Icaza—were evaluated solely based on their perceived readiness and willingness to fight the drug trade. Barclay reiterates this emphasis when he analyzes, on December 21, just weeks after Calderón's presidency began, the impressive "deft hand" that Calderón had shown by ordering the arrest in Oaxaca of leaders of a leftist civil protest and by ordering an "historically large counternarcotics operation" in Michoacán, his home state.[7] In both cases, Barclay clearly shows the ideological tenor and US-centric understanding of these issues. He lauds Calderón for arresting four of the leaders of the Oaxaca protests who were visiting Mexico City on December 4 to engage in conversations with the government.[8] In the following paragraph, he compliments Calderón's deployment of seven thousand troops in Michoacán, unconcerned about engaging the military against its own people and undisturbed by the fact that the military was being asked to do police work that they were not trained to do. When he mentions critics of the military deployment, Barclay quickly belittles their arguments and moves on. He concludes: "Certainly we are heartened that [Calderón] has demonstrated a willingness to use the full authority and resources of the presidency in the war on drug cartels, even if it remains unclear whether his earliest tactics will produce results."[9]

These records indicate that the use of military tactics was approved by the United States. By using them, Calderón was able to solidify his leadership and create consensus at a time in which Mexico's democratic pluralism had constituted significant rifts between political parties and in civil society.

To US state agencies, it mattered little that the Mexican Armed Forces were being deployed against their own people. To many, including myself, this is the greatest symbol of Mexico's geopolitical conundrum, one that Mexicans express in the common saying "Pobre de México, tan lejos de Dios y tan cerca de Estados Unidos" (Poor Mexico, so far from God and so close to the United States).

CONCLUSION

Structures take time to build. They become calcified formations, repositories of practices, ways of doing, saying, and believing. They are also the lasting memory of conflicts, negotiations, and solutions. In the case of the contemporary illicit drug trade in Mexico and the DCOs that we associate with them, their structuring obeys a historical progression that began with colonialism; continued with the early criminalization of marijuana, which gave weaponry to colonial anti-Indian racism and classist tendencies; then moved on to the criminalization of heroin, the normalization of Mexican sinophobia, and the marginalization of rural northern serranos, all of which depends on displaced populations in and outside Mexico. But their structuring is also a history of the solutions—ideological, political, legal, and military—that have normalized, over time, the particular type of antagonistic relationship between DCOs and DCOs and the Mexican state.

The structuring of the drug trade is the history of two conflicts, and for that reason, it has given way to two distinctive types of publicity that are meant to address publics in two different ways and with different goals in mind. One, obeying the logic of the illicit, uses micropublicity as a way of negotiating hyperlocalized conflict and local authority. The other, which obeys the logic of the national and political, uses mass publicity as a way of legitimizing state practices, however unsavory they may be. This chapter showed both publicity tactics at work, and it also highlighted how the Mexican state's tactics were likely shaped by foreign pressures, in particular those of the US government. Even in working democracies that use electoral systems, political decisions are crafted as the result of public consensus even if their animus began in backrooms, dark alleys, or what Erving Goffman (1971) calls the back stage.

The digital transformation of information and communication have nonetheless added a new dimension to our understanding of the back stage and, of necessity, performance and publicity. The very metaphor of the back stage Goffman uses to talk about performance depends on the idea of *opacity*, the physical capacity of a thing to clearly separate front stage from back. In this dramaturgical metaphor, the "audience" cannot see what is behind curtains and walls. Just as important, what is behind the opaque walls separating stages allows secrets to be exchanged without trace and concern. Typically, we imagine criminals acting in secrecy and politicians in public, but the events that we call the drug wars show complications worth noting. Some of the DCOs' violence is secret, but some is public, even if at a micro level. For this micropublicity, the audience includes the citizens of Mexico that they rule and oppress, and the competing DCOs and state officials they fight against. The state requires publicity, and the audience of this publicity is the Mexican middle and upper classes, the readers of newspapers like *El Universal*, readers who franchise the militarization of the war on drugs and the international governments that depend on the success of the war. This militarization was a backstage arrangement between US and Mexican government officials, one that would have remained a secret without WikiLeaks, an organization set on proving that betting on opacity in the digital age is foolish.

Digital technologies, with their highly capable encoding mechanisms and firewalls, have tricked some into believing that digital communication can also be imagined through Goffman's metaphor of the back stage and the front stage. As WikiLeaks has shown repeatedly, the metaphor does not work in the digital realm, where things are recorded, kept, encrypted, walled, and made secure by not-quite-opaque methods. Thus, communiqués can be stolen and decrypted, and walls can be opened, even if briefly. In the digital world, what is private and what is secret cannot be quite separated from what is public and open. To Mexicans, WikiLeaks provided a glimpse into the drug war as a one-sided partnership between a strong United States and a weakly led Mexican state. It also hinted that US and Mexican government officials were smart enough to know that militarizing the conflict against the DCOs could only lead to the end of innocent lives and an escalation of human rights abuses. Even after more than three thousand people arguably "disappeared" by state agents and more than eight thousand complaints of human rights abuses in Mexico, the war moves forward like an unrelenting wave of destruction.

To further problematize this US-Mexico "partnership," the next chapter will investigate US-centric approaches to thinking about the conflict in Mexico, particularly under the discourse of state failure. Ironically, when the Mexican state militarized the war against the DCOs, Mexico's problems became international problems and the violence became a matter of US national security. This prompted a debate in 2009 and 2010 about whether Mexico was a failing state in need of intervention, a debate that, as I show next, could only happen within the confines of a state-centric discourse about life and society. What is the root of this state-centrism? And what does trafficking have to do with it?

2

Almost Failing

VIOLENCE, SPACE, AND DISCOURSE

So that in the nature of man, we find three principal causes of quarrel.
First, Competition; Secondly, Diffidence; Thirdly, Glory.

The first maketh men invade for Gain; the second, for Safety; and the
third, Reputation. The first use Violence to make themselves Masters of
other men's persons, wives, children, and cattle; the second, to defend
them; the third, for trifles, as a word, a smile, a different opinion, and any
other sign of undervalue, either direct in their Persons, or by reflexion in
their Kindred, their Friends, their Nation, their Profession, or their Name.

Hereby it is manifest, that during the time men live without a common
Power to keep them all in awe, they are in that condition which is called
War; and such a war, as is of every man, against every man.
—Thomas Hobbes, *Leviathan*

On November 25, 2008, the Mexican political establishment shuddered.
A US Joint Forces Command report had labeled Mexico a state in risk of
"rapid and sudden collapse" (US Joint Forces Command 2008: 36). The report reproduced an idea circulated days earlier by Stratfor, a conservative
think tank based in Texas with an investment in defense spending. The
potential repercussions were worrisome, as the Joint Forces report recom-
mended that if the Mexican state failed, the United States would have to
act immediately to avoid general chaos and violence: "Any descent by . . .
Mexico into chaos would demand an American response based on the serious implications for homeland security alone" (US Joint Forces Command
2008: 36). That recommendation could mean only one thing: the US would,

again, invade Mexico, a possibility that revived the national trauma of 1849 when, after a US invasion, Mexico was forced to cede half its territory to the liberal democracy that Mexicans routinely call the US empire. The report generated a widespread debate in Mexico and the United States about whether it was proper to use the term *failed state* to describe Mexico's present or immediate future. Regardless of the wisdom of the term, everybody knew why it was used: Mexico was bleeding, and state authorities were unable to deal with the violence, which by the end of 2008 seemed to grow by the minute.

It is a long-standing Mexican tradition to question the state, criticize it, and deem it wanting. Drug-related violence has only intensified this tradition. Today, as always, the Mexican public sphere is full of sophisticated analyses of the weaknesses of the Mexican government. You can read any newspaper or famed newsmagazines like *Proceso, Zeta, Vértigo Político, Siempre!,* or *La Verdad* and find high-quality critical work about Mexican politics. It is impossible to be in Mexico and not routinely engage in penetrating discussions about politics and the government, but it is telling that when the pronouncement that Mexico was becoming a failed state came from the United States, Mexicans—intellectuals, politicians, professors, journalists, and other public figures—came to the state's defense. The reasons were obvious: the first was nationalism, which pushes us to defend even a bad state; the second was the awareness that when the US starts talking about failed states, it is paving the way ideologically to legitimize intervention.

This chapter engages one important way in which criminal drug violence structures the US public spheres, one that quickly and, potentially dramatically, connects to Mexico's: the idea of a failed state and its links to violence and international intervention. Although the view that Mexico is becoming a failed state is not hegemonic in Mexico or in the United States, this view has been tactically used in both countries to cast the problem of drug violence and trafficking into a geo-problem that can and should be solved by Mexico quickly "or else," as the *Joint Operating Environment* report (US Joint Forces Command 2008) implies. The issue is not simply whether the US will intervene in Mexico's affairs. As the previous chapter shows, it already does. The issue is the ideological nature of the discourse of failed states, what the discourse hides and what it shows.

This chapter investigates the discourses of failed states and its corresponding other orderly states. This discourse analysis describes the deployment of a particularly powerful concept, one that, I argue, is centered on a poorly demarcated idea of disorder. The chapter points toward implicit assumptions about order within the discourse of failed states, then delves into an examination of the political economy of the concept of order that, implicitly and uncritically, animates the discourse.

The chapter is divided in two sections. The first section interrogates how the term *failed state* is deployed in relation to Mexico in the US majoritarian public sphere, represented here by the mainstream press. This analysis sheds light on the ideological biases, semantic dispositions, and hermeneutic tactics common among cultural elites. Evidence comes from print and digital reports and opinion pieces published from 1990 to the end of 2013 in three powerful US publications: *USA Today*, the *New York Times*, and the *Washington Post*.[1]

The analysis reveals a strong continuity in the discursive treatment of crisis in Mexico and other nations, such as Somalia, Congo, and Haiti. There is, however, one significant difference. In regard to other nations, the idea of a failed state is applied to crises due to political issues including ethnic or religious divisions, territorial occupation, and economic problems due to policies, to name a few. Post-2008 references to Mexico failing are due chiefly to criminal activity. A crisis is a crisis, yet, I ask, are all crises equal? Are criminal and political crises equal? Aren't crises constructed in language? If so, what is the origin of the discourse of crisis that allows a tool for political evaluation to be applied to criminal instances? What does the criminal and political equivalence tell us about the discourse of failed states?

The second section answers these questions by noting a troubling continuity between this US discourse of violence in Mexico and early modern ideas about the state, a continuity that helps constitute a dangerous reductionism in our understanding of violence. This section shows that these equivalences are possible only if the state is defined through and by its relationship to violence and spatial sovereignty. Thus defined, I argue, politics is emptied from its genealogical connections to democracy and liberalism; it becomes the politics of absolutism and even fascism. In these political imaginaries, as in the political imaginary at root in the failed-state discourse, the state is order; its failure is disorder. Where do these ideas about order come from? The answer to this question reveals that contemporary ideas about orderly states and state failure cannot be understood without reference to the genealogy of order and its political economy. As Mark Neocleous (2006) has noted, this is one of Marx's lessons in *Capital*: order is not simply a normative value, but the outcome of particular ways of organizing political power and the economy. In the histories with which this chapter engages, these particular ways of organizing political power and the economy are intertwined with the histories of colonialism and the racial and ethnic ideologies this colonialism depended on.

Although "failed state" is not a stable concept, most popular uses of the term share two elements borrowed from scholastic uses. First, as proposed by Michael Ignatieff (2002: 117), a failed state is one that cannot exercise control over its territory (see also Rubio 2009: 1). As William Zartman puts it, a failed state is one in which "the basic functions of the state are no longer performed" (1995: 5). Second, the particular state collapse engenders violence, and constitutes a failed state in the Weberian manner through an "inability to maintain a monopoly of the internal means of violence" (Ignatieff 2002; Rubio 2009: 2). Robert Rotberg combines both elements when he argues that a state is strong or weak "according to the levels of their effective delivery of the most crucial political goods," and, he continues, security is the most important political good. Security often implies policing and securitizing territorial borders (2003: 3). Most academic definitions, like Rotberg's, Ignatieff's, and Zartman's, include both elements, making space (territory) and violence the central cogs of the idea of state failure and, ergo, of state success.

A discourse analysis of failed states is meant to change the process of inquiry and to question a failed state's relationship to other terms, concepts, and ideas. This approach is not common. Most inquiries into failed states, even if critical, engage the concept as one that describes a reality. My question is, simply, whether the concept of failed states is being used to describe the proper reality. In these approaches, which treat the concept as a given, to be critical of the concept is to highlight how it connects or fails to connect to reality, to a referent (Jones 2008: 181). To study the language and the linguistic processes that semantically animate the concept itself is so rare that Mary Manjikian (2008: 336) argued that there were only two such analyses of failed states besides hers. If Norman Fairclough (1992) is correct when he argues that discourse not only describes the world, but also actually constructs the world in meaning, then approaching the label of failed state from a discursive perspective is critical to making sense of contemporary transborder interventions.

Academics may use and even create some of the ideas that sustain the concept of failed states, but the concept exists broadly in the US public sphere, including in political speeches, in common political parlance, in the words of scholars, in media that specialize in politics, in political think tanks, and in state institutions. However the concept is defined, the different uses of *failed state* present some consistencies that suggest that the failed state is anchored in a particular cluster of propositions that give it certain stability over time, space, and social milieu.

Researchers have found that the discourse of failed states tends to legitimize interventions (Bilgin and Morton 2002; Call 2008; Hill 2005; Jones 2008; Manjikian 2008; Morton 2012). Although details varied, the process of legitimization relied on using the discourse to construct a hierarchy between at least two states, which typically legitimizes Western nations or institutions as intervening forces. This hierarchical discourse is constructed through the idea of crises, which becomes the powerful and ethical reason to intervene in the affairs of the powerless. The crisis is manifested as a lack of control over territory and people, and this lack of control produces chaos and violence. The nation in crisis is often blamed, and as Branwen Gruffydd Jones (2008) notes, the particular way in which crisis is defined is based on Western notions of state success that are both ahistorical and Western-centric. Each of these studies also locates a metanarrative, such as colonialism, imperialism, Cold War ideologies, race, and/or ethnocentrism, that helped to normalize the failed-state concept, the hierarchies the concept relies on, and the ethics of intervention. Mexicans, including President Calderón, were perhaps correct in sounding the alarm when an institution connected to the US military labeled Mexico at risk of failure, for, having used the term *failed state*, this institution began moving the discursive, and therefore the ethical and epistemic, machinery of intervention forward.

These discursive elements are joined together as a system, which is essential. As Michel Foucault (1972: 102) would note, a group of propositions are effective because they work together.[2] One proposition sounds convincing, rings true, because it connects to other propositions that also sound convincing. Together, they form the system we call a discourse. The writers of the US Joint Forces report may have started with the observation that Mexico is experiencing violence like Pakistan, and thus, as in the case of Pakistan, we should recognize in Mexico a national crisis that may lead Mexico toward failure. Without an assumption of a similar hierarchy between the United States and Mexico as between the United States and Pakistan, the discursive analogy would not work. Here as elsewhere, though, the overall effect of discourse is truth, or what Foucault would call a "truth effect," which is always dependent on the system of statements—the discourse—never on one particular definition. "Failed state" does not have a single definition, but the concept often has the similar effect of justifying international interventions. The truth effect depends, clearly, on a pattern of statements clustered around what constitutes a "failed state," even if the concept may also have connections to other elements of and ideas about politics.

Jones (2008), who produces one of the most compelling discourse analyses of the term, believes that the international community does need ways of theorizing and assessing crises around the world, but that the concept of failed states does a terrible job. Jones's main reasons for this argument are that the concept lacks explanatory power and is deeply ahistorical. Instead of analyses, the failed-state discourse uses tautological terminology such as "weak, fragile, failing, imploding, disintegrating, failed or collapsed," which is always self-referential, instead of true historical and social analysis. Even more troubling is the fact that "'state failure' is characterized as being primarily of local origin" (Jones 2008: 184). This is troubling in the case of Mexico, for, as I noted in the previous chapter, the reasons for violence are transnational and connected to the particular relationship between Mexico and the US. Predictably, scholars as prominent as Rotberg and Zartman often locate reasons for failure at the level of leadership. According to Jones, blaming the victim is part of an ahistorical and Western-centric understanding of state success. "By absenting the history of imperial structures and practices in the very creation of the conditions attributed to internal 'state failure,' the reproduction and entrenchment of imperial structures and interventions is legitimized and normalized" (Jones 2008: 184).

Given that each of these researchers found that the discourse of failed states constructs hierarchies, justifies the need for intervention, and frames these two issues under a metanarrative that serves as ideological support for intervention, it is reasonable to think that these same discursive characteristics will be found in the US discussion of Mexico as a failed state. The next section tests this hypothesis, first by showing the pattern of use of the term *failed state* in relation to Mexico, and second by analyzing whether the term is used to construct hierarchies between nation-states that justify interventions.

Discourse Analysis

USA Today, the *Washington Post*, and the *New York Times* are three of the most widely read print and digitally distributed newspapers in the United States. They are all considered, for different reasons, journalistic leaders that have the rare quality of having survived and even thrived in the age of digital distribution of news. They cater to different readerships. *USA Today*, with its flashy, graphic-centered design, and relatively brief written content, has catered, since its inception in 1981, toward youth, businesspeople, and people "on-the-go" (Pratte 2013: 675). While critics like Ben Bagdikian (2004: 136) have claimed this newspaper functions more like a five-day magazine that does not carry serious news, even Bagdikian recognizes *USA Today* continues to succeed as a news disseminator and has become one of the two most widely read newspapers in the US (it is tied with the *Wall Street Journal*). The *Washington Post* has more of a regional than a national presence, but because it caters to upscale, educated, and powerful readerships, it is widely considered one of the most influential papers in the nation (Baranowski 2013: 12). Distributed from the seat of political power, the *Post* has significant political credibility among politically savvy national readers. The *New York Times*, like the *Post*, trumpets its ability to attract wealthy, educated, and powerful readers. As its media kit reveals, the *Times* readers are "white collar employed" and "twice as likely to be in professional/managerial occupations" than the general US population (Martin 2013: 31). The *Times* has the notable distinction of being widely considered the paper of record, which routinely publishes high-quality journalism and has received more Pulitzers (US journalism's most coveted prize) than any other paper in the nation. The *Times* operates as an agenda setter for other papers and news outlets (Dearing and Rogers 1996: 32; McCombs 2014: 113). Like the *Post*, within the US the *Times* is regarded as a left-of-center paper.

From 1990 to November 2013, these three publications connected the concept of a "failed state" to Mexico fifty-two times. This attribution was present in only three reports from *USA Today*; the other forty-nine references were almost perfectly divided between the *Post* (twenty-four references) and the *Times* (twenty-five references), suggesting that the *Times* and the *Post* are papers quite active in shaping the failed-state discourse in the US press. Although the number of references is not huge, the references are significant for two reasons. First, they were not randomly distributed throughout the twenty-three years. As I show below, references appeared only at specific, junctural times and thus provided specific frames of interpretation for very important events. Second, the elite status of the *Times* and the *Post* magnifies the influence of what they publish. They are agenda setters because their news pieces are regularly cited and even reprinted in other newspapers.

In terms of temporal distribution Mexico was linked to the idea of failed states only three times during the 1990s, once in each paper. Two of these references cast Mexico alongside arguments about chaos and national security, connecting it to corruption or political and military insurrection. For Jeremy Rosner of the *Post* (1994), Mexico is the counterexample to other nations that were failing. In Tom Squitieri's journalistic piece for *USA Today* (1998), Mexico is listed with Russia as two nations that may falter in the near future due to corruption, economic crises, and, in the case of Mexico, the ongoing Zapatista insurrection in the Chiapas. Thomas Friedman (1995), a *Times* columnist, treats both Mexico and Haiti as examples of two nations in which the rich have little regard for the poor; this fact, Friedman argues, will likely inhibit Mexico's path toward democracy. In a particularly crude performance of jingoism, Friedman credits the United States' "altruistic" foreign policy initiatives in Mexico with rescuing the southern neighbor from becoming a failed state. Committed to ahistoricity, he does not specify which policies performed this savior role, or when these US altruistic efforts were directed toward Mexico.

The discursive field of international politics and conflict was dramatically reshaped after 9/11. In the 1990s, terrorism was only one of the contexts motivating the invocation of "failed state" in these publications, contexts that also included, importantly, wars like the US interventions in the Balkans, Somalia, and Iraq. Mexico, unsurprisingly, was rarely mentioned. After September 11, though, terrorism became the preeminent international event inciting the use of the discourse of the failed state (Jones 2008). Nations that seem to "harbor" anti-US terrorism groups were often evaluated in terms of the failed- or weak-state discourse. Not only did the use of the term undergo a reinflection through its articulation with terrorism, but its usage also intensified. From 1990 to September 2001, the *Post* published seventy news stories engaging with the concept of failed state. The use of the concept in the *Post* multiplied more than 770 percent (up to 539 references) after 2001, a huge statistical jump signaling that the concept of the failed state became ensconced in the post-9/11 political culture, which was characterized by the perceived need for military engagements in the name of national security.

From 9/11 to November 2013, references to Mexico in the three newspapers need to be divided into two periods in order to draw out how the idea of the failed state was deployed against it. Before 2008, Mexico was linked to the idea of failed states ten times, a significant increase if we compare it to only three mentions in the 1990s. These references to Mexico as a failed state were not connected to a single issue, but instead were political and therefore connected to the policy decisions of US governmental institutions. The references were in reports about environmental degradation, immigration and foreign aid, chaotic cities, and the drug war in Colombia. This broad, politically random spectrum of references suggests that, in this period, the increase in references had more to do with the general overuse of the idea of failed states in the US press than with Mexico's particular and internal state affairs. Things changed in 2008 in two significant ways. First, starting in November 2008, the number of references to Mexico as a failing state ballooned and stayed high for roughly eighteen months. Second, instead of referencing political issues, post-2008 US media references to Mexico as a failing state are chiefly about criminal violence. These two points deserve further elaboration.

Earlier, in 2006, Felipe Calderón had won a highly disputed presidential election. He started his presidential term on December 1, 2006, with an immediate increase in police and military actions against drug cartels in Michoacán, his home state (Anguiano 2012; Maldonado Aranda 2012). Throughout 2007, Calderón further militarized the antidrug efforts by sending military forces to Michoacán, Ciudad Juárez, Tijuana, and other affected regions and cities. Confrontations between state forces and drug cartels multiplied thereafter, as did deadly clashes between cartels fighting over territory and influence. Drug-related killings doubled from 2007 to 2008, and general violence skyrocketed from 2009 onward (Molzahn, Rodriguez Fernandez, and Shirk 2013: 15). To make matters worse, issues of corruption among security forces in Baja California, which was controlled by the Tijuana Cartel but always in dispute, came to light in April 2008, bringing controversy to President Calderón's already unpopular antidrug strategy. This is the immediate context to the transnational debate over Mexico's risk of failure in 2008. How did this debate come to be?

Although the US Joint Forces Command report that labeled Mexico as a state at risk of "rapid and sudden collapse" was released in November 2008, the first influential reference to this troubling idea came earlier, on May 13 of the same year, when Stratfor, a private intelligence organization and publisher, released a report written by George Friedman, the company's founder and chairman. Friedman argued that the lack of security at any and all levels and the overwhelming drug violence in Mexico justified the question of whether Mexico was on the path to failure. Stratfor, based in Austin, Texas, sells global security reports to a secret list of subscribers. Founded by Friedman and Fred Burton, two notorious Cold War fossils and former affiliates of the State Department and defense apparatus, the company publishes some of its least secret findings and assessments in its digital magazine, Stratfor.com. On December 4, 2008, *Forbes*, a print and digital magazine influential among business elites, essentially rehashed the Stratfor report in an article written by Jesse Bogan, Kerry Dolan, Christopher Helman, and Nathan Veradi. The authors adopted Friedman's argument and forwarded the same question: Is Mexico on the path to failure? A week later, the Mexican newspaper *El Norte* published a column by the popular political columnist M. A. Kiavelo in which the anonymous journalist cited the *Forbes* article. Although at this point the US Joint Forces Command report was no longer referenced, Kiavelo ended with a similar inference that linked the state failure in Mexico to United States security risks, signaling an inevitable intervention.

On January 15, 2009, shortly after Kiavelo's piece was printed, *Stars and Stripes*, a print and digital newspaper published by the US Department of Defense, released the key findings of the US Joint Forces Command report. From that moment on, a public debate ensued in Mexico and the United States over whether Mexico was at risk of failing. In Mexico, newspapers attempted to critically engage with the issue through the expert and legitimated voices of intellectuals like Enrique Krauze, Carlos Pascual, Luis Rubio, and Jorge Castañeda Gutman. These Mexican intellectuals often cited the *Forbes* article as the instigator of the debate. In the United States, the *Post*, the *Times*, and, to a lesser degree, *USA Today* joined the controversy. Most likely because *Forbes* is in direct competition with these elite papers, the majority of the newspaper reports did not cite *Forbes*: they cited *Stars and Stripes*. In 2009, the *Post* and the *Times* ran twenty-five articles that linked Mexico to the concept of "failed state." As in a bell curve, this number decreased quickly with each year that followed. There were no references in 2012 and only one in 2013. As far as US news media were concerned, the idea had lost its luster in 2012, when the main story about Mexico became the Mexican federal and state elections. Failure would have to wait.

Identifying the historical pattern, the link between the use of the term *failed state* and concerns about terrorism and, later, with drug violence, is only part of this analysis. In the Mexico case, almost invariably, the failed-state label is connected to hierarchical statements that tautologically demonstrate US superiority, Mexican weakness, and the need to intervene if US security is threatened. Breaking from this pattern, however, post-2008 uses of the failed-state discourse are about challenges to the state brought by criminal, not political, causes.

For instance, in the *Times* on March 1, 2009, Marc Lacey writes a Mexico-friendly piece in which he touches on whether Mexico is indeed a failing state but leaves the question unresolved. Reporting about Ciudad Juárez's security difficulties, which at the time were gigantic, he broaches the issue by contrasting the hellish Ciudad Juárez with heavenly El Paso, Texas. He points out that Juárez's mayor, Jose Reyes, lives in El Paso, where security is possible. The hierarchical stage does not end there. He constructs a hierarchy based on US police work. Simply put, El Paso's police force can do what Juárez's cannot. They can, for instance, provide security to the mayor and his family: "In an interview in his wood-paneled office overlooking the United States, Mr. Reyes, 46, whose father was mayor in the early 1980s, said he was not going to allow criminals to run the city, despite the inroads they are making." One can only imagine the longing, loving, and respectful eyes of the mayor lingering on the US landscape across the river while speaking to Lacey.

What's more, in *USA Today* on February 10, 2010, Chris Hawley reports that there are good reasons to believe that Mexico is failing, at least in some rather large geographical areas, including the state of Michoacán. Hawley's report, like most others, establishes hierarchies between the US and Mexico. Hawley does this by citing different US state agencies and think tanks as sources of information that he believes are trustworthy. These include the US Treasury, the Milken Institute, the US Department of Justice, the US Government Accountability Office, the US Joint Forces Command, and US former drug czar Barry McCaffrey. By contrast, President Calderón is cited only to be proven wrong. The only Mexican cited as an expert is Columbia University law professor Edgardo Buscaglia, who asserts that one can no longer ignore the weakening Mexican state. In Hawley's piece, US superiority is evident in the sources that are chosen, and the politics of citation do the ideological work.

Echoing previous research on the discourse of failed states, these examples establish a binary opposition between the United States and Mexico. The hierarchy frames the savior nation as the United States and justifies the use of ethical intervention in the country that needs saving—in this case, Mexico. From giving Mexicans temporary work visas to lending the expertise of police protection, these articles suggest that US institutions are both necessary and honorable. They cast their argument in terms of a crisis that that they suggest was caused by Mexico's internal politics and weak institutions. The overarching reason for the crises, the hierarchy, and the need to intervene are based on either globalization, as when arguing for a global economy that is pushing immigrants north, or "neoliberalism," as when arguing that US insecurity due to drug violence ought to be addressed through an intervention.

Yet there is one significant difference in the application and use of the failed-state discourse regarding Mexico after 2008. Prior to the 2008 and 2009 upswing in the use of the failed-state rhetoric in relation specifically to drug violence, the idea that Mexico was a "failed state" was framed in broader political terms and included the economic disparity that pushed people to migrate in great numbers to the United States; environmental degradation due to lax environmental policies; and politico-military insurrections such as the Zapatista rebellion, which began in 1994. However, after the spike in drug violence that correlated with the upswing in the use of the term, the crisis justifying intervention was largely seen as criminal violence.

The failed-state literature (for instance, Ignatieff, Zartman, and Rotberg) is not typically concerned with crises due to criminality. Even in the Colombian case, which in some ways resembles that of Mexico, arguments about Colombia as a failing state were always connected to the power of the leftist guerrillas (FARC and ELN) that controlled, and continue to control, huge swaths of Colombian territory. Although FARC and ELN are connected to criminal activity, the public goal of their uprising is to challenge the legitimacy of the Colombian state. The Mexican case after 2008 is quite different, and this difference is important. Jones argues: "The problem with the 'failed state' discourse is not with the empirical identification of social, economic and political crisis as such, but in the manner of characterizing and, above all, explaining the nature and production of such a condition" (Jones 2008: 182). If the Mexican crisis is criminal, should not the nature and production of such criminality be the chief issue attended by those analyzing it?

Drug violence is a form of criminal activity and is not politically motivated. DCOs do not typically want votes or territory. They want wealth, which can only be acquired through trafficking. Except in places like Michoacán, where La Familia and, later, the Knights Templar have tried to replace the state and government institutions, most DCOs in Mexico do not show a desire to take over the state or systematically challenge its legitimacy. Rather, either cartels direct their violence toward particular targets that try to stop their efforts or they work on placing corruptible politicians who will support their economic agenda in locations of power. The violence shapes politics, but it is not politically motivated. The violence is evidence of a desire for wealth that can only be achieved through illegal means.

What difference does it make whether the failure or weakness that plagues a state is due to economic or political activity? The question is obscured by the discourse of failed states, which uncritically posits an equivalence among phenomena deemed crises and failures. What makes this equivalence possible? What discourse made credible the debate over whether Mexico could fail? In what discursive universe are criminal economies and political crises equivalent?

FAILED STATES AND THE HOBBESIAN IMAGINARY

An equivalence between criminal/economic and political crises is possible if their social effects, widespread violence, and loss of spatial control are considered more important than the production of the conditions of the crisis. Based solely on the effects of violence and loss of spatial control, Mexico is indeed similar to Pakistan, Somalia, Colombia, and Haiti. Yet Mexico's crises coincided with the strengthening of the nation's political structures, an invigoration of its democratic commitments, and the welcoming of political pluralism. Thus, the debate about whether the Mexican state was failing was based on a particular notion of politics and the state, one in which the state is simply defined in relation to violence and territorial sovereignty—in other words, one in which the state represents a type of politics *absent* from any commitment to democracy and liberalism.

This type of political discourse has a history in Western modernity, a history that connects the failed-state concept to the absolutist state of the sixteenth and seventeenth centuries—and, more recently, to the fascist state—not to the post-Enlightenment modern nation-state. Indeed, the metaphors employed in the US news discourse are limited in part by underlying assumptions about the relationship of violence to the state. The idea that a functioning state is, preeminently, one that maintains order by banishing violence, understood as the worst face of disorder, within its physical boundaries underlies the discourse of the failed state as it is applied to Mexico. This idea allows violence to appear as an undifferentiated experience, making possible the equation of the very different conflicts in Mexico and Pakistan.

This definition of the state, and of violence as the state's other, originates at the onset of modernity, the point at which European feudalism was giving way to capitalism and the political ideas that would constitute the early modern state. Unpacking parts of this history helps shed light on the Western vantage point employed by the failed-state discourse. The discourse bears the imprint of its historical roots in Europe and the particular violence that dominated the sixteenth and seventeenth centuries there. This history included painful religious wars within—and, through colonialism and anti-Islamic rhetoric, without; the birth of the Enlightenment; and the political problems (or tools) and economic promises of colonialism. The history of the key ideas that give form to the failed-state discourse, therefore, can also help us trace the ideas of order that legitimize the nation-state and that normalize engaging social problems such as Mexico's almost exclusively from the perspective of the state as an issue of order. In other words, the order that is seen to falter in the failed state exists not in a state of nature, as Thomas Hobbes would frame it, but in a political economy. It is to this political economy that I now turn.

Crisis versus Order

When Hobbes wrote *Leviathan* ([1651] 1965), he could not have predicted that his argument for a centralized state woven by contracts, with enough power to quench internal violence, would stand as the most common argument in favor of the modern nation-state.[3] But he probably had a sense of this idea's power, as he was rearticulating a principle of ancient Roman law that structured civil society through a complex legal code of property and rights (Pagden 1990: 15).[4] Over the following three centuries since *Leviathan*, monarchies, which still dominated the world of the seventeenth century, would change dramatically or disappear. Kingdoms would either become ornamental institutions administered by national governments, as in the case of the United Kingdom or Spain, or they would go the way of the czars.[5]

Hobbes has been critiqued exhaustively—he was, after all, trying to solve the very particular problems of religious strife, unrest in Scotland and Ireland, and the questioning of the legitimacy of the monarchy vis-à-vis the pope, that England was experiencing at the time—and many consider John Locke the most relevant thinker to contemporary liberal politics. However, some of Hobbes's central propositions, which he inherited from novels and political and legal ideas of the time, have become traditional political thinking. Of these, John Barclay's 1621 allegory *Argenis* stands out for its influence and power to concretize commonly held opinions. Barclay challenged the monarch to answer the question of religious violence in a manner that would later be associated with Cardinal Richelieu and Hobbes, who were avid readers of Barclay's work: "Either give the people back their freedom or assure the domestic tranquility for whose sake they relinquished that freedom" (Barclay quoted in Koselleck 1988: 18; see also Strydom 2000: 129).

Inspired by thinkers like Barclay, Hobbes's enduring proposals about the state, which were first embodied in the absolutist European states, can be synthesized as follows: the state exists (1) to eliminate violence, (2) to provide security to the citizenry, and (3) to bring order to a space.[6] These three propositions become political axioms, and their goal is order. They are the ground on which the discourse of successful protomodern states were built and, ergo, the ground on which discourse about failed states also grew. Order and violence are the fundamental dialectic constituting politics and the basis for the idea of a failed state, a concept almost always applied toward states that, like Congo, Mexico, or Somalia, are in violent and/or chaotic disarray.

In Hobbes, order had very specific meanings and metaphorical origins. Order was a response to the bloody violence of the Wars of the Three Kingdoms, which placed into question the legitimacy of an English monarch over England, Scotland, Ireland, and the pope (Havercroft 2012: 130; Strydom 2000: 129). Order was achieved by establishing clear and inalienable rights of the sovereign over its people, a move that echoed the solution provided by the Treaty of Westphalia to the savage intrastate conflict of the Thirty Years' War (Koselleck 1988: 46–50). This treaty, often credited with initiating the principle of nonintervention across national boundaries, depended on a spatial, not just political, notion of sovereignty, a principle that marks the beginning of the current international order. Sovereignty was relational here, in that governments claiming territorial sovereignty implicitly had to agree to the rights of other governments over their territories: *Rex est imperator in regno suo* (Each king is an emperor of his own realm).[7] It is this mutual recognition of sovereignty that could potentially secure order.

Just as the Treaty of Westphalia began to normalize a notion of state sovereignty that could be the basis of the international order, *Leviathan* (Hobbes [1651] 1965) introduced or reanimated political ideas that could bring order within the state. Like Westphalia, in the Hobbesian discourse on politics, the elimination of violence is necessary to provide security for the citizenry, and internal security is metaphorically crafted chiefly through movement and space. As noted in the epigraph, Hobbes states: "Competition . . . maketh men invade for Gain." Hobbes continues discussing "the time of warre," which he argues is inevitable without a superior power to bring order, and he discusses this warring time using the same metaphor of invasion (96): "It may seem strange to some man, that has not well weighed these things; that Nature should thus dissociate, and render men apt to invade, and destroy one another: and he may therefore, not trusting to this Inference, made from the Passions, desire perhaps to have the same confirmed by Experience" (97). Passions may be the core problem of our state of nature, but these passions are manifested when invading someone's land, someone's place, and, as thievery, when taking over someone's wife, cattle, or children. If violence is metaphorically defined as invasion, the state, which Hobbes referred to as the Commonwealth, is ordered space, a type of homogenized location that allows for a shared language, shared truth, reason, science, and the virtues needed to live in order (Arendt 1958: 135–47; Koselleck 1988: 24; Shaw 2009).

The clustering of terms is here quite important. George Lakoff and Mark Johnson (1980), Otto Santa Ana (2002), and John Urry (2000), among others, have argued for the importance of metaphors in the way we construct reality and behave in the world. Concepts can only be defined metaphorically, hence, our theoretical minds can only comprehend the world through metaphoric systems, ideas that stand for other ideas or experiences. So when I note that the concept of violence in Hobbes is metaphorically connected to invasion, I am arguing that the very definition of violence is part of a metaphorical system that is spatial and dynamic and fundamentally rooted in the normative idea of spatial order, place, and sovereignty, here metaphorically defined as lording over territory and the things and people within. I am also noting that our definitions of the state, already active in Mexico at the end of the nineteenth century, during Diaz's presidency, insofar as they are legitimized based on order and the absence of violence, are part of the same metaphoric system. Thus, the core metaphor of violence as invasion makes productive very specific ideas about state success and failure.

To avoid the warring, violent state of nature, a life of "invasions" and of invading, Hobbes proposes that we must live under a Common Power, a sovereign that can inspire us and, when necessary, coerce us toward good. This idea is not particular to Hobbes, as other thinkers including John Calvin and Jean Bodin had argued that the only way toward peace and, in Calvin, religious freedom, was to stop the wars of religion that had dominated Europe. This could only be accomplished by consolidating political sovereignty. The sovereign is Hobbes's answer to this same problem.

When it comes to violence, political sovereignty is born out of an intrinsic contradiction that can again be traced back to Hobbes. In *Leviathan*, order is not simply about the elimination of violence, but also about its regulation. The sovereign is the only legitimate agent of violence, and it is the sovereign's duty to overpower those subjects who act violently or those foreigners who threaten the security of the state (Kössler 2003: 19). Max Weber takes this proposition to its natural extension when he writes, "The state . . . lays claim to the *monopoly of legitimate physical violence* within a particular territory" ([1919] 2004: 33, emphasis in the original). Is state violence not an invasion? It is, but it is a type of legal invasion, a sort of termination of private property rights for the good of the many. This too has become a political axiom, an anchor for most modern political cultures, which find stability through the strange belief that violence is a state's right. It is, very simply, a belief that some power can be exercised legitimately through violence and that protecting the citizens and the state is of greater interest than the rights of the few that undermine that security. Most violence by nonstate agents is seen to be illegitimate; all too often, state violence is deemed legitimate. Channeling Walter Benjamin's 1921 metaphoric work on the topic, nonstate violence is the violence of sin, but the state's is the violence of just retribution.

This means that the state, in this strand of proto-Enlightenment thought, has a structural, epistemic, and aesthetic identity partly based on a contrast to illegitimate violence, and it is dependent on political cultures that accept the state's right to legitimate violence and on the recognition of property boundaries that may or may not be crossed depending on the crosser's connection or disconnection from the state.

These sets of concerns and political ideas have different manifestations in different contexts. In post-Independence Mexico, Joshua Lund (2012) shows, disorder was the norm. The nineteenth century was full of conflict and open warfare. Religious, monarchic, democratic, liberal, and conservative political values, and clashes between urban and rural forces were reasons for regular conflict. Mexico also had to engage in open warfare with the United States and France and withstand the spatial and political challenge of making a nation out of the vast territory that comprised Mexico, even after losing half its territory to the US Empire. Consolidation was achieved only when the military, in the form of General Porfirio Díaz, took power in the last decades of the nineteenth century. Only at that point did the state have a chance to monopolize violence and engage in governmental programs with the help of the armed forces. Lund narrates this process as follows: "Out of this problem the old idea of 'colonization' returned as a strategy for social and political consolidation, becoming a substantial topic of debate, especially during Díaz's long presidency. Not to be confused with the overseas expansion of imperial sovereignty that constitutes traditional colonialism, colonización exerts its force domestically as a rigorous national project. Indeed, a major impetus for its promotion was the consolidation of the northern territories against the possibility of further annexation by the United States" (Lund 2012: 4).

Hobbes's ideas are obvious here, marking Mexico's early liberal political culture and defining the terms by which the Mexican state would be deemed successful. This political heritage continues. If illegitimate violence precludes us from recognizing a functioning state, as in Mexico's case, we place blame on the debilitated political, social, and economic structures that yielded space to the rise and normalization of nonstate militias, which in turn further weakened Mexico's ability to exercise legitimate violence against the wrongdoers and trespassers or invaders. It is not simply that the Mexican state allows illegitimate violence to go on, but that the Mexican state cannot or is not willing to match this force with legitimate violence. Thus, it is possible to claim that Mexico is a failed state in part because we claim we know and recognize the structure of a working state, as Jones (2008) has argued. The notion of a failed state is thus a structural and epistemic claim.

But there is more to this claim than a claim to knowledge. It is a contingent claim grounded in a Westphalian and Hobbesian logic in which order is more important than other political goods, including justice, equality, transparency, and true sovereignty. When Mexico, ruled for decades by one single party, was economically on the rise and mostly peaceful and orderly, many Mexicans and foreigners believed that what they were experiencing was a well-run and functioning state, not the most efficient one-party dictatorship of the twentieth century. Mexico was perceived as a healthier state with the PRI than it is in this post-PRI period of drug violence. This is evidenced in the use of the failed-state discourse regarding Mexico after 2008; it is correlated to the rise in criminal violence, not to the lack of strong democratic institutions common before the democratic opening of 2000.

Today the Mexican state may have a healthier, even if messier, political system, but it cannot avoid widespread violence or the debate over failed statehood. Semantics? Not really. If, in the post-Westphalian world system, violence defines the legitimacy of the state, then a state's capacity does not. Whether a state is a functioning dictatorship or a liberal democracy is irrelevant to whether a state functions or not. As Sarat and Kearns have argued, in *Leviathan* Hobbes promises "a way of taming violence by producing, through social organization, an economy of violence" (1991: 223). In the Hobbesian imaginary, then, the identity of a state is dependent on the management, production, and distribution of violence. The state is centrally concerned with invasions, spatial transgressions, and movement.

Space, Movement, Violence, and Culture

In the powerful Hobbesian imaginary, order is the absence of violence and/or chaos in a particular place, and order is the most important good the state offers to its citizens. The failed state is a counterexample, monumentally erected by current political cultures, to this Westphalia-inflected Hobbesian view of the state and of politics. But there is more to order than the recognition of its historical specificity. Order is part of a contingent mindset that normalized mercantilism and colonialism, and this means that contemporary uses of the failed-state concept also inherited the materialistic values of mercantilism and the jingoism of colonialism. I make this point because it is easy to find not one but two paths connecting the present discourse of failed states back to the Hobbesian order principle.

One of these paths predictably connects order to state and international relations. The other, less obvious but as important, connects order to citizenship and culture. Order connects to culture through Westphalian-inspired theories of space, the national territory or kingdom, and movement through said spaces; order connects to citizenship through theories of property applied to self-identity. Analyzing both paths together goes to the heart of why the notion of failed states is applied to states suffering violence, regardless of where that violence originates. The synthetic analysis of these two paths shows that only when violence is defined from a Hobbesian perspective can it be used as evidence of a failed state. And, troublingly, the Hobbesian perspective is not simply socially reductive; it is also constructed in alterity to the colonial other. Hence, the perspective from which violence and loss of spatial control are evidence of state failure is partly anchored in the colonial mindset *and* in spatialized ideas of violence. Let's begin with space and move from space to the colonial.

In *The Production of Space*, Henri Lefebvre (1991) theorizes how space is subject to control and power. His approach can help us reconceptualize the discourse of failed states and its reliance on violence, space, and movement. Like Hobbes, Lefebvre sees the state as a Leviathan, a thing that produces order but at a very high cost. According to Lefebvre, the state is a giant monstrosity transformed into normality, a machinery of homogenization that flattens social, temporal, and cultural differences. "This modern state promotes and imposes itself as the stable center—definitively—of (national) societies and spaces" (Lefebvre 1991: 23). A machinery set on producing spaces of domination and knowledge, the state is a human organization anchored to the principle of the knowability and ownability of space through geography, the survey, the grid, and property (Blomley 2003; Harvey 1990;

Lefebvre 1991). Difference is erased or flattened to more easily make difference subject to administration. Whether it is Canada, South Africa, or Bulgaria, most nation-states have been ruled by a Manifest Destiny, a shared sense that a people has a civilizing mission and that this mission is accomplished by, through, and for the state, both over space and only subsequently over people. The logic of the jurisdiction is not about people.[8] By and large, the jurisdiction follows the logic of administered space.

Expansion need not be westward, as in the colonialist US example; it may simply go deeper into the territory, allowing multicultural nations like Canada, Mexico, South Africa, and Bulgaria to rationalize conflictive space, partition it, divide it, make it knowable and accountable. That is Lund's (2012) argument about Mexico. But stability, Lefebvre (1991) notes, is never total:

> In this same space there are, however, other forces on the boil, because the rationality of the state, of its techniques, plans and programmes, provokes opposition. The violence of power is answered by the violence of subversion. With its wars and revolutions, defeats and victories, confrontation and turbulence, the modern world corresponds precisely to Nietzsche's tragic vision. State-imposed normality makes permanent transgression inevitable. As for time and negativity, whenever they re-emerge, as they must, they do so explosively. This is a new negativity, a tragic negativity which manifests itself as incessant violence. These seething forces are still capable of rattling the lid of the cauldron of the state and its space, for differences can never be totally quieted. Though defeated, they live on, and from time to time they begin fighting ferociously to reassert themselves and transform themselves through struggle. (23)

The state is thus never finished, sovereignty is never total, and the fears Hobbes uses as inspiration to justify his Leviathan are never fully squelched. Repressed, they lurk behind each social tension, reminding us that control over territory is temporary, frail, and perhaps even chimerical. Place is never finished. Order is a chimera. There is always someone out there piling up guns and harboring fantasies of invasion and overthrow.

The national space, the territory, the state, is thus the outcome of continual work. It is produced and reproduced every day in the repetitive and even traditional social practices that glue together in relative harmony a group of people often too large and diverse to be kin. The work is not simply the work of humans in their fleshy liveliness. It is also the work of people from our past, their memories, experiences, and physical and social battles. The national space is the future of the past, the dreams, fears, and compromises of some Founding Fathers, some caudillos or revolutionaries, the dreamers, the fighters, and the lawyers of some past who won the day, back in time, over the other dreamers, fighters, and lawyers from the other sides. The national space is thus always an imprint of the past in durable means that organize us and discipline us. The national space is in the strictest sense the product of culture and of mediation: embodied practices are one such mediation (Lefebvre 1991). The discourses that help people make moral choices are another. But institutions and legal cultures are the source of perhaps the most prominent mediations, as these account for the continued franchising of some embodied practices and discourses over others. Order may be a chimera, but it is the lifeblood of institutions and legal cultures.

In Western antiquity, Hannah Arendt reminds us, order was already the outcome of property logic: "Even Plato, whose political plans foresaw the abolition of private property and an extension of the public sphere to the point of annihilating private life altogether, still speaks with great reverence of Zeus Herkeios, the protector of border lines, and calls the *horoi*, the boundaries between one estate and another, divine, without seeing any contradiction" (1958: 30). In a sense, Westphalia continued the reverence for the *horoi* and produced an order that depended on the notion that a territory should be treated as property. A kingdom was possessed and could be exploited according to the sovereign's wishes. Movement across borders would be restricted, controlled, and administered. Western-centric at their core, Hobbesian and Westphalian thought helped constitute modern political thinking, the core metaphors of order and the state, and in this thinking, the right to sovereignty was expanded from states to citizens, constituting the basis for orderly societies anchored on, like the Westphalia Treaty itself, the principles of sovereignty over territory and over movement. The rights of the sovereign at the individual level became property rights. These rights became more socially meaningful as they became more common, and as a transition from feudal land arrangements gave way to enclosure (early enclosures needed not be private) and to private landownership (Marx [1867] 1977: 503; Strydom 2000: 99).

It is not Hobbes but Locke who reflects better on this evolving order. From the early 1700s, England became a geography defined by enclosed parcels, spaces structured by law, culture, protoliberal politics, and colonialism.[9] These different elements were at play in discussions about the nation-state in Locke's *Second Treatise of Civil Government*, in which he laid out ideas about property alongside basic ideas about labor (Greer 2012: 366–67). Locke, a champion of private property, the commodification of labor, and colonialism, used the open and, he believed, wasteful common spaces of the Americas as warning tales about the poverty that would ensue if England were to revert back to the commons, to nature. Private property, he believed, was socially responsible, for it produced the personal incentives to enhance productivity, and thus it was the legal tool by which a state could meet and exceed its needs.

In Locke, the order principle is constituted through a web of contracts that make property the legal avatar for order. His vision has taken roots. Ours, Carol Rose (1994) would argue, is a property regime. The centrality of property, thus, cannot be understood in isolation from Europe's transition from feudalism to mercantilism, colonialism, and capitalism. Property is a way of organizing space, and in this way it becomes the spatial logic behind the legitimation of the state as a sovereign territory, and law becomes the conceptual mechanism to theorize violence and order. Yet it is important to remember that property, like most other political and legal concepts, was defined in alterity to the colonial other. By alterity here I am referring to the epistemic practice of defining self in relation to a colonial other, and using racialized discourse to justify the superiority of moral and social practices that in other contexts could not be evaluated. When confronted with this history, the truism "My home is my kingdom" takes on a new meaning.[10]

Anchoring order on property is a dangerous proposition when we consider that property is, in mercantilism, colonialism, and capitalism, something to be coveted, to the point that property always has to be defended. Property is desired, and, these economic systems tell us, this desire is natural. In the name of the desire for property, colonizers were willing to wipe out entire civilizations. In the name of capitalism, today we justify war and strife. *Desire and invasion* are the implicit metaphorical roots connecting violence to the state in Westernized political cultures. These roots operate around a spatial and dynamic logic that has engendered some periods of lasting international peace and some successful and sustainable orderly societies around the world. Failures, too, are common, as war and colonialism, the most dramatic examples of desire and invasion, have characterized European and North American international relations, Westphalia notwithstanding.

The lessons of Westphalia are lessons of citizenship, too, as modern political cultures have appropriated these international lessons, and the logic of property, to bring peace to neighborhoods. Since the Romans, as Anthony Pagden reminds us, "civil society was, by definition, a society based upon property, and property relations were what constituted the basis for all exchanges between truly civil men" (1990: 15). The Romans' use of property to structure civil society has brought discursive complications to the host of things that are designated property. In Latin, *proprietatem* (nominative *proprietas*) can refer to owned land, ownership in general, or a particular characteristic of a thing, propriety, or a quality. In Pagden (1990, quoted above), for instance, property refers to landed property, but the last part of the sentence, "truly civil men," already refers back to property as proprietary. The French and later the English inherited all of these meanings. Since the Romans, then, property has connected land to commodities, morality, and science, engendering the term's multidiscursive inflections or what a literary scholar may call the term's highly evocative character, or its polysemy (Alexander 1997: 69). Thus, property itself is always a complex metaphor in which meaning transverses from economics to law to ethics to politics to science.

Arendt corroborates and pushes further: "[Hobbes's] *Leviathan* was not concerned with idle speculation about new political principles or the old search for reason as it governs the community of men; it was strictly a 'reckoning of the consequences' that follow from the rise of a new class in society whose existence is essentially tied up with property as a dynamic, new property-producing device" (1973: 145). Since then order between citizens has been correlated to the ability of citizens to rely on a legal system that would help them protect their private property—first their land, and later anything that can be owned. Echoing Locke, James Madison famously wrote about this expanding order principle of modern governmentality in 1792: "Government is instituted to protect property of every sort; as well [as] that which lies in the various rights of individuals, as that which the term particularly expresses. This being the end of government, that alone is a *just* government, which *impartially* secures to every man, whatever is his *own*" (Hutchinson and Rachal 1962: 267).

For an order principle based on property to work, property has to be central to life. Madison, echoing Hobbes and Locke, found no problem arguing for this centrality as he rhetorically made property an even broader concept that included not only material things but also freedom, religion, our profession, and every right: "In its larger and juster meaning, [property] embraces every thing to which a man may attach a value and have a right" (Hutchinson and Rachal 1962: 266). Madison pushed the metaphor beyond its traditional limits because, in his argument—shared by other Federalists, like James Wilson and Daniel Webster—property acquired still more meanings. It also reflected a conception of individual liberty that saw in property the mechanism for social stability; the means by which liberty could be exercised in the public sphere (Alexander 1997: 68). In the process, this economic and legal view of property expanded what under traditional English law, and previously Roman, had been a material and spatial sense of property. That is, in English common law, land was the root metaphor for property, and, accordingly, property rights evolved to cover things other than land—in fact, anything that could be owned—but with attention to the practices first established regarding land. For instance, the general category of property was divided into "real property," which tended to include land and buildings, and "private property," which included everything else that could be owned. Real property, historically, began using church registries to regulate ownership, inheritances, and sales. The use of registries has expanded from real property, and today we use registries for a substantial number of private property items, including cars and computers.

The relevance of land in property rights goes beyond registries. In the early history of the British colonies in the Americas, and at the outset of the formation of the United States, property and property rights always referred to land, even if political theorists like Madison were making broader and more complex claims and profiting from the term's metaphoric richness (Ely 1992). By the time of the Federalists, property law was expanding the notion of property to include "imaginary," nontangible goods, which were best exemplified in financial concepts that involved future interests ("reminders," "reversions," and "executionary interests") and other types of rather abstract things such as "incorporeal hereditations," or what today lawyers call "easements" (Alexander 1997: 69–70). Cheryl Harris has even convincingly shown that in the US American context, whiteness itself was treated as property in this juridical tradition: "In ways so embedded that it is rarely apparent, the set of assumptions, privileges, and benefits that accompany the status of being white have become a valuable asset that whites sought to protect and that those who passed sought to attain—by fraud if necessary. Whites have come to expect and rely on these benefits and over time these expectations have been affirmed, legitimated, and protected by the law" (1997: 5). From land to the things needed to function freely in the public sphere, even whiteness, property became the logic of life and the central technique for securing order.

Carol Rose makes a similar point when she argues that property became a type of narrative of justice and self-ownership at the root of law *and* social norms of public interaction. In her most insightful contribution to the subject, she notes the intermixing of the words *property* and *propriety*, arguing that there are substantive reasons to believe that a property regime has the goal of dispensing that which is "'proper' or appropriate . . . to keep good order in the commonwealth or body politic" (1994: 58). Gregory Alexander would add: "Property was central to this plan of social stability. It anchored the citizen to his (for in this premodern vision, the citizen-freeholder could only be a man) rightful place in the proper social hierarchy. Property . . . was more than wealth; it was authority" (1997: 4).

It is tempting to think that in the evolution of property from land to commodities and other abstract goods, property has become despatialized, but the opposite is true. Commodities, abstract rights such as whiteness and freedom, and intangible goods such as intellectual property have become metaphorically defined with a spatial and even material logic that, for instance, obstructs legal practitioners from abandoning the idea that taking away a property right such as whiteness, as Harris argued, would yield a net loss to the individual and a net gain to others. This happens even in cases such as intellectual property, which Lawrence Lessig (1999: 131) argues is a type of property that is nonrivalrous. A nonrivalrous good is one that can be used by two or more people (e.g., a book, a movie in a theater) without harming each other's experience. Yet even intellectual property, as Lessig critically notes, tends to be legally defined as rivalrous and assumed to be the property of one, for at least a length of time that coincides with the property's most profitable years. In each of these cases, commodities, rights, and intangible goods are legally imagined first as landed property, a material possession relying on a registry to regulate its transference and exploitation. The metaphors for property and its opposite, invasion, partly tell the story. Rights become *possessions*; illegality becomes *trans*gression; goods are *rivalrous*; and, the mother of all metaphors, commodities become *property*.

The history of these important metaphors, discursive equivalences, and socio-legal practices tells us that landed property, owned space, and the subsequent and expansive property regime that defined first mercantilism and then capitalism shared similar roots and traits. Connecting back to bloody times, dreams of order became political theories and eventually normalized ways of seeing our political reality. Connected through powerful and insidious metaphors, the political and legal concepts that sustain the state, land, and commodities have become part of our material and civic lives, making them part of our economic and political identities.

When we seek and praise orderly societies today, we do not often reflect on what that means. The discourse of order depends on a Hobbesian definition of the state that cannot be separated from the property regime and its injustices. Order is thus a fantastically rich and potentially dangerous notion, and it is from this notion that an expansive idea of crisis that allows for the otherwise puzzling equivalence of political and criminal violence to be discursively spread. The dangers of the order principle, however, are more expansive.

Desire and Invasion

According to Arendt (1973), the political economy of order is a never-ending cycle of property accumulation. In Hobbes, she writes, property is power, and order based on property necessitates more property to reproduce itself:

> Since power is essentially only a means to an end a community based solely on power must decay in the calm of order and stability; its complete security reveals that it is built on sand. Only by acquiring more power can it guarantee the status quo; only by constantly extending its authority and only through the process of power accumulation can it remain stable. . . . This process of never-ending accumulation of power necessary for the protection of a never-ending accumulation of capital determined the "progressive" ideology of the late nineteenth century and foreshadowed the rise of imperialism. (142–43)

The wars of empire, which in the sixteenth and seventeenth centuries were already redefining the European political imaginary, would serve, Arendt here argues, to further justify territorial expansion. But they did more than justify present and future actions. They also provided the ideological ground for expansion by anachronistically evaluating the immediate colonial past based on emerging legal principles of property and race and, in the process, used history to justify past violence and genocide.

The connection of the property regime to colonialism is quite clear, as part of the political imaginary of Hobbes and Locke depended on the constitution of a European subject distinctly capable of using property for the establishment of order. They did this partly by drawing differences between the West and the colonial other, which were imagined in alterity—the former as capable of encompassing successful societies, the latter as incapable. In the same section of *Leviathan* in which Hobbes argues for a common power that would end violence and war, he provides a short but vivid description of its nasty alternative: "It may peradventure be thought, there was never such a time, nor condition of warre as this; and I believe it was never generally so, over all the world: but there are many places, where they live so now. For the savage people in many places of America, except the government of small Families, the concord whereof dependeth on naturall lust, have no government at all; and live at this day in that brutish manner, as I said before" ([1651] 1965: 97). His vision was not unique. "In the beginning," Locke hyperbolically stated, modifying the book of Genesis, "all was *America*" (1689: §49). With the rhetorical equation of America to waste and chaos, he disqualified those social orders that did not use European concepts of property or otherwise resemble European social organization. Subjecting the indigenous land and populations to European property regimes was, in their imaginary, establishing order (Armitage 2000: 63; Greer 2012: 367).

The European property regime also provided legal justification and techniques for colonialism. Pertinent to Mexico, the early arguments Spanish jurists such as Palacios Rubios and Matías de Paz used to argue for Spain's right to take over property in the Americas depended on Westernized notions of property that were hardly applicable to the American context. They argued that communities in the Antilles, in particular, had not formed what Rubios and de Paz, via Roman law, called civil society and could not be understood as owners of property, even if they lived there. The Aztecs and the Incas, whose empires were political communities based on property, presented a challenge. Rubios's and de Paz's arguments did not fully work, and instead they had to resort to declaring all Americans heretics and thus incapable of "dominium," the right of ownership, including self-ownership.[11] Based on their ungodly state, Spain had a right, indeed a duty, to proselytize and, with the encomienda, Spain gained the right to dispossess. The whole edifice of colonialism in the Americas rested on the argument that "political, and hence also property, rights could be held only by civil men in civil communities" (Pagden 1990: 27). Heresy precluded natives from both.

The English and French used similar logic in their colonies across the Atlantic, arguing that Native Americans were neither owners nor responsible keepers of the land. Generations of English monarchs, from Henry VII and Elizabeth I to James I, used the notion that the Americas were not owned by a Christian monarch and were thus empty. Robert Miller notes that King James I gave settlers property rights in America because the lands were "not now actually possessed by any Christian Prince of People" and "there is noe other the Subjects of any Christian King or State . . . actually in Possession . . . whereby any Right, Claim, Interest, or Title, may . . . by that

Means accrue" (James I quoted in Miller 2006: 19). Vicki Hsueh (2006) has shown that Locke and the others were fundamentally wrong (see also Greer 2012). Many of the legal mechanisms of enclosure were part of precolonial societies, albeit in that enclosure was also part of what Hsueh calls inner commons. Not that this would have mattered, as Europeans and, later, the United States have used all sorts of legal contortions to justify, apropos Westphalia, shameful colonization and transnational interventions (Marx [1867] 1977: 296). Mexicans know this well: the United States manufactured a war with Mexico that ended in Mexico's loss of half of its territory, a tactic that the US repeated in the Spanish-American War, which ended with the annexation of Puerto Rico and a neocolonial arrangement with Cuba, the Philippines, and Guam (Leonard 2000: 148; Pinheiro 2007: 151; Pletcher 1973: 254, 478). In all of these cases, the violent wars of dispossession that shaped the North American continent were legal as the property regime had instituted what Rose notes were the basic rules of ethics and morality toward others.

Mexico's independence did not mean a break from these ideas. In fact, one can argue that Mexico served as a laboratory for the mixture of liberal, racist, and imperialistic ideas common in Europe in the context of a multiethnic nation. When Mexico's internal colonization became the answer to the concretion of an orderly and governable state at the end of the nineteenth century, property was at the center. Lund (2012) explains as follows:

> The idea driving the colonization campaign was that rural Mexico represented a mass of bottled-up capital waiting to be liberated in the name of national progress. Colonization, then, referred to the recruitment of immigrants and nationals for settlement in and development of unoccupied lands, either purchased by the government or appropriated after being declared *terrenos baldíos*. *Baldío* is a Spanish legal term connoting land that is untilled or fallow but also vacant. A major impediment to the colonization plan was that much of the land on which it had designs was not, in fact, unoccupied or even untilled but often represented the homes of existent rural communities . . . understood to be indigenous in the ethnocultural sense. (4)

What was happening in Mexico is more than an echo of Locke's ideas. The history of the Mexican state shows that the Lockean ideas of order that justified US imperialism against Mexico had also become a common way of imagining Mexican governmentality—that is, by using ethno-racial ideas to justify external and internal colonialism. The "Indian problem" in

Mexico and its ambivalent and ambiguous resolution in the form of racially exclusionary legal and political practices by a state that at the same time embraced *indigenismo* as a pillar of national identity became emblematic of the type of political contortionism needed in multinational and multiracial contemporary states. One can easily find parallels between this process in Mexico and Brazil's claims of "racial democracy" and the United States' contemporary era of color blindness and new racism. It is doubtful whether one can understand modern liberalism without acknowledging the central role of the property regime to the modern liberal nation-state and the project of Western modernity itself.

Possession is one element of the property regime, granting certain property rights that typically include the rights of exploitation and wealth extraction. It is these processes of colonial extraction that helped sustain the property regime, mercantilism, early capitalism, and the order principle in Europe (Arendt 1973: 143). Eduardo Galeano (1997) aphoristically titled his political study of these economies of extraction by Europe in the Americas *Open Veins of Latin America*. This study of the plundering that animated the European economies shows also the profound dislocation between the principles of order common in England and Europe and colonial principles. Joseph Inikori (2002) goes further, showing how England's Industrial Revolution was furnished by colonialism in Africa and the Americas.[12] At its root were not only the processes of exploitative extraction, but also the manner in which Africa and the Americas were brought into the capitalistic Atlantic trade. From Madeira's sugar in the fifteenth century, to the slaves needed to operate the sugar plantations, to the gold and silver that ultimately supported the colonial structure, trade allowed the growth of European wealth and population and provided the material basis for industrialization and the rise of the modern nation-state.

The political economy of order is the political economy of colonialism. The issue is not simply that plundering happened, but that the wealth extracted paved the way for and funded the property regime and the order principle. On this, Daron Acemoglu, Simon Johnson, and James Robinson (2005) present one of the most persuasive arguments about European growth after 1500. Their economic analysis of the rise of Europe shows that Western European nations grew much faster than Eastern European nations and that the nations with Atlantic trade and access to colonies grew the fastest. From 1500 to 1800, Atlantic Western Europe's GDP per capita practically doubled. The rest of Europe experienced growth of only around 30 percent. What is significant is that there is another split within Atlantic

Western nations, one that separates the Netherlands and England from Spain, Portugal, and, to a lesser degree, France (Acemoglu, Johnson, and Robinson 2005). The former group grew much faster, and this growth was made possible by changes in the property regime; the latter grew, but their growth was tempered by relationships with the Catholic Church that extended the aristocracy's grip on property, hence reducing the new wealth's effect on society. In France and on the Iberian peninsula, monarchs and those close to them kept most of the wealth from the Atlantic trade. England and the Netherlands were different. "Rapid economic development did not begin until the emergence of *political institutions* providing secure property rights to a broader segment of society and allowing free entry into profitable businesses" (Acemoglu, Johnson, and Robinson 2005: 55, emphasis in the original).

The lesson here is not simply that liberal secularism was better for the early modern European economy but that the growth of the property regime correlated with the excess wealth that circulated in England and the Netherlands due to colonial extraction. Colonialism and the property regime were thus the two most significant factors in Western European growth.

Today, in the discourse of failed states, order seems to be simply the application of good economic principles, good law, and good political leadership. But order has a political economy; it is costly, it takes time, and it is often the result of state violence within or without. Just as the principle of order based on property was emerging as the core of the political discourse of Europe, the historically contingent seeds of crises were being planted there and elsewhere. The processes of extraction that characterized colonialism and that continued under neocolonialism meant that the regions of what Immanuel Wallerstein (1974) calls the "periphery" experienced chronic poverty, and only very recently have some of these economies—more precisely, Eastern Europe—begun to catch up. In the Americas, the GDP per capita (PPP) of Chile, Argentina, Uruguay, Panama, Mexico, Venezuela, and Brazil has passed that of some Eastern European nations, such as Montenegro, which is at the bottom of Europe in terms of GDP. Moreover, the PPP of Chile and Argentina will likely pass that of Portugal, one of the original Atlantic trade nations, within the next three to four years. These are momentous events in modernity, but the PPP hides the manner in which lack of wealth distribution characterizes these growing American economies, including those of Chile, Argentina, Brazil, Venezuela, Uruguay, and Mexico.

Can inequality breed order?

The political economy of order also includes the particular costs and po-litical logic that today constitute the contemporary securitization of the state. The costs alone are instructive. In 2014, the Institute for Econom-ics and Peace released its annual report, which showed that in 2013 alone Mexico spent $172.7 billion fighting DCOs. Its methodology accounts for military expenditure, homicides, internal security, crime, private security, incarceration costs, and GDP losses from conflict, among other expenses. The $172.7 billion cost is staggering. This is more than twice Mexico's foreign debt ($73 billion), 9.4 percent of Mexico's GDP, and roughly $1,430 per capita. The United States, a so-called partner in Mexico's war on drugs, has, under the auspices of the Mérida Initiative, committed only $2.3 billion since 2008. All this wealth used and wasted in the war on drugs is wealth not invested in Mexican schools, technological development, or infrastructure.

In the United States, the drug crisis is also growing increasingly bad. Although crime rates have been falling for the last few decades, criminal justice expenditures have multiplied. Murder rates, for instance, spiked to a rate of around 10 per 100,000 people during the 1980s, but since then, the rate has declined by more than half, falling to below 5 per 100,000. Since 1982, though, criminal justice expenditures have gone up 600 percent, from $35 billion to over $180 billion in 2003 and $213 billion in 2007, making the US criminal justice system by far the most expensive in the world (Cuéllar 2008: 954). Considering that more than half of the US inmate population was convicted for drug-related charges and that the majority of inmates are black or Latino, the internal cost of the US war on drugs is not only dra-matic. It is also a modern investment in coloniality.

In the United States, the property regime is extremely costly. According to the Stockholm International Peace Research Institute, in 2013 the US spent $617 billion on defense, an amount equivalent to 47 percent of the world's military expenditure. If we add to these already astronomical figures the budget of the Department of Homeland Security (around $60 billion), the cost of civil courts, the training of lawyers, judges, clerks, police officers, and other specialists at the service of the courts or police departments, as well as the cost of the technological infrastructure keeping it all together, sustaining order becomes a gigantic economic enterprise. With that price tag in mind, perhaps the question of why these states suffer so much vio-lence should be accompanied by the question "Can Mexico, Somalia, Haiti, or Colombia afford order?" Can Mexico afford its law-and-order strategy against the cartels much longer? What's more, is it fair to evaluate the success or failure of a state and society on the basis of its ability to order and control space to such an absolute and Hobbesian extent?

CONCLUSION

The popularity of the failed-state concept is instructive of the type of geopolitical narratives welcomed in the US public sphere. The concept began to be widely used in the 1990s in the United States and the rest of the Western world. It quickly became a tool for assessing different types of national crises, most of them in the developing world. The 9/11 attacks on the US provided even more opportunities for its use, particularly to assess nations like Pakistan, Sudan, Libya, and South Yemen. Critics of the concept such as Jones (2008) and Manjikian (2008) correctly point to the fact that the term is used to justify interventions using ahistorical, neocolonial, and Western-centric arguments.

But in this chapter I have shown that the term's problems are greater than that. When the majoritarian US public sphere gave space to the debate on whether Mexico was, like Pakistan, at risk of failure, users of the concept showed that the discourse of state failure could easily be applied to nations suffering from crises due to criminal, not political, activity. This was unusual. The concept, rooted in politics, had been applied to nations suffering from violence and chaos originating in politics. In most of these crises, politically defined groups like FARC (Colombia), religiously defined groups like the Islamist militant groups Hizbul-Islam, al-Shabaab, and Ahlu Sunna Waljama'a (Somalia), or ethnically defined groups like the Mayan Zapatistas (Mexico) violently oppose central governments and take control of territory. In Mexico, however, the majority of violence and chaos caused by DCOs was motivated by profit, not political power. That the nature of the DCO crises did not matter showed that users of the failed-state concept regarded crises, not their nature, to be sufficient evidence of whether a state was failing.

How was this possible? The clues are in the deep history of the discourse of state failure. I show that an early modern political discourse that undergirded colonialism, in particular the thought of Thomas Hobbes and John Locke, continues to animate today's concept of state failure and, by default, state success. A successful state is orderly. It is a state that controls violence and territory. Just as the Treaty of Westphalia depended on the idea of the territory to constitute a legal international order, Hobbes's vision imagined an orderly society based on property and contracts, a property regime that would be at the basis of a materialist (and republican) notion of citizenship. As Rose (1994) and Alexander (1997) suggest, civic order would be within reach if citizens were invested in a property regime. These were and have been strong bases for a society of order. And this is also where things break apart.

Order has a political economy, a history, and a counterhistory. Its history is, in a sense, the basis of the contemporary discourse of state success and failure, a discourse that has generated powerful normative ideas of the relationship between capitalism, state, law, and order. Mexico, like any other state, is evaluated against these normative notions, particularly as criminal violence seems rampant and at times capable of breaking down the fundamental state institutions of order.

But a counterhistory of the discourse of order, based on an examination of the political economy of order and the metaphors it relies on, reveals that order's historicity and discursive power is tied to the particular contextual conditions of seventeenth-century England, mercantilism, the rise of capitalism, the expansion of property rights, and colonialism. Order was constructed in alterity to a colonial other, the inhabitants of the Americas, who served as a warning tale about the state of nature and the lack of property rights. In addition, the order principle was constructed partly through the processes of wealth extraction made possible by the jingoistic application of the property regime in the Americas.

This counterhistory of order instructs us on how to interpret the public debate regarding Mexico's failing state. Leading US news institutions have equated criminal and political crises, and in so doing, they have normalized profoundly ideological theories of society, politics, and people. These leading news institutions normalized the assumption that order is the measure of state success—a standard so low that it is considered pre-Enlightenment. This definition of state success belongs to the political ecosystem of the absolutist state or, more recently, to fascism; it is a definition that betrays any commitment to equality, justice, and democracy.

In doing so, these leading news institutions avoided asking the tough questions pertinent to the nature of Mexico's crisis. When members of DCOs justify their violence in terms of their desire to acquire wealth using whatever means necessary, their desire for wealth is never subject to critical questioning. It is taken as natural, as part of being human. We may criticize the means that narcos use, but not their goal. The goal is, after all, shared by most. It is the central ingredient of advanced capitalism and neoliberalism. Is it natural to desire wealth? No. This desire has a history and a political economy, some of which is explored here under the notion of the property regime, one of the grounds of order in the West. Is it surprising that the desire for wealth is treated as the desire for justice, representation, and equality that compels, however misguidedly, FARC, Hizbul-Islam, or the Zapatistas? It is not surprising in a US political ecosystem in which the search for order justifies the massive growth of the US carceral system, military expenditure, the rise of anti-Latino nativism and xenophobia, the killing of black citizens at the hands of police, and the success of the gun lobby. A political ecosystem of order depends on the property regime; together they energize the legal extremism that allows wealth to be the biggest predictor of political success and political influence.

Hobbes is weeping in his grave. He saw an Ouroboros, a serpent biting its own tail; he saw a world of religious morality destroying itself, and, in attempting to disrupt the cycle, he imagined peace based not on a moral but on a material basis. The Ouroboros, impervious to such change, has continued to re-create itself. An order based on property, as Marx, Arendt, Wallerstein, and many others have argued, can only normalize invasion. If we cannot even see the current cycle, we are fools to think we can do anything to disrupt it. We can do nothing if we are blinded or desensitized to the historicity of our absurd desire for extreme wealth that drives the current Ouroboros.

3

Censoring Narcoculture

MEXICAN REPUBLICANISM AND PUBLICITY

The songs narrating the fortunes of narco-traffickers are the rage in the radio and dance clubs, the phenomenon belongs to a Narcoculture that penetrates deep in our nation's society, especially with Mexican children and youth. The narcocorridos offer the other face of the quotidian in their stanzas; the traffic of drugs is not the most dangerous threat to National Security, rather the lifestyle of a few hardened individuals, more or less despicable, who know how to play tough.

—Congress of the State of San Luis Potosí, April 24, 2001

The public sphere is the metonymic figure of the successful modern nation-state discussed in the last chapter. Just as the successful state is a sovereign space in which orderly processes of power distribution are structured through the orderly ethos of the property regime, the public sphere is a political space in which concerns about the many—political concerns—are shared, debated, and perhaps even negotiated and agreed on. Space *and* order here are essential.[1] Theories of publicity may differ on many things, but they have in common the assumption that, within the space of publicity, order rules. Although today's complex societies show a significant diversity of public spheres, from which spring different theorizations, communicational practices within these spheres are conceived and understood as orderly ways of performing social criticism and thus integral to a healthy political culture. These communicational practices are, simply, core elements of democratic political principles.

There are exceptions to the rule of order, and, as is common, these exceptions illuminate things differently, highlighting typically unseen textures and shadows. Publicity, order, and democratic politics can look quite different when seen from an uncommon perspective, such as when the space of publicity is overtaken by communicational and expressive practices that threaten order and that seem to predicate violence, publicity's other. Narcoculture—narcocorridos, narco-cinema, and narco-television—has these characteristics, and the responses to its massive popularity by hegemonic forces and the Mexican state cast into relief uncommon aspects of publicity, order, and politics worth investigating.

This chapter does precisely that. It expands on previous arguments about order and violence to illuminate publicity's connections to the property regime and to colonialism. With attention to hegemonic responses to narcoculture, I show today's publicity in Mexico not simply as the Habermasian realm of the social or the Arendtian realm of the political, but as state-sanctioned sociocultural spaces meant to foster civic behavior through the franchising of orderly ways of criticizing the state. In these spaces, people learn to be orderly citizens. Publicity is thus part of governmentality, of the way nation-states perform modern ways of doing government.

This description of the structure of publicity in contemporary Mexico is clearest when one looks at the censorship and the regulation of what state actors and community leaders perceive as bad and dangerous public culture. Censorship cases make evident some of the social and political expectations regarding publicity and insinuate rarely acknowledged normative aspects of publicity in the modern nation-state: the public spheres are training grounds for nonviolent social protest and are thus essential to the orderly running of a nation. As Habermas reminds us, "The political task of the bourgeois public sphere was the regulation of civil society" (1989: 52). And the benefits of this political task were not simply giving a voice to citizens versus the state. The benefits were also for the state, which would have an orderly population, citizens less likely to take up arms against their rulers. This means that public spheres are several things at the same time: they are citizen-run spaces key to expressing and debating public matters, but they are also spaces regulated by the state, which uses them to craft peaceful citizens. The censorship of narcoculture clearly illuminates the latter, but it also throws into relief the former.

The history and practices of censorship of narcoculture in Mexico are rich. Calls for the banning of narcoculture in Mexico have been common for decades, but these calls have intensified since the democratic opening of 2000. The majority of the censoring efforts have targeted narcocorridos, songs narrating the fortunes of narco-traffickers, the lives and deeds of fictional and real drug cartel members. Hugely popular in northern Mexico and most areas affected by the violence (as well as among Mexican Americans in the United States), narcocorridos have repeatedly been singled out as the largest cultural threat to the nation. Different state institutions have issued calls for their censorship, as exemplified by this chapter's epigraph. In this 2001 case, the Congress of San Luis Potosí appealed to the state-level Chamber of the Radio and Television Industry (CIRT) to ask broadcasters to stop playing the notorious genre. Censoring tactics can be also quite creative. For instance, on May 2, 2011, Mario López Valdez, governor of the state of Sinaloa, promulgated a decree with the goal of censoring narcocorridos. He used the power of his office to, among other things, take away the liquor licenses of bars and public venues playing the violent music or related music videos. The decision, which echoed city ordinances in Tijuana, BC, was replicated in Chihuahua.[2]

The most common argument in these political, legal, and legislative processes of censorship is that the music has the power to constitute bad and disorderly citizens and that this power is in direct opposition to the goals of the state. As public culture, narcocorridos betray the political task of the public sphere, making civil society more difficult to regulate. The political task, which is one aim of the Mexican government (as I show below), can be defined as the "authoring" of, the giving shape to, good citizens. Francisco I. Madero, the first president after the Mexican Revolution of 1910, famously implied this goal as follows: "Un buen gobierno solamente puede existir cuando hay buenos ciudadanos" (A good government can exist only when there are good citizens) (Rosas and Villalpando 2001: 140). And good citizens don't appear out of thin air. Good citizens are shaped, constructed, convinced, disciplined, cajoled, or all of these things at the same time. Public education plays a significant part in this crafting of civic beings, but so does public culture, which functions not simply as a content provider of proper ideas, but also as a space for proper civic behavior.

This chapter argues that a key task of the public sphere is censorial and authorial. It is censorial because the public sphere privileges ideas of order, orderly debate, and proper civic behavior, hence constructing boundaries to public culture. This censorial capacity is what Habermas refers to as the political task of the public sphere. It is political because the beneficiaries are the state and hegemonic forces (e.g., mainstream media industries), which also provide the regulatory framework for censorship. This censorial capacity of the state and media industries, which provides the normative value of order to the public sphere, is productive: it has the capacity to author citizens. Below I show that these capacities are not hidden but central to the way many in Mexico see the Mexican state, and also important to the way the state sees itself. I show these features of Mexican political culture through a discourse analysis of the contemporary debates about censorship in Mexico and of the way state and federal lawmakers have discussed the problem of narcocorridos.

In addition to showing that the political task of the public sphere is aligned with the censorial capacity of the state and the crafting of citizens, the chapter shows that these features of contemporary political culture in Mexico depend on agrarian theories of culture that have been central to republican ideals. This argument locates these features within the long history of constituting governable citizens in the modern nation-state. It also continues building on the counterhistory of the discourse of order, its political economy, and the metaphors and concepts that animate it, particularly in relation to culture and media.[3]

SITUATING THE PROBLEM

Attempts to prohibit narcocorridos in Mexico go as far back as thirty years, when musical groups like Los Tigres del Norte began to succeed with songs such as "La banda del carro rojo" and "Contrabando y traición" (Wald 2001). Luis Astorga (2005) documents how the state's governor, Francisco Labastida Ochoa, requested censorship of these groups but failed to get it. The market won (Astorga 2005: 146; Simonett 2001b: 334). However, things changed. During the last two decades or so, there has been a marked increase in calls for censorship and actual censorship. These government actions are in tension with liberal and market-driven Mexican political traditions. These propose, respectively, that freedom of expression is a central cultural and civic right and that cultural trade should be regulated by the public, not the state. But as *Excelsior*'s columnist Pascal Beltrán del Rio (2011) argues in what has become a common view in powerful civic circles, no freedom is absolute, and the context of violence is such that it merits extraordinary measures, including censorship. The political and legal debates about narcocorridos illuminate important ideas about the role of public culture in society, and provide a window into culture as a hegemonic theoretical construct in Mexican political circles. They also show the recentering of republicanism in Mexican politics.

As Astorga (2005) notes, the first official attempt to censor narcocorridos were in 1987 in Sinaloa, the cradle of Mexico's drug trade and the imaginary

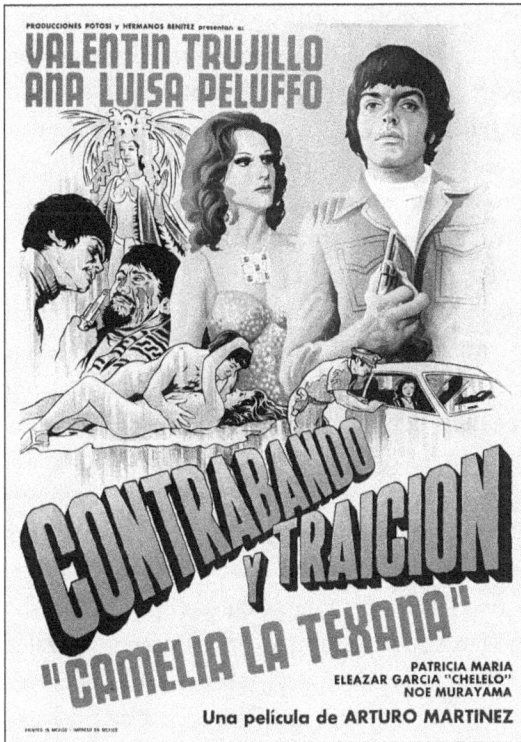

Figure 3.1. The song "Contrabando y traición" was made into a film directed by Arturo Martinéz in 1977.

cradle of narcocorridos (see this book's introduction). Labastida Ochoa, governor of Sinaloa from 1987 to 1992, became one of Mexico's most prominent politicians. He was the secretary of energy during the presidency of Miguel de la Madrid (1982–88); the secretary of agriculture and secretary of interior during the presidency of Ernesto Zedillo (1994–2000); and the presidential candidate for the Institutional Revolutionary Party (PRI) in 1999. He lost to the National Action Party (PAN) candidate, Vicente Fox. Although he was properly credited with trying to prohibit narcocorridos as governor of Sinaloa, the CIA revealed documents accusing Labastida Ochoa of collaborating with the drug cartels, bringing to the fore the degree to which the PRI constituted an orderly relation to drug cartels at the expense of legality (*Washington Times*, February 1998). On November 11, 1998, Sinaloa senator Jorge Alfonso Calderón Salazar discussed in front of the Senate of the Republic another instance of this orderly arrangement. He argued that politicians belonging to the PRI in Sinaloa used narcocorridos in their campaigns as a way of proselytizing. He requested a ban at the federal level on narcocorridos in electoral campaigns. Other calls for censorship also failed during the 1990s, including one by the director of the Michoacán Chamber of Radio and Television Industry (CIRT), Arturo Herrera Cornejo. With the support of Governor Lázaro Cárdenas Batel, Herrera Cornejo proposed a ban of narcocorridos in 1996, but the measure failed (Astorga 2005: 154).

Though narcocorridos were very popular in the north of Mexico in the 1990s, they became a common target of regulation after Fox took office in 2000. Fox's presidency, as part of the PAN party—probusiness, conservative, and right-wing—provided a better stage for these debates at the federal level, and in the early 2000s calls for censorship multiplied. The initiatives themselves came from members of different political parties. Only days after the beginning of Fox's term, in December 2000, the Chamber of Deputies, led by members of the PRI, was already proposing a law for the rights of youth that included the prohibition of damaging culture, including narcocorridos. The music genre was the only type of culture specified by the law. Three months later, in March 2001, Senator Yolanda Eugenia González Hernández (PRI) requested a study to understand the proliferation of narcocorridos and to suggest ways to restrict their circulation. Setting the bases for the way narcocorridos would be interpreted in future censorship processes, she argued that these songs are "apologies of crimes against health and other crimes that are part of the Federal Law against organized crime." In using the term *apology*, González Hernández referenced Article 63 of the Federal Law on Radio and Television (FLRT), which stated that any broadcasts "apologizing for violence or crime" were prohibited. Her proposal was approved.

In April of the same year, González Hernández presented to the Commission of Public Education and the Commission of Culture, Recreation and Sport of San Luis Potosí a resolution asking the secretary of government and the CIRT to prohibit the broadcasting of narcocorridos. This resolution defined narcoculture as "the subset of cultural elements, including material and immaterial (values, knowledge, language, norms of behavior, lifestyle, work-tools)" used by a community regarding narcotraffic. It also defines narcoculture as the result of a society that "has lost its values." In 2001, the most important type of narcoculture was "narcocorridos." Citing the FLRT, in particular Article 63, the resolution argues that the youth of this state were "induced" by the concepts central to these narratives, and in some cases these concepts become examples of behavior. The world they depict, the central concepts these legislators focused on, included "the world of familial allegiances, of escaping poverty, of the code of honor and the punishment to traitors."

Censorship has been discussed at the federal level, but it has actually occurred in states and cities affected heavily by the violence. Sinaloa, for instance, has prohibited the broadcasting and sale of narcocorridos, on and off, for roughly two decades. In March 2001, Sinaloa's CIRT voluntarily stopped the playing of the notorious genre. The same month, Sinaloa announced the ban of live performances of narcocorridos. Following Sinaloa's lead, politicians in Baja California, began calling for similar bans. San Luis Potosí's Senator Yolanda González Hernández justified these bans with the following comments: "Though we are absolutely convinced of the fundamental rights to freedom of expression, guaranteed by the sixth and seventh articles of our constitution, we also firmly believe that this freedom of ideas has certain limits in the case of attacks on morals, the rights of third parties, and provocations to crime or distress to the public" (González Hernández, quoted in Torres and Guarneros 2001). The same year, there were federal calls for the genre to be banned altogether, but the ones that succeeded were state-based initiatives. The new wave of bans is thus a continuation and an exacerbation of common and accepted state practice in Mexico. Although not without opposition, politicians in states affected by the violence have typically succeeded in making a case for censorship that calls attention to the supposed unusual power of the popular genre to, in the words of politicians, "incite violence," "make heroes out of narcos," spread "corrupt language," and in general incite "young people to lose interest in studying, work, and family values," so that they become "lured by easy money, depravity and vice."[4]

Between June 2001 and May 2007, different states' legislatures debated the censoring of narcocorridos; reached agreements to ask the secretary of government, the official who heads the General Direction of Radio, Television, and Cinematography (RTC), to apply Articles 63 and 64 of the FLRT to narcocorridos; and pressured state CIRTs to have their affiliates stop playing the controversial genre. These included Coahuila (December 2001), Chihuahua (debated in December 2001), Nuevo León (2002), Querétaro (June 2002), Guanajuato (2002), Durango (December 2002), Michoacán (June 2005), Oaxaca (May 2005), Chihuahua (approval of censorship in April 2011), Sinaloa (May 2011), and Sonora (December 2012).

The Commission of Communication and Transportation (CCT), in charge of regulating all federal communication technologies, recognized the problem of narcocorridos in a report in 2001 that detailed the commission's official position. Echoing almost every complaint about narcocorridos before and after the report, the document argued that narcocorridos are the concern of different social groups and that they are an "apology for the violence generated by organized crime" and "promote pseudo-values foreign to those aspired for society, in particular for kids and adolescents." Although the CCT is in charge of granting broadcasting licenses, it does not oversee the application of the FLRT, which is under the jurisdiction of RTC and the secretary of government.

In July 2009, the Director's Board of the CIRT (Cámara Nacional de la Industria de Radio y Televisión) stated that the RTC had registered sixty-three instances of "apologies for the violence, crime, vices, narco-traffic, and the corruption of the language" on different television and radio stations throughout the country in the past five months. The report added that from 2002 to 2009, the RTC had opened 134 administrative cases against broadcast stations.

The CIRT, an industry organization in charge of advising local and federal legislatures on matters related to broadcasting, is chartered by the state to regulate the industry in matters other than those under the FLRT. This may include regulating copyright, the rights of users and consumers, health communication, matters related to elections, and so on. It has a code of ethics that regulates issues of technology, practices related to journalism, social and representational equality, and rights of children. The code of ethics also has an entire section on how to cover violence, but nothing in particular about prior censorship of music or cultural work, even if violence is the reason for the policy. Regardless, at different times, state-level CIRTs have cooperated with state legislators, as in the case of Sinaloa and Michoacán, and city mayors, as in the case of Tijuana, BC, to ban narcocorridos from the radio in specific localities or states.

Although the majority of attempts to censor violent culture target the broadcasting of narcocorridos, procensorship law and policy makers have attempted other tactics to try to muzzle narcoculture in general. In 2005, Deputy José Francisco Landero Gutiérrez presented a proposal to the secretary of public education to eliminate from public school libraries any material that references narcocorridos. The resolution was tabled. The same year, Sinaloa's educational minister banned from school libraries the book *Cien corridos: Alma de la canción mexicana* for including lyrics to five narcocorridos (Wald 2001). In 2010, Deputy Óscar Martín Arce Paniagua (PAN) proposed a change to the criminal code and the Federal Law against

Organized Crime that would make performing narcocorridos, as well as displaying narcomantas (cloth banners containing threats or explanations by the cartels), a felony punishable with a hefty fine and six months to six years in jail. Arce Paniagua has repeatedly presented proposals with the goal of censoring communication forms, including some uses of social media that can be construed as apologies for organized crime. A modified version of the proposal was approved by the chamber's Commission of Justice in September 2011 (Justice in Mexico 2011). In 2012, the Sonoran legislature proposed to change policies governing the behavior of public servants, who would be forbidden from using public funds to reproduce any media, music, music videos, or performances at public events, festivals, and dances of music that could incite crime. It was not approved at the federal level.

In 2016, a music video by narcocorrido star Gerardo Ortiz was censored by the federal legislature for depicting crimes against women. The video included scenes in which a woman is tortured and then burned alive. The Senate approved this censorship measure on March 19, 2016, and to signal the seriousness with which the Mexican state was treating the censorship of his music video, Ortiz was briefly arrested after he arrived in Guadalajara. Last, beginning in October 2016, the presidents of Radio y Television of the Cámara de Diputados and the senate began a campaign against narcoseries for breaking Articles 223, 226, and 228 of FLRT. Narcoseries are telenovelas that center on drug and criminal activity; they are arguably the most successful television currently produced in Mexico. The articles referred to in the complaints were all about the protection of children, and the proposals called for moving narcoseries to air after midnight.

Social media have also been the target of a few harsh governmental restrictions. For instance, in August 2011 a judge in Veracruz sent two Twitter users to prison under the charge of terrorism. Although freed after twenty-nine days, Gilberto Martínez Vera and María de la Luz Bravo Pagola were prosecuted for posting to Twitter that different schools were under different threats (Miglierini 2011; Soberanes 2011). Echoing the zeal with which the Veracruz courts behaved, in October 2015 Martín Juárez Campos was detained and briefly jailed in Jalisco for claiming to be "M Juárez," the leader of the Cartel Jalisco Nueva Generación. He had used Facebook to stage his claims. Although the police were able to corroborate that his claims were false—that is, that he was not the leader of this cartel—Juárez Campos was prosecuted for being an "apologist of organized crime using social networks" (Martínez 2015). These instances do not have the same governmental coherence as calls for censorship against narcocorridos, but they have set the legal stage for future censorship of social media.[5]

The sheer multiplication of calls for censorship since the democratic opening of 2000, their regional proliferation, and the efforts by lawmakers and politicians to situate "narcoculture" and other communication technologies at the center of the fight against violence make censorship an important and even urgent object of study. Given this urgency, it is tempting to write about censorship descriptively, to recount and simply document what is going on in Mexico. But I believe that more can be gained by critically situating the calls for prohibition in a broader and deeper framework that would help us understand not simply current censorship, but the current and changing landscape of Mexican political culture. So, aware of the importance of the context surrounding each use of censorship, I continue the analysis below in terms of the overall goal of this book: to amplify the historical and philosophical range that we use to study contemporary violence and publicity. In that spirit, I engage the calls for censorship in Mexico in terms of the deep history of Mexico's political economy of symbolic order, including the influence of Roman censorial practices, Enlightenment republicanism, and colonial Inquisition practices in public debates on censoring narcoculture. The next section explores traces of these past principles of order in today's context. I argue that these traces of the past are particularly evident in Mexico's political culture and are strong evidence of the resurgence of Mexican republicanism in the new millennium. It is under the theoretical logic of this republicanism that the Mexican government defines the political task of publicity in the context of the current violence.

CENSORSHIP IN MEXICO

In the epigraph at the beginning of the chapter, the Congress of San Luis Potosí expressed concern about "a Narcoculture that penetrates deep in our nation's society, especially with Mexican children and youth." The concern is for the well-being of society, in particular society's most vulnerable members, and it assumes that this narcoculture, exemplified by narcocorridos, is likely to do some ideological and moral damage. In other words, the Congress of San Luis Potosí believed that it was its duty to protect its citizens from culture that could damage their civic lives and values. This way of understanding the role of the state in people's lives is republican at its core. Republicanism refers to normative ideas about the state and citizens that emphasize civic virtue and a contractual relation between the state and its citizens. Philip Pettit succinctly argues that this "republican position . . . sees the people as trustor, both individually and collectively, and sees the state as trustee" (1999: 8). Republican ideals have been part of human history for the last two millennia, and although they are not the only way of imagining politics—others include liberalism, fascism, libertarianism, and communism—republican ideals become particularly attractive in times of violence, insecurity, and heightened social vulnerability. This republicanism is what gives space to the censorial, even if the contractual character of republicanism makes it a political form potentially unfriendly to the authoritarianism of, for instance, the censoring ban. Authoritarianism would betray the trust needed for the social contract to remain balanced, yet the republican emphasis on civic virtue makes it potentially friendly to censorship's concerns with virtue and morality, and it is the lack of virtue or lack of morality that many blame for violence and illegality. This central ambiguity of republicanism, the authoritarianism of the censorial, has been constant since Classical Rome, during the Enlightenment, and in the present, and it has been part of Mexico's political history.

Madero's famous political republican axiom ("A good government can exist only when there are good citizens") follows a line of political thinking common in nineteenth-century Mexico.[6] The first decades after independence are often termed Mexico's first republicanism (1824–35), and the decades following the fall of Maximilian, in which the country was led by Benito Juárez (1861–72), are often called Mexico's liberal republicanism. Besides the macroperiodizations that hint at the grand principles behind federalism and independence, republicanism with a small r was part of the transformation of society at the granular level. The examples are many. Republican order and ideas were part of the ongoing process of suturing northern Mexico to the federal order. Republicanism was also a central theoretical trope among the growing number of educated Mexicans who saw the liberal republicanism of Mexico, imbued in the Atlantic world of revolution, as an example to European monarchies of the time, and who, as James Sanders (2011) argues, located Latin America's modernity as the future of Europe.[7] The values of republican order matched well with the way order was imagined during the Inquisition in that it helped organize politics, society, and culture in the New Spain until the end of the colony. While ideas about democratic participation and pluralist politics central to republicanism diminished during the decades following the Mexican Revolution (as they did with most other republicanisms), the era of Mexican authoritarianism relied heavily on ideas of traditional order and civic virtue and, as the twentieth century progressed, peaceful civic dissent.

With the democratic opening of 2000, republicanism quickly reclaimed center stage in Mexico's political culture, and perhaps nowhere is this clearer than in the Law of the Rights of Youth, which I referenced above. This law, which was introduced to the Chamber of Deputies by the PRI Deputy Jaime Cleofas Martínez Veloz, establishes a system of rights that is balanced by a system of duties. Article 2, which designates the orientation of the law, states:

The present law is oriented to:

I. Establish, guarantee, and promote the rights of youth;
II. Propitiate the integral development of youth, including educational, physical, sociological, social, and spiritual;
III. Establish their rights, the guaranteed defense of these rights, and the promotion of their interests;
IV. Determine the obligations that each young person has toward herself or himself, toward family, toward society, and toward the nation.

Contractual at its heart, this law balances rights with duties, which include duties toward the nation. The same law, in chapter 3, article 136, proposes: "Youth have the right to be protected against all situations that threaten their physical, moral, intellectual, or spiritual integrity, or that block or limit their wholesome development, including damaging public culture that foments alcohol and tobacco consumption, the broadcasting on television, radio, and other media of programs or images with highly sexual and violent content, and the dissemination of songs that apologize for anti-values, like those called 'narcocorridos.'" In this law, as in many instances of official republicanism, youth are given particular rights as a class, but they are also given particular responsibilities and duties. Just as important, youth are deemed vulnerable to psychological threats by bad culture that threatens their "wholesome development." Perhaps unsurprisingly under a presidency that began an offensive campaign to dismantle or at least weaken drug criminal organizations (DCOs), the law singled out narcocorridos as the best and clearest example of bad culture. This law is a textbook case of republicanism: it is contractual; establishes an expectation of civic virtue; and promotes censorship as a valid way of protecting (vulnerable) citizens. This law also highlights the political task of the public sphere and the need to regulate it.

These features of republicanism are not new or particularly modern, and examining their origins give us clues about the discursive traditions behind each of them. The twenty-first century may be far from classical antiquity, but it is not divorced from antiquity's love of force. And while the contingent character of Mexico's current challenges cannot be dismissed, solutions to current problems are not necessarily new. Solutions to the problems of massive social disorder and violence have included the use of republican principles and censorial governmental techniques and are thus projects of order that start at the symbolic level. Below I show that the history of these solutions to Mexico's violence at the level of public culture runs parallel to the history of the political task of publicity, and it is thus potentially useful to think about cases of publicity in and beyond Mexico.

The Authorial State

Madero's axiom may have been common in nineteenth-century Mexico, but it is actually much older. At least since Roman times, those in power have understood that social order depended on structuring a symbolic field, a culture in the modern sense, that would help citizens live orderly lives. Evidence of these ideas about the symbolic field are found in the shared root of the Latin verb *censeo*, to proclaim solemnly and with authority, and the noun *censor*, which refers to a magistrate during Roman times (Salazar 2004: 6). The Roman *censor* was tasked with helping administer farmland, collect taxes, and cultivate good morals. According to Emile Benveniste, the authority of the censor's words (*auctoritas*) connects to the "divine in principle" (cf. *augur*), of "causing to exist" ([1939] 1973: 423). The word *augeo* (authorship), like *cultivation* (as in culture as cultivation), connects the censor both to the authorial—the capacity to bring things into existence (*augur*)—and to the agrarian—as in the power to grow plants (*augere*). These connections to religious creation and arboreal growth make institutional authorship and culture as cultivation ideal centerpieces in agrarian and traditional political discursive systems and are used in mostly republican systems of concepts and political metaphors that normalize an idealized vision of order and politics.

In Classical Rome (from the Empire to the Republic), the *censor* achieved his goals by performing several key functions, which have remained central to republicanism all the way to the modern state. The *censor* made a roll of the citizens (a function replicated by contemporary census practices); he evaluated the private wealth of each citizen and assigned them classes (a function replicated in the first article of the US Constitution, which both creates the census and does so for taxation purposes); he recruited the Senate, hence he constituted the representative side of the Roman government; he supervised the morals of the citizens and was thus an arbiter of morality; and he allocated contracts of public works and helped in the regulation of farming contracts. The censor hence fixed citizens to their proper place in society, while helping regulate a property regime that was key to the taxation strategies of the Roman kingdom and, later, the Republic.[8] Importantly, giving fixity to citizens was not simply about economics, but also about the social life of Rome, its morals, and the cultivation of the proper behaviors for politics.[9]

If the noun *censor* relates to tasks assigned to a magistrate, the verb *censeo* designates an act of solemn judgment or speech. Benveniste starts his chapter on the subject with these startling and rich sentences: "If the Roman magistrate with specifically normative functions is called *censor* and if the senators whom he enrolls formally register their authoritative opinion by saying '*censeo*,' this is because the Indo-European **kens-* strictly meant 'to affirm a truth (which becomes law) with authority.' This authority—*auctoritas*—with which a man must be invested for his utterances to have the force of law is not, as is often stated, the power of promoting growth (*augere*), but the force (Skt. *ojaḥ*), divine in principle (cf. *augur*), of 'causing to exist'" ([1939] 1973). *Censeo* is at the epicenter of a republican political discourse connecting the bureaucratic and administrative roles of the magistrate to the political and economic needs of the Republic. As discussed in note 9, however, this political discourse becomes even more powerful. Benveniste shows *censeo* connected to authoritative speech, judgments that can become law and that can bring things into existence, as if these judgments and their speakers were touched by the divine. *Censeo* hence points toward the authorial capacity of the state, the capacity to bring moral citizens into existence, and it is through this authorial capacity that someone like Madero, a modern political thinker, can expect to fulfill the political desire of having a good government. If this was not enough, the authorial capacity of the state also irons out the republican contradiction of authoritarian censorship, which informs the Law of the Rights of Youth. The power of the censor is productive, generative: it is not totalitarian.

Although old in its origins, this authorial capacity of the state is not some abstract principle behind the contemporary censoring of narcocorridos. This authorial capacity is clearly manifested in two ways. First, it is the metaphoric base of the theory of culture behind the censorial, one that connects culture to cultivation. Just as John Durham Peters points out for broadcasting, culture as cultivation adopts an agricultural metaphor to describe culture. To cultivate is both to grow and to trim; to nurture and to weed out; to allow passage and to stop; to let free and to prohibit. Censoring is thus part of cultivation. It is also this notion of culture as cultivation that connects back to authorship, authority, and *augeo*: the creative capacity that Benveniste defines as the power to make plants grow, but also the power of laws to bring something into existence ([1939] 1973: 423). Culture as cultivation is part of the conceptual tree in which states are imagined as having the capacity and duty to author citizens.

Second, the authorial capacity of the state is manifested in practically every contemporary call for censorship in Mexico, particularly among lawmakers. It is expressed in different ways. In an interview in 2007, Deputy Jorge Zermeño Infante, a leader of the Fifteenth Legislature in Mexico, referred to the issue of the authorial capacity of the state in paternalistic ways. To a question regarding an attack likely sponsored by drug cartels, Zermeño Infante responded that "public safety is an issue that involves all of us as parents, the media, the churches, schools, teachers. Together we generate a better culture of respecting the rights of others, the life of others." He added that public safety is "not simply about repression, persecution, jailing felons, or giving felons the harshest sentences." It is about generating "a culture of values." One may rephrase this to point out that the censorial is not simply about trimming—it is also about fertilizing and growing. He finishes by reminding the interviewers that the media play a relevant role and at times apologize for crime through the broadcasting of narcocorridos or narcofilms.[10] Deputy Irineo Mendoza Mendoza requested regulations in 2008 that would compel radio and television broadcasters to issue warnings before they played narcocorrido music or music videos, as well as to restrict the times at which they were broadcast. In this request, Mendoza spoke about regulation as a moral necessity. He argued that it was troublesome that something that should be regulated was instead a source of ratings for radio broadcasters and sales for the music industry. He continued by declaring that it is the responsibility of the federal government, which controls radio stations and music sales, to regulate.[11]

The words of these Mexican legislators are not unusual. They represent a powerful orthodoxy in Mexico that believes, like the Romans did, that the generative power of the censorship is the proper governmental technique for authoring good citizens. It is through the proper cultivation of the symbolic order that the state can hope to harvest the political outcome of good government. Clues as to the principles of the censorial and their application in Mexico can be found in the critical history connecting Roman republicanism to the Enlightenment, the Inquisition in New Spain, and independent Mexico. Below I show that the principles of the censorial in these different historical periods were not simply empty political values. They were part of the state's legal and regulatory apparatus in charge of regulating the symbolic order.

COUNTERTHEORIZING CENSORSHIP AND PUBLICITY

From Rome to the present, the genealogy of censorship historically bifurcated in the sixteenth century, the time of the colonization of the Americas, Reformation, and the printing press. In some cases, mostly in northern Europe and England, censorship became part of the republican imagination that would engender the Enlightenment. Reformation, after all, needed to be argued as something other than heresy, and the censoring tool needed to change to fit the new political and legal environment. In other cases, particularly in the kingdoms of Castile and Aragon, which dominated the Iberian Peninsula, censorship became a tool for state and religious coercion. This bifurcation in the uses of censorship originated in Europe but deeply affected the New World: while the thirteen British American colonies were ruled by an empire gradually moving from a relatively weak absolutism— the Magna Carta of 1215 had already reduced the power of the monarchy— toward parliamentary democracy, New Spain was dominated by a state in which absolutism grew stronger from the fifteenth to the eighteenth centuries (Cañeque 2004: 5). This does not mean that New Spain, as a stage for political ideas and theories, was totally different from the British colonies or from Europe. Books and broadsheets traveled and influenced New Spain's urban centers. However, the growth of absolutism does mean that New Spain and, later, independent Mexico had a distinctive political history in their connection to republicanism, particularly as it pertains to the censorial character of the state. Mexico's engagement with censorship is the product of these two traditions: the republicanism of the Enlightenment, and the centuries of the Inquisition, which aimed to shape the moral life of the colony and left a deep imprint on what would eventually become Mexican political culture.

The bifurcation in the uses of censorship in the body politic is related to the rise of the absolutist state, the political formation that gave precedent to the modern nation-state. It is also in the absolutist state that we find first evidence of new republican uses of censorship that would depend on the boundary between the private and the public. This new republicanism arises in part because of new communication technologies and in part because of violence. The transition from feudal societies ruled by kings and the church to modern secular states that, first in England and later in Europe and North America, were partly energized by the discursive proliferation brought about by the printing press. In most of Europe, this new discursive paradigm, rich, complex, and plural, fueled religious wars that ravaged the British Isles and the Continent from the mid-sixteenth century onward. In England first, the result of these wars was a new understanding of the state as a secular political institution independent from the Church. As shown in the work of Hobbes, understanding the state as above the Church could be possible only if the power of the state was deemed absolute, so his Leviathan is a properly monstrous metaphor of absolute sovereignty. "The princely State," Reinhart Koselleck argues, "supported by the military and the bureaucracy, developed a supra-religious, rationalistic field of action which, unlike its other aspects, was defined by the policies of the State" (1988: 16). Caught between religious morality and the expanded power of the sovereign, individuals had few choices. "A State order—in so far as it is secured from above—can only exist if the plurality of parties and individuals also finds itself in a morality that accepts the ruler's absolute political sovereignty as a moral necessity" (Koselleck 1988: 31). In the absolutist state, public actions were absolutely subject to state priorities. Privacy, on the other hand, was a sphere of relative freedom. Koselleck continues: "Hobbes's man is fractured, split into private and public halves: his actions are totally subject to the law of the land while his mind remains free, 'in secret free'" (37). This split between private freedom and public subjection gives rise to three things: first, the bourgeois understanding of a free public sphere, which I address in the next chapter; second, the rise of public anonymity as a political value, which I address in chapter 5; and third, a new type of censorship and *censura* articulated in the word *criticism*.

Enlightenment forms of republicanism, such as those of John Locke and Jean-Jacques Rousseau, present censorship as a legitimate need of contractual societies. Locke points to the direction that the new understanding of censorship would work in these discourse-rich societies, particularly as they were transitioning, again, from absolutist states toward modern nation-states (1670). In his *Essay concerning Human Understanding*, Locke identifies a new type of law governing the social. Sometimes called "The Philosophical Law of the Measure of Virtue and Vice," or "The Law of Opinion or Reputation," or the "Law of Private Censure," this law was anchored on the realm of consciousness and asserted that thought remained private and free from state intervention under the absolutist imagination ([1689] 1764: 10–13). The citizens retained the power to pass judgment and used this power to construct, through processes of social consent, ideas about vice and virtue that could hinder or aid a person's reputation. Unlike the laws of the state, which are punished with physical and material coercion, the law of public censure works through pressure in the form of public praise and blame, which would determine an individual's social and even political standing. On this, Koselleck writes: "Civic morality becomes a public power, one that works only intellectually but which has political effects, forcing the citizen to adapt his actions not just to State law but simultaneously, and principally, to the law of public opinion" (1988: 59–60). Contrary to Habermasian publicity, which is a central expression of nascent liberalism, in Locke and Koselleck public censure is a regulatory technique that helps discipline individuals to behave in proper ways.

Rousseau discussed censorship early in his trajectory as a political philosopher, in particular in his *Letter to D'Alembert* ([1758] 1889). In this letter he argues that it is a legitimate measure to control science, art, and literature and the dangerous tendency of these fields of expression to disregard their role in shaping morality and politics (Day 1997; D. Porter 1995: 108). This position may seem surprising when we consider that Rousseau himself was subjected to brutal censorship and persecution, but it is consistent with his contractual and republican view of politics and the individual. In what some (chiefly Louis Althusser) consider an early use of the notion of hegemony, Rousseau blames the sciences, literature, and the arts for participating in humanity's seduction, in helping hide the "chains that weigh men down." This seduction happened through different means, but Rousseau seems more concerned with those relying on aesthetics, in particular the theater, and the genres of tragedy and comedy. His views on the matter echoed those of Plato, but his understanding of the power of the theater was more in tune with contemporary cultural theory. As Patrick Day notes, Rousseau did not believe that tragedy or comedy offered useful moral lessons to the audience. "On the contrary, Rousseau believed that state representations . . . inspired only the semblance of sympathy and identification between the audience and the actors on stage . . . and that the spectators felt that they had fulfilled their moral responsibility simply by having seen immoral actors portrayed by actors on the stage" (Day 1997: 144). Rousseau ([1758] 1889: 44, 52, 60, 64), skeptical of most redeeming qualities of these popular genres, repeatedly noted different censurable elements of the comedies of Molière, in particular *The Misanthrope*. In a manner closely resembling contemporary Mexican debates on narcocorridos, which center on the effects on audiences, Rousseau writes: "Public entertainments are made for the people, and it is only by their effects on them that we can determine their absolute qualities" (1759: 13). When their effects are negative, "we [had] better renounce such kind of entertainment" (13 n. a). Matters of morality, however, are "not regulated like those of particular justice and strict right, by laws and edict" (84). Like Locke, Rousseau understood that shaping manners and morality would have to be through public opinion: "Nothing appears good or desirable to private people, but what the public has judged [as] such" (85). Insofar as public opinion is entrusted with the shaping of morality and civic life, it is given a political task central to republicanism; yet insofar as it is the citizens, not state actors, who are the censoring agents, this enlightened republicanism marks a departure not only from Roman practices but also from the common practices of the ancien régime.

These influential political philosophers had no problem prioritizing the well-being of the body politic over people's individual expressive freedoms, and in the public sphere they saw possibilities seldom accounted for by contemporary public sphere scholars. Public culture could foment civic life, but it could just as easily erode it and thus needed to be kept in check. The mechanism to check public culture was public opinion (or public censure, as Locke called it), a form of social criticism that horizontally targeted other citizens and their public expressions and that had the power to censor them. This was not simply a process of expressive Darwinism, which would guarantee that the best opinions and expressions rose to the top, but a more effective means of censorship. Rousseau, for instance, spends several pages trying to figure out the best way for the state to use public opinion. In his *Letter*, the use of public opinion is not simply about empowering citizens to use their critical capacities for the well-being of the state. It is about finding the best state processes to manipulate opinion (1758: 85–95). This is truly far from what Habermas and others would see as publicity during the Enlightenment—quite different from the salons and cafes in which social criticism emerged as a force for liberalism. Locke and Rousseau espoused a form of publicity that could be used to govern better. They believed that the political task of publicity was the reason for the existence of the public realm. This political task would later be part of what Michel Foucault calls modern governmentality, understood as social techniques that help individuals interiorize juridical culture, crafting law-abiding citizens entrusted with monitoring each other (in a panopticon) and using public culture to regulate the social.

The lessons distilled from Rousseau's concerns about freedom and public opinion are also lessons about how to govern complex societies. On the issue of freedom, Mexicans have no problem arguing that freedom has its limits. Repeatedly, state officials have embraced a pragmatic vision of freedom that sees the good of society as freedom's natural boundary. For instance, the most common censorship measure in Mexico occurs when state officials convince or pressure specific broadcasters or a state's Cámara de la Industria de Radio y Televisión (CIRT)—the Mexican equivalent of the US Federal Communications Commission—to "voluntarily" stop the playing of certain genres. In 2002, for instance, Arturo Herrera, president of Michoacán's CIRT, proposed banning narcocorridos and declared in perhaps paradoxical fashion: "Esto no representa de ninguna manera una actitud de prohibición, ni una actitud en contra de los autores de este tipo de melodías, sino que simplemente es un ejercicio de autorregulación" (This does not represent an attitude of prohibiting, nor an attitude to suppress the authors of these melodies. This simply is an exercise of self-regulation) (qtd. in *La Jornada* 2002). Here self-regulation is used as a virtuous practice, for it considers first the well-being of the citizenry, even if the rights of authors and performers are trampled in the process. In 2012, Luis Alfonso Leal Valenzuela, the person in charge of the legal processes of Sinaloa's State Commission on Human Rights, published a report about music in which he addresses music as a human right but also argued that narcocorrido composers and singers do not have the right to express themselves, because the music is harmful to others: "The enjoyment of music, as any other exercise of a right, involves the obligation to not affect others. For instance, if we enjoy listening to music too loud[ly] and we live in a condo, it is likely that we will disturb the right of peace and quiet of others. We cannot lose sight that the exercise of a right cannot damage the right of others" (Leal Valenzuela 2012, 26). In April 2011 Deputy Boone Salmón (PRI) presented a formal request to the legislature of Chihuahua to ask people and organizations involved in the diffusion of narcocorridos to stop. He argued that the way to secure our personal freedom is to use it responsibly. Freedom here is republican, not liberal.

Republican freedom is freedom with a small *f*, but people accept it and even defend it because of the contractual promise of republicanism. In exchange, the state is committed to the well-being of society and acts as trustee of the social contract, and according to this contract, state actions have to be performed in the name of pastoralism or paternalism. Like a shepherd taking care of its sheep, or a father taking care of his children, the state can justify almost anything, including censorship, based on the necessity to protect. This type of statecraft has been the norm in cases of state-sponsored censorship of narcoculture. Even though the banning of music may fall within the realm of authoritarian state actions, the performance of pastoralism makes it hard to argue that censorship is simply authoritarian.

The rhetoric used in these performances attempts to define censorial actions as a way of caring for citizens, particularly for the well-being of children and youth. For instance, when in 2001 the San Luis Potosí legislature debated narcocorridos, legislators argued that narcocorridos transgress the prohibition stipulated in Article 63 of the FLRT, that narcocorridos were an apology for crime, and, as importantly, that these songs induced youth and children to follow the narcotraffickers' example.[12] Similarly, in 2005 the Official Diary of the Michoacán Legislature presented an argument describing the "counterculture of the narco-traffic," especially narcocorridos, as constituting the life models and goals of children and youth. The concern again is the shaping of young people's minds, their values and aspirations. In 2008, in the petition referenced above, Mendoza also argued that the narcocorridos are a threat to both public safety and public health, in particular for minors, who receive from the music a false idea of what reality is. "For that reason," he continues, "I believe that these songs must be regulated, because in these songs the felon is treated as a reason for national pride, when in reality they are the scourge of society."[13] In 2011, Deputy Boone Salmón (PRI) added a new twist to this pastoralism. He argued that the censorship measure he requested was necessary in the fight to protect children and youth from a culture that normalizes the values of the drug trade, which include the pursuit of "easy money," overconsumption, and fashion. Narcocorridos exalt the deeds of narcos "who become heroes or people that youth want to imitate." However, expanding on his pastoral argument, he added that he was particularly concerned with people living in poverty and in communities with little access to education or employment.[14] From a pastoral perspective, legislators have also argued about the connection of narcocorridos to actual crime. In these statements, "narcoculture is a tangible reality; they tell stories about actual traffickers."[15] In 2010, Deputy Arce Paniagua (PAN) started his proposal to change the penal code with an anecdote about Víctor J. Serrano Galván, nicknamed The G-1, who in his confession narrated how he always wanted to be part of organized crime, "because he loved the corridos and when he listened to them he always dreamt of someone composing a narcocorrido for him."[16] Or lawmakers may remind us that narcocorrido singers have been killed by narcos, as when Mendoza mentioned the killings of Chalino Sánchez, Valentín Elizalde, and, recently, Sergio Gómez.[17]

In these cases, censorship of narcocorridos is meant to shove crime and criminals away from the weak.

In the case of narcocorridos, elements of pastoral and republican state-craft are also at play when Mexican lawmakers claim that their actions are in response to public opinion. Taking care of the public here means caring for their opinions, and public polls can function as evidence of the trustor and trustee's proper relationship. It is thus in the state's interests to understand and use public opinion polls on controversial issues such as censorship. The Mexican Chamber of Deputies has an office in charge of polling and gathering public opinion: the Social Studies and Public Opinion Research Center (CESOP, in Spanish). In June 2011, at the Chamber's request, CESOP released a report titled *Tendencias predominantes*, which supplies and discusses polling data about whether narcocorridos should be censored. The results, widely distributed among news organizations, show a majority of Mexicans in favor of censorship. According to the polls, 70 percent of those polled agreed with the censorship of narcocorridos in bars and dance clubs. Fifty-two percent opined that censorship was appropriate because the music promoted sympathy for narcotraffickers and their activities. Thirty-nine percent, however, believed that the music should not be censored because it was a popular expression of the reality that Mexicans have to know (CESOP 2011: 19). The majority of those polled (58 percent) believed that prohibiting narcocorridos contributed, at least a little, to the fight against narcotrafficking and organized crime (CESOP 2011: 20). In the spirit of a shared pastoralism between the state and those who were polled, CESOP asked about the vulnerability of the children. Fifty-seven percent of those polled believed that narcocorridos could set a bad example for children and youth. A majority almost as large (55 percent) believed that the narcocorrido is not a genuine expression of popular culture. By contrast, two-thirds believed that traditional corridos were indeed genuine popular culture (CESOP 2011: 21). Although 32 percent believed that narcocorridos should not be prohibited because censorship trampled over the principle of freedom of expression, a full 60 percent believed that narcocorridos should be prohibited because they "attack life and the respect for the law" (CESOP 2011: 21). Requesting this polling and sharing it widely with news organizations has allowed lawmakers to move the issue of censorship within the discourses of pastoralism and republicanism. These numbers show that on this issue, a majority of Mexicans placed republican expectations on the state and accepted censorship as a proper way of caring for their vulnerable populations. Finally, this poll also shows that, when reflecting on violent culture, most people embraced a theory of culture in the agricultural sense, as cultivation, and believed that narcocorridos had at least some negative effects on people's minds and values.

The rhetoric of pastoralism and the relevance of public polls are two contemporary manifestations of Enlightenment republicanism's concern with public opinion as governmentality. This new republicanism promised to sidestep the problem of authoritarianism by harnessing the horizontal power of vox populi, the voice of the people. As Rousseau theorized, this voice could be manipulated, and pastoralism does that. Vox populi can also be referenced as a source of state behavior, as when lawmakers justify legal measures based on polls. Yet this concern with public opinion in the seventeenth and eighteenth centuries had different weight in different contexts. In England and Holland, which moved relatively quickly from absolutism to modern nation-states, the Lockean law of private censure was part of the nascent and influential public sphere and helped constitute a social realm independent from the state, one that left an enduring mark on liberalism (Koselleck 1988: 53; Pagden 2003). Even if the political task of public opinion was to censure, adapting Habermas's original phrasing, the fact that the agents of censorship were regular citizens meant that public opinion, however republican in spirit, could be repackaged within liberalism as an exercise of personal public freedom. Already in Locke's work, the Latin word *censura* was becoming "criticism" and publicness, the nonviolent and orderly process of using communication to criticize the state or society. In this context, *censura* could be transformed into a tool for liberalism, and it is this *censura* that Habermas privileges when reflecting on publicness. From the perspective of the citizenry, the optic Habermas and most public sphere theorists prefer, the value of *censura* is attached to liberalism and the power of individuals to freely engage in criticism. From the perspective of the state or the power structure, *censura* owes its value to the republican ideal of crafting citizens engaged in orderly communication. From the perspective of the citizenry, the opposite of *censura* is privacy or selfishness. From the perspective of the state, the opposite of *censura* is violence.

REPUBLICANISM IN MEXICO

The specter of violence has cast a different shadow in different contexts. In its sixth article, the Mexican Constitution of 1917, the one in force today, establishes freedom of ideas and reads: "No judicial or administrative inquisition can be imposed on the manifestation of ideas, unless these ideas are an attack on morals, harm third parties, incite a crime, or disrupt public order; the right to information is guaranteed by the State."[18] This law quite openly establishes both the rights of freedom of expression and the legal ground for "inquisition," which in the Mexican Constitution is synonymous with censorship. This word is intimately connected to the term *inquest*, or a juridical investigation. However, words are contextual, and, in the legal and political culture of Mexico—which was inherited from Spain, where the Inquisition was abused for centuries—the word's first connotation became the prohibition, a technique central to the shaping of moral and religious behavior.

The ideas of enlightened republicanism did not enter Mexico following the same path as in northern Europe and the thirteen British colonies. In the absolutist empire that was the Iberian Peninsula and the Spanish colonies, the Inquisition dictated the connections to Enlightenment ideas, authors, and changing social mores. In the partnership of Castile and Aragon, *censura* became the Inquisition, the legal and religious tool that the kingdoms used to address, first, religious and social plurality and, later, social and political dissidence.

Yet even the Inquisition had to reckon with the changing social, cultural, and technological world of the time. Over the course of the seventeenth and eighteenth centuries, the cultural and communicational world of New Spain transformed. Although the press was chiefly controlled by the monarchy and their New World representatives, the printing world had expanded, and networks of information that used the increasingly important colonial postal service allowed residents of New Spain to share letters, manuscripts, and publications (Guerra 1992: 26). By the second half of the eighteenth century, it was common to find public lectures, even if these happened in private homes. The Enlightenment in New Spain was a public event, a source of conversation and opinion. According to Gabriel Torres Puga, the very term *public opinion* came to New Spain through Almodovar's translation of Guillaume-Thomas Raynal's *Historia filosófica y política de los establecimientos y el comercio de los europeos en las Indias Occidentales y Orientales*, a classic work written by Raynal in collaboration with other Enlightenment thinkers of the time, including Diderot, who is credited with having written a third of this famous book (Torres Puga 2010: 531).

In these centuries, thus, New Spain was experiencing both the rise of public opinion and the appearance of the Habermasian public sphere, even if the contours were quite different from northern Europe's public spheres. After all, Spain's Enlightenment, and by extension New Spain's, was shaped by the absolutist character of Spanish colonialism of the Americas, so the

Enlightenment itself was late and partial (Ciaramitaro and Souto 2012: 188). Public opinion, particularly opinion critical of the state, was relegated to private spaces, as was common in other absolutist contexts. Public culture, such as the theater, was subject to censorship or, if you prefer, prior restraint. As late as the early nineteenth century, in New Spain, the owner of a theater needed to present a list of works to be staged during the month to a "judge of the theatre," who was nominated by the viceroy, to make sure the text would not be harmful to the state or the Church (Koeninger 2014: 129). In Spain and New Spain, in response to the growing popularity of political broadsheets originating in France and republished in Spain, the Crown reactivated a rule from 1752 that forced publishers to request a license to publish any text (Soberón Mora 2014: 41). The Church continued publishing edicts prohibiting specific books, which throughout the eighteenth century included books written by Enlightenment philosophers. *Censura* thus had a second meaning throughout the Colonial Enlightenment: that of the Inquisition. The Enlightenment of Spanish Colonial America was thus a complex mix of absolutist political culture and Enlightenment ideas that nonetheless gave way to dramatic social changes, as evinced by the fact that, by 1810, the majority of Spanish America was in revolution. Social antistate criticism existed; publicity was effective, even if it was fragmented and relatively slow to take root.

Censorship in Mexican Law and Media Regulation

The European bifurcation of censorship in the sixteenth century that separated the Enlightenment republicanism from the Inquisition was reconnected in Mexico after its independence, as one can see in the complex way censorship has been carried out throughout the last couple of centuries. This is clear when analyzing the tensions on the regulatory and legal frameworks in charge of crafting Mexican symbolic and cultural fields. Mexican law and media regulation have defined freedom of the press and, later, freedom of ideas (expression) and broadcasting as contingent freedoms, freedoms limited by moral, nationalistic, and security issues. They have evolved to this point pulled forward by the force of republicanism, the moral principles of the Inquisition, and a much less sure-footed liberalism.

Mexico's first constitution was approved in 1824, but it had direct connections with Spain's new and radical Constitution of Cádiz of 1812, the first Spanish constitution showing the effects of the Enlightenment. Cádiz defined "freedom of the press as a limited freedom," to be taken away if the material printed threatened the state, the monarchy, or the social peace. It also proscribed satire, obscenity, immorality, and libel. Mexico's War of Independence had begun two years prior, but in 1812 Cádiz was the law in the nonindependent areas of Mexico, including Mexico City. This opening of freedom of the press precipitated the printing of politically radical materials, which likely shaped the remaining years of the war (Sordo Cedeño 2012: 133–34). Opposing Cádiz and embracing a liberal perspective, Mexico's Constitution of 1824 addressed freedom of the press in three articles. Article 50 established the protection of the press, but defined this freedom as political. Article 161 gave each state the obligation to protect freedom of the press. Article 171 makes freedom of press an aspect of the constitution not subject to modification. This is the only Mexican constitution in which freedom of the press is clearly liberal. It lasted less than two decades. In 1843, Mexico passed a second constitution, commonly called the Organic Basis, which was republican, pro-Church, and centralist. In this document, freedom of the press was greatly reduced. Article 196 stated: "A law will determine the cases of abuse of freedom of the press, and it will designate the punishment and trial, not pointing to abuses other than the following: against religion; against morality and proper conduct; provocation of sedition and disobedience toward authorities; attacks to the independence and form of the government that establishes this basis; and when a public functionary is slandered."

Echoing the Constitution of Cádiz, the Organic Basis established clear boundaries to freedom and morality as its central goal. Like the constitution that preceded it, the Organic Basis did not last; after a war against the dictatorship of General Antonio López de Santa Ana, President Ignacio Comonfort passed the Constitution of 1857. In this document, which remained valid until 1917, freedom of the press was again crafted following Cádiz. Article 7 established freedom of the press and the illegality of prior restraint or coercion, but it also stated the limits of this freedom, which included "respect of privacy, morality, and public peace." This article served as a basis for the Constitution of 1917, mentioned above, which forbids "judicial or administration inquisition" unless "these ideas are an attack on morals, harm third parties, incite a crime, or disrupt public order." In contemporary Mexico, this constitution makes clear, expression, culture, and information can be banned if they are immoral, harm third parties, promote crime, or threaten the harmony of society, which is safeguarded by the state. Hence, a threat to the state is also a threat to society's harmony. Similar to the US tradition, in which the state legitimately prohibited and punished obscenity, libel, and sedition up through the early twentieth century and still polices the individual states' powers to safeguard citizens' health and morality, the

Mexican tradition counterposes a system of rights to a system of prohibitions, highlighting the contractual nature of state-citizen relations. However, unlike the more liberal US Constitution, Mexico's 1917 Constitution is still concerned with morality and the crafting of a culture that promotes legal behavior and opposes criminality. It is thus a legal document concerned not only with citizens' nationalistic lives but also with their souls.

This series of Mexican constitutions shows that morality remained central to Mexico's republicanism all the way to the twentieth century, and even though secularism has marked Mexico's political culture since the liberal government of Benito Juárez, the concern with morality makes evident the ongoing influence of the Church and the spirit of the Inquisition in Mexico. This is not to say that the Inquisition lives in today's Mexico, but that Mexico's particular kind of republicanism is informed by certain theories of public life in the colonial period, including the notion that the role of the state is to shape the moral life of its citizens. The state creates the citizen, and the material that the state shapes is partly the citizens' morality. The tools to do the shaping, of course, include public culture, and during the twentieth century this meant constituting a regulatory system that would guide mass media, particularly film, radio, and television, in their established roles as agents of morality.

These new communication technologies, starting with film, were quite complex, socially influential, ideologically powerful, and economically profitable. Given that at the end of the nineteenth century, the moment when film was first introduced to Mexican society, literacy reached only 15 percent, film, and later radio and television, had the potential to reach populations previously unreachable by the news, the broadsheet, or literature. This created the necessity to have specialized forms of regulation, and over time the state developed specialized legal and policy frameworks to regulate these media. In 1911, during the Mexican Revolution, the city of Guadalajara prohibited "immoral films," including those showing thievery, for fear that people would emulate them (Peredo Castro 2015: 65). In 1913 Mexico passed the first federal law on film censorship, which was designed both to protect the image of the police and the courts and to stop the circulation of films denigrating Mexico or its Revolution (e.g., Enrique Rosas's *The Grey Automobile* in 1919) (Mercader 2009: 201). A second censorship law in 1919, called the Reglamento de Censura Cinematográfica (Cinematographic Censorship Law), was aimed at protecting the public image of the Revolution, the nation, and at shaping the moral life of Mexicans (e.g., Juan Bustillo Oro's *Nun and Married, Virgin and Martyr* in 1935).

Issues of politics continued to be important to Mexican censors, but the bulk of their efforts were directed toward the protection of the moral life of Mexicans, particularly from depictions of crime and sexuality. In the 1930s and 1940s, for instance, the Union of Mexican Catholics and the Mexican League of Decency would publish weekly bulletins about films that needed to be censored due to immorality (Peredo Castro 2015: 71). In the 1930s, these organizations adapted the 1930 US Hays Code and used it as a model for a Mexican Production Code that would regulate moral behavior in film (Zermeño Padilla 1997: 88–99). The code would regulate depictions of sexuality, crime, blood sports, homosexuality, and social conflict. A truly conservative cultural primer, the Mexican Production Code never became a central part of the Mexican film industry as the Hays Code did in the United States, but it gave censorial guidelines to these organizations and shaped production and film exhibition in Mexico.

These censorial practices and the influence of conservative civil society organizations continued to be strong throughout the 1950s and throughout the rise of Mexican counterculture. These media regulations often targeted the new musical genre of rock 'n' roll and its use in film. In 1957, the Department of Interior Affairs created a film censorship board in charge of identifying foreign and Mexican films that could endanger the moral lives of Mexicans in general and youth in particular (Zolov 1999: 55). Nudity, violence, crime, and immorality, the themes that would later characterize narco-cinema, would be forbidden.

The concerns in the 1950s for radio, the broadcasting medium more commonly censored because of narcocorridos, were slightly different than those for film. Efforts to control, contain, and censor radio were spurred by what was perceived as a crisis of values, an argument that conservative and patriarchal forces also used to organize themselves against the increasingly immoral tone of mass culture, including print, comics, film, and broadcasting. Depictions of violence and crime were central to these efforts. In fact, the catalyst for the creation of specific and limiting guidelines for radio and television broadcasting was a cultural text not too different in some ways from those limiting the narcocorridos. The catalyst was Elvis's 1958 *King Creole*, which was seen as an apology for criminal behavior that had the potential to increase crime and homicides in Mexico (Zolov 1999: 58). The debate over this film (and its music) resulted in the 1960 Federal Law of Radio and Television, a policy primer sponsored by President Adolfo López Mateos and easily passed by Congress. The fifth article of this law, which still regulates Mexican broadcasting to this day and is the legal basis for the censoring of narcocorridos, states:

> Radio and television have the social function of contributing to the strengthening of the nation and the improvement of forms of human coexistence. To this effect, its broadcasts will have the following goals:
>
> I. To affirm the respect for social morality, human dignity, and family ties;
> II. To avoid harmful or disturbing influences in the harmonic development of children and youth;
> III. To contribute to the cultural uplift of the people and to the conservation of its national characteristics, its customs, the proper use of the language, and the exaltation of the values inherent to Mexican identity;
> IV. To strengthen democratic convictions, national unity and friendship and international cooperation.[19]

Following the republican spirit of the 1917 Constitution, this 1960 broadcasting law established freedom of expression and the prohibition of prior censorship (Article 58), yet also created a primer for prior restraint and censorship. Article 63 forbids broadcasts "that corrupt language and [are] against good morals, either through malicious expressions, words, images, phrases, and scenes with a double meaning, *that are apologists to violence or crime*; forbidden too is everything that denigrates or is offensive [to] the civil respect for heroes, religious beliefs, or is racially discriminatory" (Ley Federal de Radio y Televisión 1960: 16, emphasis mine).

There is something particularly censorial, in the Roman sense, to the instituting of these Mexican broadcasting laws: that is, most of the censoring elements would be at home in Classical Rome. President López Mateos, the censor-in-chief, took note and franchised the concerns of some citizens; he evaluated citizens' private wealth and assigned them classes, differentiating between citizens who embodied the principles of the Republic, which in this case were the wealthy, educated, and conservative elites shaping civil society and the moral panic about the counterculture; he organized the political class to share his views and those of the franchised citizens; he made himself an arbiter of morality; and he constituted the policy tools that would allocate broadcasting resources to some, including the already influential Televisa, which controlled some of the most important Mexican music stars of the time, whose careers would benefit from these state policies. In short, the censor-in-chief made solemn proclamations about the role of bad culture in the moral life of Mexicans while simultaneously protecting the economic interests of the Mexican cultural and economic elites. These are not coincidental continuities, but evidence of the deep impact of Rome and the Spanish colonial legacy in contemporary republican forms of government, including Mexico's.

As I showed above, current calls for different types of censorship on narcoculture follow this pattern of concern for morality. This is why the San Luis Potosí legislature can argue that "narcoculture is evidence of a society that has lost its values. This culture 'denigrates' the good morals of Mexican society. The world depicted by narcoculture is the world of 'familiar allegiances, of escaping poverty, of the honor code and the punishment to traitors.'"[20] In practically every instance of procensorship argumentation, lawmakers establish that the material substance that the state would use to author Madero's good citizen was the moral core. Echoing Koselleck's assessment of absolutism, in Mexico morality becomes public morality, the central pillar of civic behavior, and the most characteristic element of the particularly Mexican republicanism that the drug violence has energized.

CONCLUSION

Censorship is one example of an orderly practice at home in the republican idea of the citizen—a fixed citizen, anchored on land, property, values, and the delicious and tiny freedoms without which fixity would seem coercion. This view of the citizen relies on an agricultural theory of culture based on property and cultivation. Perhaps unsurprisingly, all of these political ideas have semantic connections, as the word *censor* is connected to authority and cultivation.

The critical history presented above shows these connections. It illuminates the way in which censorship arrived in contemporary Mexico, as well as the relevant elements for discourse analysis, including concerns with the authoring capacity of the state, the importance of public opinion for modern governmentality, and the ideological power of morality. But this is not simply a critical history of censorship, for I argue that the censorial corresponds to the political task of the public sphere, which has as its central mission the regulation of civil society, as Habermas (1989) would phrase it. This is particularly clear in times of violence, when the republican promises of order and virtue tempt us into forgetting the authoritarian substratum of republicanism. In Mexico, lawmakers have foregrounded the political task of the public sphere and have reminded us that this space of civic debate must be understood as sovereign territory. It is the ground on which we cultivate the values of the good citizen. Mexican law and media policy are unambiguous on this. Article 4 of the FLRT states: "The radio and television constitute an activity of public interest, and therefore the state must protect it and overlook it so that [it fulfills] its social function." Clearly, what the legislatures of different states have argued is that the political task of public culture is to cultivate, or author, a moral society.

Perhaps nobody has made this aspect of publicity clearer than Arce Paniagua (PAN), who proposed changing the criminal code based on a theory of publicity that connects it to the expectation of order. He wanted to criminalize what FLRT calls "apologists" of crime. However, for this apology of the illicit to be criminal, it must be done publicly. He reasons that it is the public character of the apology that "perturbs indirectly public order, it produces a scandal, an alarm, a feeling of insecurity." In addition, he continues, this apology is dangerous "because it can find a receptor interested in realizing or executing the crimes" suggested by the instigators. He believes that the law cannot wait for the crimes to be committed and that the law must punish the probability of crime "publicly instigated."[21] Although his proposal was never approved, his reliance on public instigation, particularly apologies that use mass media, illuminates his expectations for the public sphere. Culture that is publicly shared must help produce order and a feeling of security. Arce Paniagua's proposal also spells out what an authorial state should do in cases of violence and disorder: "We, the legislators, are obligated to stop the deterioration of society, protecting the integrity and security . . . of the citizenry. . . . It is primordial to stop the deformation of our values avoiding the violation of norms with deplorable and illegal acts."[22] In 2011, the Justice Commission voted unanimously for a modified version of the proposal. Justice in Mexico, an organization based at the University of San Diego, reported Arce Paniagua's views after the commission's approval: "The use of the public discourse as a tool of power for criminal actors . . . is something that Mexico's legislators want to put a stop to now." To Arce Paniagua, the political task of publicity is clear.

Clarity notwithstanding, censorship has not worked. Narcocorridos are bigger than ever. Nowhere is this clearer than in the way the music moved and circulated after the ban. Instead of stopping or slowing down its traffic, for instance, in the days that followed the prohibition of narcocorridos in the state of Sinaloa, sales went up (Sánchez 2011). This increase in economic success by the banned cultural form signals the desire of young Mexicans to participate in counterhegemonic practices, particularly if these can be articulated through consumption, and the ability of narcocorrido texts to convey counterhegemonic feelings. Yet the uptick in sales also shows that the ban could not quite contain the genre's digital distribution and popularity. Bans on broadcasting and live performance are simply anachronistic when the bulk of cultural trade is happening online. The religious/agrarian vision of order at the heart of this censorship is in tension with the social, economic, and cultural forces of mobility and new media technologies.

The ban is, predictably, ineffective because this negative censorship exists in a worldview of politics and culture meant to be blind to the increasing centrality of three manifestations of excess: transnationalism, new technologies of cultural production and distribution, and immigration. When accounting for these three types of excess, censorship's inefficiency *is* productive, for it yields new spaces for cultural value, surplus value, and profit. On this point, Gilles Deleuze and Félix Guattari comment: "The more the capitalist machine deterritorializes, decoding and axiomatizing flows in order to extract surplus value from them, the more its ancillary apparatuses, such as government bureaucracies and the forces of law and order, do their utmost to reterritorialize, absorbing in the process a larger and larger share of surplus value" (1983: 37). Though the state is here described as ancillary, it is also a pillar of the capitalist socius, for the processes of reterritorialization—the order principle that I have discussed in this and the preceding chapter—provide the orderly, if always incomplete, ground for capital to profit. The order principle codifies what will be decoded and grounds what will be deterritorialized.

Censorship may be a governmental measure more at home in a socius of political order and economic stability than in deterritorialized, transnational, mobile, multiethnic, Twitter-friendly, evanescent, and flash-mob societies. Censorship may belong to a Fordist political imagination of civic productivity that relies on the rationalization of political culture to craft docile individuals (Jay 2010). Censorship may depend on citizens fixed to a territory, a location, and to a way of telling that locale's history, but capitalism depends on the censor's orderly ideal, even if only to destroy it, market it, and consume it. Could there be newness without the old? Could there be innovation without tradition? Could there be freedom without order? Could there be trafficking and displacement without fixity? In 1989, two years after Labastida Ochoa tried to censor narcocorridos in Sinaloa for the first time, Los Tigres del Norte—the creators of the narcocorrido genre,

Sinaloa's favorite band, and a truly transnational Californian product—recorded the album *Corridos prohibidos,* one of the best-selling albums of all time in Mexico. The ban had become the brand. Since then, censorship has been worn by narcocorrido musicians like a badge of honor.

Censoring narcocorridos has not worked in Mexico. Narcocorridos are bigger than ever. They have become popular not only in northern Mexico, but everywhere in the nation. They are huge in central Mexico, and as the next chapter shows, they are also huge in the United States. *La Jornada*—based in Mexico City, the cosmopolitan center of Mexican pop and all things rock—goes so far as to declare narcocorridos "the sound of modern Mexico" (*La Jornada* 2014). I believe that.

4

Narcocorridos in the USA

DETERRITORIALIZATION AND THE BUSINESS OF AUTHENTICITY

La violencia engendra violencia, como se sabe; pero también engendra ganancias para la industria de la violencia, que la vende como espectáculo y la convierte en objeto de consumo.

(Violence engenders violence, as we know; but it also engenders profits for the industries of violence, which package violence as a spectacle and an object of consumption.)

—Eduardo Galeano, *Patas arriba: La escuela del mundo al revés*

On February 21, 2013, the Lo Nuestro Awards awarded narcocorrido star Gerardo Ortiz the prizes for Best Regional Mexican Song and Best Norteño Artist. The Lo Nuestro Awards were created in 1989 by Univision and *Billboard* as a way of recognizing the best Spanish-language music in the United States. Since then, the ceremony has been televised on Univision, the number one Spanish-language media corporation in the United States (Amaya 2013; Perlman 2016; Wilkinson 2016). That Thursday in 2013, Ortiz performed, to roaring cheers, his hit "Dámaso," a first-person narrative of the life of wealth, sex, and violence of Dámaso López, alias "el Mini Lic," the second-in-command of the Sinaloa Cartel, the biggest criminal drug organization in the world, and the person who at the time was presumed to be the successor to El Chapo Guzmán.[1] In other words, Lo Nuestro Awards, branded by Univision as an opportunity to highlight the reasons to be proud of Latino music and artists, showcased a song about the life and exploits of Dámaso López, whom the FBI and the DEA undoubtedly considered one of the worst enemies of the United States.

Something extraordinary has happened with narcocorridos in their dual existence in Mexico and the United States. In Mexico, narcocorridos are routinely censored and persecuted by state representatives. Although Mexican fans love them, Mexican elites fear them. Because of this fear, narcocorridos have become part of the Mexican political lexicon, objects of censorship and regulation. The opposite happens in the United States, where narcocorridos are treated as profitable, harmless culture that mainstream media can use to symbolize the best of Mexican American life and culture. The same violent texts are transformed depending on their place of production and consumption. This conversion from politics to commerce is not unique to narcocorridos but instead part of the capacities inherent in deterritorialization and capitalism, the two forces shaping the production, distribution, and aesthetic characteristics of the music genre in the United States.

This chapter is an analysis of the process of conversion, which depends, I argue, on the genre's ability to reconstruct the codes of narcocorrido authenticity. Here I examine the narcocorrido careers in the United States of three of the genre's biggest stars, the now-deceased Dolores Janney Rivera Saavedra ("Jenni Rivera"), Gerardo Ortiz, and Alfredo Rios ("El Komander"). These artists have commonalities: for example, they have all been based in California, and their success was rooted in the United States before being exported to Mexico. Most importantly, they have also existed in similar media cultures and profited from similar evolutions in the genre.

Through a historical analysis of the genre's aesthetic and production characteristics, the first section will show that the corrido has evolved into the narcocorrido using three codes of authenticity: violence, place, and the counterhegemonic. This section also shows that changing recording and distribution technologies have fostered a different relationship between the genre, place, and audiences, which also changes the meaning of place and of the counterhegemonic. Through a media industries approach, the second section examines how contemporary media cultures and production structures use branding techniques to reconstitute the codes of authenticity for today's narcocorrido. The third section argues that in order to recreate codes of authenticity, contemporary narcocorridos use the codes of violence, place, and the counterhegemonic to simulate the experience of life in DCOs, the primary reason for the first-person narrative modality that characterizes today's narcocorridos. An overarching argument in the chapter is that the crafting of authenticity also helps media industries, which use the narcocorrido claims of authenticity to strengthen their own. Narcocorrido stars like Rivera, Rios, and Ortiz have been mainstays in Spanish-language broadcasting and music, shaping and leading the music market in the important category of Regional Mexican Music, which is in turn authenticated by the stars' personas.

DETERRITORIALIZING THE POPULAR

One cannot explain the rise of narcocorrido stars like Rivera, Ortiz, and Rios without first observing how deterritorialization and capitalism have given new meanings to narcocorridos north of the Rio Grande. "Deterritorialization" is part of a cluster of concepts that, like hybridity, transculturation, and mobility, help us understand globalization in terms of advanced capitalism (García Canclini 2001; Kraidy 2005). It is meant to be a tool for the critical description of movement across and within nations brought about by the economic and technological conditions that characterize modernity today. This cluster of concepts often implies a fundamental critique of territorial modernity and the nation-state, yet violence is a specter haunting all of these concepts, as violence is itself a sort of phenomenological critique of the sedentary theory of society and politics at the root of territorial modernity. In a Weberian fashion, Charles Maier succinctly writes: "Territory is the premise of state sovereignty" (2006: 34). Nonstate violence is its antithesis. Predictably, violence is often the root of deterritorialization and the reason for immigration and for seeking refuge. This is certainly true about narcocorridos and the US-based fans that support the genre. Social, political, criminal, and economic violence are the reasons for most recent migrations north of the Rio Grande.

The deterritorialization of populations supporting narcocorridos is a disrupting force that has shaped the genre's standing in the United States, but it is not the only one. The globalized forces of capitalism also give the genre shape and meaning, for the issue is not simply that narcocorridos exist and are produced north of the US-Mexico border; more importantly, the issue is that they have thrived. Just as violence in late capitalism can quickly become a commodity to be traded, as Galeano describes in the epigraph, deterritorialization may produce conditions for the success and profitability of violent culture. This at least is what Deleuze and Guattari imply in their early, influential, and synthetic analysis of the challenges to order brought about by territorially unbound modes of production:

> The prime function incumbent upon the socius, has always been to codify the flows of desire, to inscribe them, to record them, to see to it that

no flow exists that is not properly dammed up, channeled, regulated. When the primitive territorial machine proved inadequate to the task, the *despotic machine* set up a kind of overcoding system. But the *capitalist machine,* insofar as it was built on the ruins of a despotic State more or less far removed in time, finds itself in a totally new situation: it is faced with the task of decoding and deterritorializing the flows. Capitalism does not confront this situation from the outside, since it experiences it as the very fabric of its existence, as both its primary determinant and its fundamental raw material, its form and its function, and deliberately perpetuates it, in all its violence, with all the powers at its command. Its sovereign production and repression can be achieved in no other way. Capitalism is in fact born of the encounter of two sorts of flows: the decoded flows of production in the form of money-capital, and the decoded flows of labor in the form of the "free worker." Hence, unlike previous social machines, the capitalist machine is incapable of providing a code that will apply to the whole of the social field. By substituting money for the very notion of a code, it has created an axiomatic of abstract quantities that keeps moving further and further in the direction of the deterritorialization of the socius. (1983: 33)

Deleuze and Guattari start with order as the central goal of the socius, which in their work is a reference to Althusser's "society effect," or the forms of social production, a political goal that in societies not dominated by capitalism is implicitly connected to the state and to the orderly regulation of movement. Capitalism, as a socius centered on money and profit, is by contrast a contradictory or, if you prefer, a schizophrenic socius that moves toward order but depends, for profit, on the disruption of the established. One of the key order-disrupting tactics in capitalism's arsenal is the deterritorialization of flows, the unlatching of workers from their place, the detaching of commodities from their market, and the transplanting of processes from their socio-legal regimes. In Deleuze and Guattari's seminal work on deterritorialization, capitalism is built on its ability to understand, manipulate, and destroy codes, even its own, and on its ability to transform patterns of movement between production and labor.

The recording and performing careers of Rivera, Ortiz, and Rios are examples of a deterritorialized mode of production in which the artists have benefited from their standing in two societies, with two fan bases, two affective structures, and two regulatory systems. Rios's career, for instance, began in Mexico but took off only after he joined El Movimiento Alterado (EMA), a narcocorrido brand that originated in California and has gained popularity in the United States and Mexico since the violence spiked in Mexico in 2007. Although EMA is a US brand, it specializes in distributing narcocorridos dealing with the violence in Mexico.[2] Similarly, Ortiz and Rivera have used their links with Mexico to build recording careers in the United States that benefit from the violent narcocorrido brand. Their success in the United States has paved the way to the Mexican market. At the time of her death, Rivera, for instance, was one of the judges on the Mexican version of *La Voz . . . México* and was seen by millions in Mexico every week (Cobo 2013). Like Rivera toward the end of her career, Rios and Ortiz constantly tour in Mexico.

There is something particularly counterintuitive about succeeding as a narcocorrido performer in the United States. The reason is simple. The narcocorrido is a particularly demanding genre that depends heavily on authenticity. In the case of narcocorridos, authenticity means the ability to connect to the folk history of the corrido, as well as to the Mexican territory and the rural values of the Sinaloan Sierras, the place of origin of the oldest cartels. So Rivera, Rios, and Ortiz are more than examples of the deep connections between deterritorialization, music industries, distribution technologies, and brands. Their careers and performances also illustrate a solution to the riddle of simultaneously using deterritorialization to connect to Mexican Americans while embracing a music genre heavily dependent on authenticity.

From Corridos to Narcocorridos

Although few terms have elicited more theoretical commentary in disciplines concerned with expressive culture (i.e., art history, literary studies, music studies, and media studies) than "authenticity," today's scholars have moved away from the controversial question of "What is authentic?" to questions such as "What is the nature of authenticity?" and, more central to my endeavors in this chapter, "How is authenticity coded?" This last question allows for a great deal of flexibility as to the nature of authenticity, while also allowing for authenticity to be discursively and historically constructed. Personally, I favor a hermeneutic view of authenticity and thus presume that authenticity is created in the interplay between producer(s), text, and audience or viewer (Gadamer 1975). Contrary to constructivist views of authenticity, which rely on authorities to corroborate some features of a work, I prefer what Véronique Lacoste, Jakob R. E. Leimgruber, and Thiemo Breyer refer to as authenticity's *"performative mode* where authenticity is staged by creating 'reality effects,' that is an enactment via credibility of performance and content" (2014: xii, italics in the original). This useful definition of authenticity has two temporal dimensions: a performance of authenticity is both synchronic and staged. Yet the reality effects tend to be diachronic: they have a history. This section details how the diachronic elements, the indexes of authenticity for today's narcocorridos, came to be accumulated throughout the genre's history. It concentrates on three indexes or, as Lacoste and colleagues term them, "reality effects": (1) violence, (2) place or territory, and (3) the counterhegemonic standpoint.

The narcocorrido is the latest evolution of a centuries-old music genre that originated first in Spain as "the romance" and that arrived in Mexico and the US Southwest in the nineteenth century and became the corrido. This evolution ripped away the music genre from "the primitive territorial machine," as Deleuze and Guattari so colorfully phrased it, and slowly brought it into the sphere of capital. From its origins, the corrido has experienced several distinctive transformations, each of which has moved the corrido further from the genre's oldest roots. These transformations started with the lyrical element of the romance (Valenzuela Arce 2010: 11). Reaching back centuries to Spanish narrative traditions, the romance originated as an oral form for memorializing events and people, telling the heroic tales of warriors and aristocrats.

In its move to northern Mexico, the romance retained some of these factual and mythic storytelling characteristics, albeit in a situation in which state logic and nationalism were becoming dominant. In this setting, the romance became the corrido, which served to capture the struggles of common people against the landowner or the state. In the US Southwest, Américo Paredes (1958) shows that the corrido was used after 1848 to memorialize the struggles and conflicts between Mexicans and Anglos (see also Burgos Dávila 2011: 98). In simple and memorable poetic form, corridos told stories that mattered, and they became what Jesús Martín-Barbero (1993) would call a popular form of media: they originated among the popular classes and constructed and reconstructed a version of reality from their standpoint. In the terms of Deleuze and Guattari (1983), corridos codified the desire for power of the rural and immigrant communities, inscribing them into a memorable form with counterhegemonic potential.

Against the backdrop of place, corridos recorded violent events endured by the poor and the immigrant, and thus they functioned, like scars, as ways of remembering injury and death. Even if popular understandings of kinship in the nineteenth century were no longer feudal as in the Spanish romance, understandings of violence echoed feudal exchanges. "The Ballad of

Gregorio Cortez," a famous corrido from Texas, tells the story of Gregorio, who is wanted for killing the sheriff. In the song, Gregorio defends the killing as retaliation, because the sheriff killed Gregorio's brother. As with the European *weregild*, a blood debt can be repaid only with blood. The context is different than in feudal settings in that the argument of the song justifies the killing of sheriffs. In Texas, though, the state functions by a different logic, and the Texas Rangers took Gregorio into custody on June 22, 1901. Soon after, the anonymous corrido showed up and helped construct the myth even as Cortez languished in jail. Singers of the corrido were often beaten and jailed themselves, but the corrido served its purpose, making Cortez a folk hero and forcing the Texas courts to treat him gingerly. At a time when death penalties were common, he was sentenced to life in prison. The corrido remains as a classic narrative of the conflicts between Mexicans and Anglos and reminds us that even at the turn of the twentieth century, blood constituted a debt that could only be repaid with blood.

The index or reality effect of violence has continued. Today narcocorrido performances are often honor ballads that narrate stories of violence and revenge. Rios's song "Caceria" ("The Hunt") is a first-person narrative of a hunt for a traitor, someone who committed a breach of honor and will therefore meet certain death. In the music video for Ortiz's "Fuiste mía" ("You Were Mine"), a man discovers his woman with another man and proceeds to kill them both. The classic song "Contrabando y traición" by Los Tigres del Norte is a story of betrayal that is resolved when Camelia empties her revolver into Emilio (see this book's introduction). In each of these songs, violence is the result of challenges to honor: violence becomes the right thing to do. These songs are indexical reminders of narcocorrido roots, and even though today they are often based on fictional stories, they continue to function as ways of establishing community through the symbolic remembrance of death.

The brutal honor code often displayed by these narratives has been linked to the serranos, the group that often symbolizes the narco life. The serranos, the inhabitants of the Sierra Madre, have become emblems of most of the values that characterize organized crime. As Gabriela Polit Dueñas notes, "The *serrano*, or highlander . . . is an emblematic northern character described as a party-lover, a hard worker, a rebel, and a *machista*. For the serrano, disobeying the law is a question of honor" (2013: 16, italics in the original). Honor, in fact, is a common currency in serrano life, and differences of all sorts are often settled by reference to it. Honor is not simply a value; it is a way of connecting to the past, to Mexico's history; it is also a symbol of place, of the way life is lived in the harsh, rural setting of the Sierra Madre.

Communities in northern Mexico and the US Southwest have used corridos to memorialize violence, but violent events always take place somewhere, so the history of the corrido is as dependent on ideas of place as it is on ideas of violence. This is partly because the rural is always a spatial construction and partly because the struggles of immigrants are partly about place and territory. Yet narrative forms like the corrido are bound to their distribution technologies and systems, and advances in media technologies have often fostered the deterritorialization of the genre. As an oral form, corridos were indebted to the values and interests of a geographical region. They were responsive to locality. But by the nineteenth century corridos were published on sheets of paper and sold by the musicians that composed them. The publishing of corridos gave these narratives a new reach and greater cultural potential. Paper reaches farther than the singer's voice and lasts longer; publishing thus delinked the corrido from orality, locality, and from the present (Hernández 1992: 326). The record player engendered further transformation. Corridos became vehicles for stardom, and their narrative conventions multiplied. Instead of being narrowly defined by the local, as early corridos were, or by the epic, a common style during wartime, corridos were also written to tell the lives and deeds of both common people and of criminals in their struggles against the law.

Over time, the forces of capitalism and deterritorialization have preyed upon the index of place and territory, transforming it significantly. If corridos, like the events they memorialized, could happen anywhere in the Mexican North or the US Southwest, the range of places that narcocorridos describe has narrowed to the point that only a few places—those that gave origin to the narco trade (e.g., Sinaloa), or those with extreme violence (e.g., Ciudad Juárez)—are mentioned regularly. As I argue in the next section, place has changed from an index meant to simply specify where violence happened to an index meant to symbolize the violence itself.

Capitalism and deterritorialization have also dramatically transformed the index of the counterhegemonic. Early corrido narratives, which were often about the hardships of the poor and the immigrant—at the hands of the landowning classes and the Anglos, respectively—had a clear counterhegemonic, popular standpoint. By the mid-twentieth century, industrially produced corridos regularly narrated struggles against the law without the political framework of early corridos. "El ojo de vidrio" ("The Glass-Eyed Bandit"), written by Víctor Cordero, a popular Mexico City composer and one of the most prolific composers of postrevolutionary corridos, was a hit thanks to the interpretations by corrido and ranchero recording stars such as Eulalio González ("El Piporro") and Antonio Aguilar.[3] Void of any political framework, this famous corrido is the story of a bandit who dresses like a poor person to rob people in the road. In the postrevolutionary corrido, this celebration of banditry often stood in for the counterhegemonic, and it is this substitution of the political for the illegal that narcocorridos inherit.

Corridos involving the trafficking of drugs began to appear in the 1930s with titles like "Maldita droga" and "Por morfina y cocaina" (Ramírez-Pimienta 2011: 13).[4] These early narcocorridos carried forward the three indexes of authenticity that had been codified early in the corrido genre: that is, they were inspired by the territorial challenges of moving illicit drugs across borders and were stories told from the antistate perspective of criminals. By exploring the moral life and deeds of drug dealers, the narcocorrido portrays a world from the point of view of the outlaw, including fantasies against traditional social mores and against the state (Valenzuela Arce 1992: 20). The subgenre did not immediately succeed commercially. It took a few decades for the music to become popular. It was not until the 1970s, when Mexican drug cartels had grown and consolidated their influence around the growth, sale, and traffic of marijuana and heroin, that this lurid genre gained broad popularity. In 1972, the little-known norteño band Los Tigres del Norte recorded their album *Contrabando y traición* in Los Angeles, and the title track, also known as "La Camelia," became one of the biggest hits in the history of norteño music (see this book's introduction). With narcocorridos, Los Tigres del Norte became arguably the most influential Mexican regional band in history and redefined the narcocorrido genre, making it a cultural phenomenon that expanded from California, where they lived, worked, and recorded, to northern Mexico, where they became akin to matinee idols (Kun 2007; Wald 2001).

Since a significant portion of drug culture and power has been located in Chihuahua and Sinaloa, most narcocorridos today are put to music in either "norteño" or "banda" style. This means that narcocorrido music is indexical of place and territory. Norteño music, the style used by Los Tigres, is also known as conjunto and closely linked to Tejano music across the border. It is organized around the accordion, an instrument of German origin, and the guitar, of Spanish origin. Rooted in Chihuahua and Texas, norteño music is a hybrid style that may also include, as in the case of Los Tigres, in addition to vocals, an accordion, electric bass, saxophone, *bajo sexto*, and drums. Though Los Tigres are from Sinaloa, the success of norteño music beyond

Chihuahua created deep and old influences in other regions. Significantly, norteño music has a shared history with Tejano music, the slightly slower, rhythmic polka-based style of Mexican Americans in Texas, which is often played with more virtuosity and today is also influenced by other US styles like swing and country-and-western (Ragland 2009: 4). By the time Los Tigres del Norte entered the narcorrido scene in the 1970s, norteño was a music genre that had been industrially absorbed. It had a star system; it was recorded broadly both in Mexico and the United States; it had a northern Mexican geographical brand, but it could be listened to and bought all over Mexico; and it was successful and profitable in the United States, particularly as post-1960s migrations from Mexico were increasing each year.

In Sinaloa, early norteño fused with another popular style, *jaranas*, to form what today we recognize as banda music. Like norteño music, the *banda sinaloense* is a particular subgenre of Mexican polka. Also known in Sinaloa and Sonora as *tambora*, after the distinctive large bass drum that is often the ensemble's only percussion, banda is a brass and woodwind ensemble that includes at least a trumpet and often a clarinet. La Banda El Recodo is a perfect example of contemporary tambora: it includes four clarinets, three trumpets, a tambora, a tuba, three trombones, a *tarola* (or snare drum), and two singers.

I grew up in Navojoa, a city at the crossroads of Sinaloa, Sonora, and Chihuahua. In my town, itinerant musicians, the kind that played on public buses or the street, were typically tambora or norteño ensembles. The tambora, with as few as two musicians, always included the large bass drum and perhaps a clarinet, guitar, trumpet, or even a violin. For norteño, all you needed was an accordion. When I was a kid, norteño was already huge, dominating radio broadcasts and music stores. By contrast, tambora was still the regional music of the working classes and rural people in Sinaloa and Sonora. Today tambora is arguably as big as norteño; this is partly due to the fact that they have encountered a transnational market that allows them to have significant reach within relatively wealthy Mexican American migrant communities. The tambora band Banda El Recodo has played in Monterey, California; Nashville, Tennessee; and Johannesburg, South Africa, where El Recodo had one of the key concerts during the 2010 World Cup. Their overwhelming success has even reshaped the name of the genre, transforming the old name, tambora, into the more generic name banda.

The rise of banda music and its significance in the narcocorrido genre marks a particular transition and coding of the index of place and territory through the use of serrano rural and agrarian motifs. As Helena Simonett

(2001a: 93) has shown, traditional banda music is eminently rural, connecting the values of rural communities to particular places and to particular identities. Traditional Sinaloan bandas have deep connections to their villages and perform musical narratives that idealize the values of honor and tradition engendered by the long-lasting bonds between people and their land.

Migration from rural Mexico, and Sinaloa in particular, made possible the northern movement of the banda sound. They created new music scenes different from the norteño one, with their dance halls, concert halls, recording businesses, radio programming, and even new US-organized bandas. Simonett's (2001a) careful ethnographic observations of Los Angeles's recent Mexican immigrants indicate how the rural genre's scene is used for nostalgic and political reasons. The music facilitates immigrant connections with their places of origin and reenergizes agrarian values in the midst of the second-largest city in the United States. Banda music also reenergized political and ethnic identities. Bringing people together at dances and concerts, the banda scene helped Mexican immigrants connect to each other and to feel the power of their togetherness at a time, during the 1980s and 1990s, when anti-immigrant forces in California were vocal and mainstream. The popularity of banda music in the United States, then, is more than an example of deterritorialization. It also shows how nostalgia for agrarian values can be an essential ingredient in the reterritorialization of a musical genre. Counterintuitively, these agrarian values give meaning to new and complexly modern forms of crafting political and ethnic identities.

Banda's closer connection to rural life and to folklore is important to the contemporary genre of the narcocorrido, but this importance is relatively recent. The commercial consolidation and mainstreaming of the narcocorrido lyrical genre happened alongside the rise of commercial norteño music and the massification engendered by commercial and technological innovation that transformed the corrido's lyrical form throughout the twentieth century. Banda has brought another, more recent transformation, reactivating the narcocorrido connection to the rural, to nostalgia, and to the reshaping of Latino ethnic identity. The results can be aesthetically remarkable. One case in point is the music video for Banda El Recodo's song "Vas a llorar por mí" ("You're Going to Cry for Me"), which has over 215 million views on Vevo as of March 2017. Directed by LGA Productions, the music video has high production values and is set in New York. The lyrics are basically a romantic ballad, but the video, to remind us of the connection between the musical genre and narco imagery, tells the story of a mafia deal against the backdrop of a love triangle. Violence, place, and antistate symbols, the three indexes of authenticity, are perfectly performed against the profile of New York's skyscrapers, in restaurants, and in other beautiful, glitzy architectural spaces. In doing so, the song's traditional instrumentation resignifies the cosmopolitan environment. It connects Manhattan to the rural values of honor and virtue of the Sinaloan sierras and normalizes the presence in the city of the Spanish language and of Mexico's folklore. The symbolic dissonances between the old and the new, the local and the cosmopolitan, the rural and the urban, the Mexican and the US American, are ironed out by the incredible success of Banda El Recodo, which is one of the biggest musical acts in Mexico and the United States, yet a musical group that most non–Spanish speakers in the US would not even recognize.

I began this section by noting that commercialism detached the corrido from "the primitive territorial machine," a phrase that Deleuze and Guattari use to alert us to a historical move away from the modes of kinship and cultural encoding preceding the formation of a state. But what the history of the narcocorrido shows is how the genre has managed to encode the three indexes of authenticity at each turn of its evolution. The next sections expand on this insight by further analyzing the industrial, performative, and symbolic tactics used in the encoding of the indexes of authenticity in today's narcocorrido genre. These sections are the synchronic counterpart to the diachronic analysis performed above.

MEDIA CULTURES OF NARCOCORRIDO PRODUCTION

Ortiz's success at 2013's Lo Nuestro Awards was not his first. On October 20, 2011, *Billboard* put together the first annual Billboard Mexican Music Awards. The event was co-organized with Telemundo, the second-largest Spanish-language television network in the United States. The awards would recognize excellence in *Billboard*'s Regional Mexican Music category. Prior to 2011, Regional Mexican Music was recognized during the Billboard Latin Music Awards, but as a testament to the sheer power of the Regional Mexican category, *Billboard* and Telemundo bet that the standalone ceremony would be a television and marketing success. They were correct. Five million people, almost 2.8 million adults in the coveted 18–49 demographic, saw the show. The ceremony also became one of the five highest-ranked entertainment shows of 2011 for Telemundo, and won the ratings war in Los Angeles and Miami among men between the ages of eighteen and thirty-four (Cobo 2011). *Billboard*'s Regional Mexican category refers to a radio format that includes banda, norteño, mariachi, *grupero*, and *ranchera* music. This format is the most popular among Mexican Americans in the United States, due in part to the large number of immigrants from northern Mexico who reside in the US. Cementing the category's relevance is the fact that Regional Mexican accounts for more than 60 percent of sales in *Billboard*'s broader Latin Music category. By all these accounts and by its success in Los Angeles, a city dominated by Mexican Americans, and Miami, a city dominated by Cuban Americans, Puerto Ricans, and immigrants from other Latin American nations, this ceremony was of huge significance to Latinos in the United States and to the media industries that court them.

In 2011, the big winners of the Mexican Music Awards were Gerardo Ortiz, who took the six major awards, including the Artist of the Year Award, and Jenni Rivera, who took home the Female Artist of the Year Award and a special award, El Premio de la Estrella, for her positive influence beyond music. Ortiz's awards were garnered for two very successful albums named after two narcocorrido hits: "Ni hoy ni mañana" ("Neither Today nor Tomorrow") and "Morir y existir" ("To Die and to Exist"). Rivera got her awards for the imprint she made throughout her career and for a double-disc collection called *Joyas prestadas* (Fonovisa/Universal) in which she reinterpreted iconic Mexican ballads banda style.

Ortiz and Rivera also dominated the 2012 Billboard Mexican Music Award ceremony. That year Ortiz received seven more Billboard awards, including Artist of the Year. Rivera's 2012 appearance was also successful, winning the Female Artist of the Year back to back and receiving two other awards. In 2013, Gerardo Ortiz again received seven awards, and Rivera posthumously received four. Rivera died in a plane crash in Mexico on December 9, 2012, and since then her music sales have skyrocketed. At the moment of her death, Rivera was the highest-selling artist of the powerful, multinational label Fonovisa and "the highest-selling female artist in regional Mexican music" (Cobo 2013: 5). In 2014, the Mexican Music Awards were folded back into the Billboard Latin Music Awards and Gerardo Ortiz won one more award, while Rivera, almost two years after her death, won three. The same was repeated in 2015, with Ortiz and Rivera winning one and three awards, respectively. In 2016, Ortiz again won an award, and for the first time, Alfredo "El Komander" Rios won the Regional Mexican Artist of the Year—Solo category.

The star personas of Rios, Ortiz, and Rivera are tied to narcocorridos and violence. Today Ortiz remains one of the most important narcocorrido singers, though Rios is closing the gap. Rivera also began her career as a narcocorrido singer; though over time she shed some of her connections to the

Figure 4.1. Gerardo Ortiz at the 2016 Billboard Latin Music Awards. Source: *Billboard* digital magazine.

narco imaginary, her original success stemmed from her ability to sing the narcocorrido from a female standpoint. The standing of these performers in these award ceremonies, which track sales and distribution (e.g., downloads), speaks to narcocorrido's commercial importance for Telemundo, Univision, and Billboard, three of the most important media corporations shaping the Spanish-speaking music world in the United States. Yet the success of these stars is due in part to the music recording and business infrastructure set up by Mexican American producers in California, who have understood the relevance of the narcocorrido brand and the best way to craft it. Deterritorialization is thus the heart of this segment of the music industry, and the challenge to the industry is to deliver a cultural product that speaks to the indexes of authenticity, or the reality effects, that have accumulated in the genre.

Deterritorialized Production

Today many narcocorrido singers are based in northern Mexico, near the places where the influence of the drug cartels is greatest. In towns and cities like Ciudad Juárez, Culiacán, Tijuana, and Nuevo Laredo, the ubiquitous presence of drug-related events has inspired complex cultural responses, including cultural forms and practices that support the cartels and others that reject them. Some narcocorridos are thus popular responses to these social conditions. Small, local banda or norteño ensembles in Sinaloa, for instance, are sometimes asked to compose a corrido in honor of someone killed in a drug-related event. The song is later performed during the funeral as a matter of respect and as a symbol of love for the deceased. Almost never recorded, these narcocorridos are an example of a popular tradition that connects people to shared experiences and to the feelings, worldviews, values, and particular challenges of existing in that place, at that point, in that context.[5]

These truly popular narcocorridos are the minority. The majority of narcocorridos are the product of a cultural-industrial apparatus dominated by the interests and needs of capitalism and transnational music companies. The vinyl record facilitated the disconnection of corrido and place and initiated a process whereby the field of music became defined and dominated by stardom, commercialism, and branding. Digital distribution technologies have increased this process, participating in the growing deterritorialization of the corrido and its contemporary and dominant subgenre, the narcocorrido. Just as Los Tigres del Norte managed to become the early stars of the narcocorrido from California, away from Mexico and the violence brought about by the drug cartels, today an increasing number of narcocorrido stars are based in the United States. In addition to those already mentioned, other narcocorrido megastars who live in the United States at least part of the year include Marco Antonio Solís, Adolfo Ángel, Pepe Aguilar, Los Huracanes del Norte, Los Tucanes de Tijuana, and Los Bravos del Norte (Ramírez-Pimienta 2011: 187). Similarly, the majority of narcocorridos are produced and recorded in the US Southwest; most are recorded in California and Texas, though a growing number come from midwestern cities like Chicago and Detroit.

The careers of Rivera, Rios, and Ortiz are examples of the process by which a deterritorialized cultural form can, with the right industrial and aesthetic moves, construct a brand of authenticity. Each of their cases also shows the importance of relying on industry leaders that can act as savvy translators of cultural codes who understand their audiences. Perhaps unsurprisingly, the personal biographies of those directing the labels that support these three stars are rather similar: each of the labels was started by immigrants from northern Mexico with a deep knowledge of the Mexican American experience and popular music.

Jenni Rivera was born in a household marked by narcocorridos (Qui-nones 2012). Her father, Pedro Rivera, a poor goatherd from Jalisco, had crossed the border to the United States without papers in the late 1960s to work in Fresno, California, picking lettuce, melons, and grapes. After decades of struggles, in 1988 Pedro Rivera founded the record label Cintas Acuario, which is credited with launching the career of the hugely famous narcocorrido singer and songwriter Chalino Sánchez. If musicians like Los Tigres del Norte have always represented the highly commercializable end of the narcocorrido, in the late 1980s and 1990s Chalino (the moniker his fans prefer) represented the popular and the authentic. His lyrics seemed to have the proper amount of rural credibility that defined the original cor-rido, and his raspy, untrained voice added authenticity to a music career that ended in violence. He was born in Badiraguato, a town and municipal-ity in the Sinaloa mountains that is notorious for being the original home of several of the most powerful drug cartels, including the Sinaloa Cartel, the biggest crime organization in the world. This rough town was the credible backdrop to Chalino's musical career, and his death cemented his fame. In 1992 Chalino became famous in Mexico and the United States when, dur-ing a concert in California, a patron neared the stage and began shooting at him. Though hit in the side, Chalino famously took out his own gun and fired back. By the end of the evening, two people had been killed, including the would-be killer. Chalino's reputation grew, but his success lasted only a few months. In May 1992 Chalino was killed execution-style in Mexico after a concert. These events proved extremely profitable to the labels that recorded Chalino, including Cintas Acuario. If Chalino was famous prior to his death, he became a rock star after it; his recordings continue to sell today.

To Pedro Rivera and Cintas Acuario, Chalino was more than a source of monetary profit. In Chalino, the music industry found the clearest example of how a narcocorrido singer from California could be read as authentic. Chalino's performances were lessons on how to encode all the indexes of corrido authenticity into the narcocorrido—including violence, place and territory, and the counterhegemonic. In fact, his influence is arguably as important to the genre's evolution as the early influence of Los Tigres del Norte. After Chalino, Cintas Acuario developed a narcocorrido brand cen-tered on authenticity, and Pedro Rivera has often referred to himself as "el patriarca del corrido" (the patriarch of the corrido) (Rivera n.d.). All of his sons and his daughter, Jenni, became musicians, and Lupillo Rivera, Jenni's brother, has climbed to the pinnacle of the music world. Today Lupillo is one of the biggest narcocorrido stars, regularly appearing in the *Billboard* rankings in the United States and in Mexico.

Alfredo Rios's production house and the banner under which he performs, El Movimiento Alterado, are the business initiative of brothers Adolfo and Omar Valenzuela Rivera, also known in the music world as "Los Twiins." Los Twiins can be seen as auteur figures who heavily imprint EMA's music with their aesthetic and creative goals. They were born in Culiacán, Sinaloa, Mexico, and migrated to California in 1992, when they were fourteen (Replogle 2011). They are the sons of musician Adolfo Valenzuela, who performed with Banda Tierra Blanca and who instructed his sons *not* to go into the music business because of the inevitability of having to deal with drug cartels. In the 1990s, banda groups, which popularized narcocorridos, already operated in connection with the power of the cartels, which often played the role of wealthy Maecenas, capable of controlling a musician's path to success. The brothers did not follow their father's advice, and soon they were playing in bandas and organizing them at all levels, from composing and playing the music, to learning the business of recording, producing, and distributing. Their big break came when Thalía, one of Mexico's most popular singers and actresses, decided to record a banda album with them. Their production business grew, and since then their San Diego studio has become the recording place for a diverse group of artists, including banda veterans such as La Banda del Recodo; new bandas like Los Tucanes de Tijuana, Banda Machos, Valentín Elizalde, and El Chapo de Sinaloa; and pop singers like Paulina Rubio, Shakira, and Chayanne (Índigo 2011). Their productions have received Grammy awards, Lo Nuestro awards, and Billboard awards, and they have established themselves on both sides of the border as leading music producers. Their fame and cultural influence is such that Telemundo put together a reality series, *Los Twiins,* that showed the professional lives of the Valenzuela brothers. *Los Twiins* aired to relative success on mun2, Telemundo's music channel (Madrigal 2011).[6]

Soon after Mexican drug violence began to grow in 2006, the Valenzuela brothers founded LA DISCO Music & Entertainment in California, a production company meant to house what they saw as the inevitable upsurge of new narcocorrido talent inspired by the violence. Sometimes called postcorrido, the new genre was partly crafted by the aesthetic and commercial ideas of the successful producers who, in 2006, branded this postcorrido genre El Movimiento Alterado (The Altered Movement). Mixing old with new and national with transnational, the new genre capitalized on the arduous process of the Mexican corrido's cultural capital accumulation, the unique abilities of new technologies to constitute star personas, and the technological possibility of advertising new media products using someone else's technological and economic resources, specifically that of Google and its star audiovideo delivery platform, YouTube.

Gerardo Ortiz's recording house, DEL Records, was founded in 2008 by Ángel del Villar, a Californian born in Zacatecas, Mexico, who made his money with a successful fencing business in Los Angeles. At that time, Ortiz was just beginning his career in Sinaloa. To publicize himself, he would upload videos of his performances to YouTube. As a ruse, in fall 2009 he traveled to Los Angeles, his home city, to do an underground performance that attracted three thousand people, including del Villar. In an interview published with *Billboard* in 2012, del Villar revealed that with little experience in the music business, he convinced Ortiz to sign with his starting label and profit from the benefit of having all the label's attention (Águila 2012: 8). The conjunction of del Villar and Ortiz proved to be fortuitous.

Practically all the musicians with DEL Records are narco-singers, and DEL Records, from its origins in 2008, began developing a narco-brand identified as Corridos Enfermos (Sick Corridos) or Enfermedad Masiva (Massive Illness). This curious use of illness as metaphor in the branding of DEL Records' music compilations is reminiscent of the narco-brand El Movimiento Alterado. Corridos Enfermos, like El Movimiento Alterado, brings together artists to record successful narcocorrido compilations. In Corridos Enfermos, Enfermedad Masiva, and El Movimiento Alterado, being out of health and being altered are metaphors that signal both the music's counterhegemonic identity and the sense that the crime world the music glorifies is an unhealthy aspect of normal, sane society. Although not as successful as El Movimiento Alterado, Corridos Enfermos strengthens DEL Records' narco-brand and introduces listeners to other singers working for the label. At this moment, Ortiz is DEL Records' most successful artist, repeatedly reaching the top of the *Billboard* rankings. As a testament to the growing influence of the music label, *Billboard* named del Villar one of the 2016 Latin Power Players (Cobo 2016). This is not bad for someone who was basically a builder of fences until 2008.

All of these music industry entrepreneurs are clearly keen observers of their audiences and of the evolution of the music business after digitization. Unlike traditional recording enterprises, these labels and recording houses bypass music stores and use the viral power of websites such as YouTube, Vimeo, and Vevo to advertise their music and direct-sell albums. Hits by Jenni Rivera, El Komander, and Gerardo Ortiz have been viewed up to 203 million times each as of the writing of this book. To make sense of these numbers, it is useful to compare them to the YouTube success of other popular narcocorridos musicians. The most-viewed video by Los Tigres del Norte, "La Reina del Sur," has been viewed 49 million times.[7] To give a general sense of the relevance of these music videos, Lady Gaga and Taylor Swift, two of the hottest pop stars of the last few years, each has only six videos on YouTube that have achieved more than 130 million views.[8]

The millions of views garnered by these music stars speak to the overall success of narcocorridos, but it is partly the result of the type of music fan they are trying to access: young, technologically savvy listeners who are invested in traditional musical forms but willing to use aesthetic variations that signal urban, as opposed to rural, identities. By contrast, Los Tigres del Norte continue cultivating musical personas that connect them to older audiences who consume their narcocorridos in relation to traditional corridos, the narcocorrido's rural roots, and who use traditional distribution venues (Polit Dueñas 2008).

Technology matters. Not only does technology facilitate new commercial and aesthetic possibilities, but online distribution is increasingly accounting for the majority of narcocorrido sales.[9] Thanks to direct sales of songs and albums, and CD distribution schemas based on websites rather than physical music stores, contemporary narcocorridos are less constrained by place and nation than vinyl recordings, cassette tapes, and CDs have been. This has meant that these stars based in California can have instant access to the rest of the US territory, a feature key to Latino artists, whose fans are increasingly located in cities and towns without a music store that specializes in Latino music. As Josh Kun writes: "Music can be of a nation, but it is never exclusively national; it always overflows, spills out, sneaks through, reaches an ear on the other side of the border line, on the other side of the sea" (2005a: 20). As importantly, digital distribution allows these artists the ability to quickly reach the Mexican market, which constitutes a sizable portion of their music and concert sales. If in the 1970s the narcocorrido had to make the arduous trip from California, where it was often recorded, as in the case of Los Tigres del Norte, to the rest of the United States and northern Mexico, digital technologies and online distribution have made this process instantaneous.

Yet technological transformations and deterritorialization have changed the political meanings of the narcocorrido in the United States. Rivera's estate has used The Orchard, a gigantic multinational company that specializes in digital distribution, to disseminate the Riveras' music since 2008

(Ben-Yehuda 2008). The Orchard, which globally controls more than 1.3 million songs and 5,000 videos, locates, places, and markets songs in hundreds of digital stores like iTunes, eMusic, Google, Rhapsody, rdio, Spotify, and Vcast. They also sell songs as ringtones to mobile carriers like Verizon, Vodafone, and Bell Canada. Digital circulation technologies have left an imprint on the corrido in general and the narcocorrido in particular, facilitating on the one hand the production and distribution of narcocorridos across nations, but also straining the genre's ability to continue connecting to a specific set of shared experiences. If at one point the corrido could be considered music for and by the people, and the corrido's appeal included the tradition of narrativizing the lives and struggles of the Mexican and immigrant working and rural classes, US narcocorridos have had to rely on new ways of encoding violence, place, and the counterhegemonic in narrative conventions and performance. The next section details the manner in which the experiential has been encoded. It shows how the experiential has been broken down into basic units of phenomenology and then encoded back using branding strategies designed to simulate the experiential.

AUTHENTICITY AND THE SIMULATION OF THE EXPERIENTIAL

Corridos codified the desire for power against the government or the landowning classes who ruled over the rural and the poor in Mexico and the US Southwest. With music and lyrics, the popular genre allowed specific communities to engrave in memory a meaningful version of a vanishing present, constituting a shared sense of history and experience. Ripped apart from its popular milieu, the narcocorrido has been reconstructed by the industrial logic that dominates it today. The preferred reconstruction tactics have included a change in the narrative modality of the narcocorrido from third person to first, a trope that helps give authenticity to brands that aim to connect fans with experiences of violence, place, and the counterhegemonic. Together these indexes help simulate the experiential and recodify it in terms of embodiment, place, and directedness. These three code modalities are not random: they correspond to the phenomenological basis of experience. Generally speaking, phenomenology helps us understand how a first-person point of view is constituted or, stated differently, helps us understand the way individuals exist in the world. It assumes that all experiences are embodied, which means they are filtered through our senses, intellect, affect, and desires. It assumes, too, that they exist in a particular time and place and that they are based on what Husserl, one of the preeminent philosophers of phenomenology, would call "intentionality," or the way in which we direct our consciousness toward particular objects in the world. Moreover, we exist in the present, but we interpret the world by reference to our past, to history, and to memory. Interpretation is what Husserl calls a "theoretical act" (1990: 5). What we call a shared experience is another theoretical act, already the result of an interpretation and past knowledge; it is partly a recognition and partly a calculation that presupposes that different individuals share not only similar presents but also similar pasts and similar memories.

I showed above that the diachronic indexes of corrido authenticity, from the romance to the narcocorrido, are violence, place, and the counterhegemonic, three indexes with a deep correlation to the axis of experience. Violence, particularly as it exists in the narcocorrido, is embodied. Place helps the song perform its theoretical act of interpreting space. The counterhegemonic explains the intentionality of "foci," the types of objects and actions to which the narrator and listener will direct their attention. These are objects that fall within the political/politicized categories of power, valor, and dispossession. In the narcocorrido, these also include the objects that pertain to illegality and the trafficking of illicit drugs. These three indexes of authenticity do more than help us recognize the history of the genre. They also reveal that, like other folk and popular genres, narcocorrido authenticity is dependent on the experiential and the genre's ability to represent, through performance and narrative, what it feels like to be amid the violence.

In an industrial setting, the task of encoding the particular type of experience narcocorridos demand (i.e., violence, place, and the counterhegemonic) is part of branding, a commercial signifying technique that uses repetition, consistency, and different planes of signification (e.g., the meaning of music, the meaning of attire, and the meaning of the song) to create semiotic redundancies that over time give heft to the meanings and effects the narco brand is meant to elicit (Oswalt 2015). It is the use of these codes, these indexes, that the brand, consumers, and media industries use to claim the authenticity of the genre.

That a brand conveys authenticity is not an oxymoron. Sarah Banet-Weiser notes the relevant connections that branding has with authenticity in contemporary culture. "[The] process of branding," she writes, "impacts the way we understand who we are, how we organize ourselves in the world, what stories we tell ourselves about ourselves" (Banet-Weiser 2012: 5). Branding has thus become essential to self-identity. Branding is intertwined with the personal and social processes by which we define our authentic selves, including the social practices, objects, and knowledge that can yield for us and, often, to us, an aura of authenticity. Banet-Weiser also points out that some categories of life are particularly susceptible to being conceived as authentic, and these categories include self-identity, politics, creativity, and religious experiences. The narco brand connects self-identity to politics by relying on the encoding of experiences of antistate and counterhegemonic violence. Because the violence is elsewhere, however, a political interpretation of the narcocorrido in the US requires the resignification of the counterhegemonic stance, one that relies on institutional support and affirmation. In the United States, the counterhegemonic stance becomes ethnic affiliation, which creates an imagined community, to use Benedict Anderson's (1991) metaphor, between Mexican Americans and Mexicans, as well as Mexican Americans in urban centers like Los Angeles, California, with Mexican Americans in rural communities like Topeka, Kansas. It is this affiliative work that defines the connection between narcocorrido performers, Mexican American urban youth, and capitalistic recording enterprises like *Billboard*. Activating it all is the branding that connects US narcocorridos to authenticity and the experiential.

The systemic branding efforts by Rivera, Rios, and Ortiz are particularly clear in the way their performances address the index of place and territory. That is, they face a signifying challenge. From the United States, they must claim to share the experiences of violence at the heart of the narco brand. To simulate proximity, performers routinely and repeatedly state their connections, real or imagined, to places embroiled in the violence. Take, for instance, Rios's performance in Pico Rivera, California, on October 15, 2013. After beginning the second song of the concert, "Los sanguinarios del MI" ("Bloodthirsty Men of the MI"), which has become a sort of anthem for EMA, he stops himself after a few verses to address the audience directly and yells a call-and-response invitation: "Si hay gente de Michoacán, de Jalisco, de Zacatecas, de Durango, o de Sinaloa . . ." (If there are people from Michoacán, Jalisco, Zacatecas, Durango, or Sinaloa . . .). Roars silence him. Each of these places is home to cartels and to cartel violence, and though some in the audience may have had to leave their homes behind because of this violence, they cheer excitedly nonetheless. At this moment, violence is not a hindrance or a source of fear and pain. It is refigured as a source of pride and community, a scar in their own biographies that reminds them all that they survived, that they are tougher than the violence.

Although many Mexican states and cities have been bloodied by drug-related violence, the branding efforts of these California stars reveal a hierarchy of places. At the top are Sinaloa, Culiacán, and Badiraguato. Rios, Ortiz, and Rivera use these claims of location in their performances repeatedly, which is notable given that only Rios is from Sinaloa. Ortiz is from Pasadena, and Rivera was from Culver City, California (often misreported as Long Beach) (Cobo 2013: 12). To add to this sense of place and experience, Rivera, Ortiz, and Rios each performs a catalog of songs that routinely narrate events, real or imagined, that happened in Mexico's violent North. In addition to the numerous references to Sinaloa in the lyrics, songs like Rivera's "Recuerdos de Sinaloa" ("Memories of Sinaloa") and "Sinaloa: Princesa norteña" ("Sinaloa: Northern Princess"), as well as Ortiz's "Ferias sinoaloenses" ("Sinaloa's State Fairs") and "Soy sinaloense" ("I Am from Sinaloa") eulogize the state and its culture, including its violence and serrano values. Although the state of Sinaloa has a diversified economy with tourism as its leading source of revenue, in these songs the state becomes the site for rural life. Rios's song "Soy de rancho" uses an expression that is hard to translate. The closest is "I come from a ranch," but the expression is not simply about place; "Soy de rancho" is a complex code where the person becomes the place and thus the expression signals the place's and the person's identity and values. It connotes that the person lacks education or social finesse, but he is honest, hardworking, and respectful, a set of connotations that Mexican American audiences will likely recognize as their own.

The song is the story of a border-crosser interrogated by a border agent who answers the question "Where you come from?" with "Venimos de Culiacán, Sinaloa" (We come from Culiacán, Sinaloa). It then proceeds to explain in the first-person perspective: "Sí, señor, yo soy de rancho, soy de botas y a caballo, soy nacido y criado en el monte" (Yes, sir, I am from a ranch, I am about boots and horses, I was born and raised in the boonies). Mixing first-person singular narration with first-person plural, the first verses work as an invitation for the listener to share an identity with the singer, one centered on the sentence "Soy de rancho." The song continues specifying the connections between place and ranch serrano values, which are anchored in poverty, family, and religion. The song is also a story of transformation in which poverty becomes wealth thanks to the profits of the drug trade: horses become fancy pickups, but importantly, the values remain the same. With these and other songs, the California-based stars, their managers, and their labels, are showing that they understand their audiences and know that these audiences demand indexes of authenticity such as place that can remind them not only where they come from but also who they are. In the narcocorrido, Sinaloa becomes a complex code that connotes place, identity, and solid rural values, even if the real or fictitious protagonists are also criminals.

These stars' efforts to simulate and emphasize location have had secondary effects at the industrial and institutional level. They have helped *Billboard* and Spanish-language radio validate their own branding strategies, which also depend on mystifying claims about place. After all, there is a clear parallel between singers who, like Rios, Ortiz, and Rivera, embody a narco-identity while claiming to be from Culiacán or Sinaloa, and *Billboard*'s use of the term *Regional Mexican* to classify and brand narcocorridos. This official term, which classifies the most successful Spanish-language radio stations and Spanish-language music in the United States, depends on a simulation of place that has become essential to a "brand culture" that hides the deterritorialized character of the music industry today. As Banet-Weiser posits, brand culture refers to the process by which the converging relationships between marketing, a product, and consumers "become cultural contexts for everyday living, individual identity, and affective relationships" (2012: 3). Claiming thus that embodiment, place, and orientation (directedness) are central to the branding of artists and media genres that give industrial meaning to the term *narcocorrido* is more than claiming that violence has become commoditized. In our contemporary culture, branding is central to the meanings we give to cultural experiences, hence branding is not only about capitalism but also, as Banet-Weiser notes and narcocorridos show, about identity. The claims of Mexicanity and the way performers like Rios, Ortiz, and Rivera have embodied the narco-brand are not only commercial tactics. They are also the means by which Mexican American urban youth, the typical consumers of narcocorridos in the US, refigure their marginalization, their directedness, through the tactical understanding of who they are vis-à-vis place and through the deployment of counterhegemonic fantasies that narcocorridos activate.

In the case of narcocorridos, the branding has paved the way for commercial success, benefiting in the process the radio and music industries. Banda and norteño music are the two leading music categories in the *Billboard* Regional Mexican Album category. They are also the leading genres in the Regional Mexican radio format. For instance, banda and norteño artists like Ortiz dominated the top five spots in Billboard's Regional Mexican Song category during the week of December 15, 2012. Rivera was in fourteenth place with her song "La misma gran señora" ("The Same Great

Lady"). These artists dominate sales with romantic ballads. This may mean that the romantic ballad remains the most important subgenre of banda and norteño, but it also means that Regional Mexican is dominated by artists whose personal brands are closely associated with narcocorridos, except for Grupo Pesado, Claudia Contreras notes (2008), which has made a public rejection of narcocorridos. This means that the rest of the top five have a musical repertory that includes narcocorridos (Contreras 2008). La Arrolladora Banda El Limón may only have a few hits related to narcoculture, but Ortiz, Rios, and Tapia are three of the most important narcocorrido singers today. Rivera's life is remembered as closely connected to the narco imaginary. The appeal of these artists, then, even while singing romantic ballads, is undisputedly bound to a brand crafted through the performance of narcocorridos.

Branding is the result of symbolic work that requires a high degree of consistency through time. Rivera, for instance, began recording in 1994, and she released her first album in 1995 (*La chacalosa*, Capitol/EMI), which sold around 1 million copies. The title song, "La chacalosa," is the story of a drug queen-pin and the song positioned, from this moment on, Rivera as a singer branded by narcoculture. In this song, Rivera performs in the first person as the daughter of a narco ("Soy hija de un traficante" [I am the daughter of a drug trafficker]), who was raised by and inherited the heroin business from her father ("Conozco bien las movidas, me crié entre la mafia grande de la major mercancia" [I know the moves well, I grew up between the big mobs and the major commodities]). The song describes her illegal poppy crops in Jalisco, her heroin labs in Sonora, and declares, from a curious feminist standpoint that would be repeated in many of her songs, that women can also become narco leaders ("y tambien las mujeres pueden" [and the women also can]). *La chacalosa* included several other tracks that furthered Rivera's narco-brand, including "Tambien las mujeres pueden," a song originally made popular by Los Tigres, and "La perra contrabandista," which literally translates as "The Trafficker Bitch." Like other narcocorrido singers, her albums also included romantic ballads; *La chacalosa* included, for instance, "Libro abierto," a ranchero standard ballad. But Rivera's identity as a powerful woman willing to defy male-dominated society depended on her drug-related songs. Although in several albums she continued the tradition of other famous Mexican women singers (e.g., *Farewell to Selena* and *Joyas prestadas*), her work can also be described as an ongoing conversation with the great ones of the narcocorrido genre. This is particularly true for her 1999 album *Reyna de reynas*, in which she is in conversation with one of the greatest narcocorrido albums, *Jefe de jefes* (1997) by Los Tigres del Norte. This narco-album reasserted Rivera's complex gender performance and invited listeners to, at least briefly, reflect on the sexism implied by the traditional, male-dominated narcocorrido subgenre.

Rios and Ortiz make no qualms that their brand is narcocorridos and has been narcocorridos since the beginning of their careers. A huge percentage of their songs deal with the drug world, and although they are not always from the point of view of the narco (Ortiz's "Sangre azul" ["Blue Blood"], for instance, is from the point of view of a policeman), the majority depict the drug war from the perspective of the cartels. Rios, whose career began in Mexico but took off in California, has always been a narcocorrido singer. His brand under EMA has become even more violent. The "K" in El Komander, for instance, is depicted with an AK-47; he goes to the stage dressed to fight, with a bulletproof vest and militarized clothing; the violence in his work is relentless, graphic, and idealized.

Ortiz's songs like "La ultima sombra," "Aquí les afirmo," "Morir y existir," and many others speak of violence, drugs, revenge, and trafficking. In addition to these classic drug-related topics, Rios and Ortiz also compose and perform narcocorridos that are about the narco-lifestyle. "El troquero locochon" and "Culiacán vs. Mazatlán," for instance, are about highly stylized (pimped, if you wish) pickup trucks and sports cars. "A la moda" is about fashion, jewelry, and material consumption. These narco-lifestyle songs and the videos that publicize them are full of young women who seem to be the sexual reward for men engaging in the proper display of excessive consumption. During the last three years, Ortiz and Rios have thus delivered a series of performances that, taken together, paint a fantastic type of masculinity bound to violence, wealth, rebellion, and traditional heteronormative sexuality.

These cases show how the narcocorrido brand is constructed around the indexes of authenticity, which the music genre reassembles based on the code modalities of the experiential. Like other popular and folk genres, the narcocorrido tries to position itself as part of the repertory of experiences shared by Mexican Americans and connect them back to the social realities of violence and power differentials in particular locations in Mexico. As I have shown, narcocorrido performances lend authenticity to the genre, to the singers who use them for branding, to the media and music institutions (e.g., Univision and Billboard) that use the moniker "Regional Mexican," which aims to classify banda and norteño as music connected to a place, Mexico, and to the flesh-and-blood communities of Mexicans, not simply to audiences. The very particular way in which authenticity is crafted through reference to the codes of the experiential, embodiment, place, and directedness, has one last powerful outcome that defines today's narcocorrido storytelling and performance: the first-person narrative modality.

In the "I" of Violence

The romance, the corrido, and early narcocorridos were third-person narratives. The singer told the story of someone else; he or she is a narrator. This is the case, for instance, in the classic song "El corrido de Pancho Villa," in which the singer/narrator places himself or herself as a witness to Villa's heroic acts. The third person is so common in the corrido that a traditional first verse is a variation of "Voy a cantar un corrido del . . ." (I am going to sing a corrido about . . .), a verse that is the equivalent of "Once upon a time" in that it points to the genre, the position of the singer as narrator, and the beginning of the story. Third-person narration remained common in early popular narcocorridos, even though these were part of an industrial mode of cultural production. For instance, the first narcocorrido megahit was on Los Tigres del Norte's album *Contrabando y traición* (1972), an album that included one narcocorrido title track, several romantic ballads, a couple of stories of immigrants (including the very famous "Chicano"), and an anti-Mexican government story about a journalist who is serving all the people by trying to investigate the truth and corruption ("Porro"). "Contrabando y traición" was a third-person narrative; the rest of the songs were narrated in the first person. Los Tigres' second album (*La banda del carro rojo*, 1975), also a huge hit, included two narcocorridos, "La banda del carro rojo" and "Ya encontraron a Camelia," both of which were in the third person. The rest of the album was not. *Corridos prohibidos* (Forbidden Corridos, 1989), an album dedicated to narcocorridos, was told entirely in the third person. Chalino was killed in 1992, and Jenni Rivera recorded her debut album, *La chacalosa*, in 1995. By the time Los Tigres recorded *Jefe de jefes* (Boss of Bosses) in 1997, the genre had changed. In this double album, five of the fourteen narcocorridos were first-person narratives, though not every song on the double album was a narcocorrido.

The change in narrative modality has continued and escalated over time. Today the narcocorrido genre is mostly sung in the first person. This applies even to songs like "Dámaso," which is based on a real person: the singer takes on the role of the central character of the story. These narcocorridos use the experiential codes to identify the singer(s) with the imaginary world the song creates. *This is a type of overcoding that compensates for the geograph-*

ical and experiential distance between singer and events that parallels the way the narco-brand circulates among Mexican American urban youth. Like gangsta rap in other youth communities, narcocorridos have become hegemonic among urban Mexican American youth who use these songs and performances to resignify the violence and poverty that too often surround them (Morrison 2008).

This narrative modality has been key to the careers and personal brands of Rivera, Ortiz, and Rios. Rivera's "La chacalosa," her first narcocorrido hit, already used this form of address ("They are looking for me for *chacalosa*; I am the daughter of a drug trafficker . . ."). Most contemporary narcocorrido singers, including all of the members of Corridos Enfermos and El Movimiento Alterado, do not typically sing descriptions of things that happen to others or moralize about the outcomes of illegal activity. They do not share the news or distribute local lore; they *are* the news and place themselves at the center of the stories. These singers, in song and performance, embody the narco-imaginary and present themselves as examples of drug-dealing success, as beneficiaries of the wealth found in drug trafficking, as those inflicting violence on others, or as those suffering the violence.

In addition to channeling the experiential, and thus helping construct the brand of authenticity, the form of address produces other narrative outcomes. A first-person narration of violence implies that the singer is singing from the position of those who survived the violence or even of those who inflicted it. Exceptions do exist, as in Ortiz's "Cara a la muerte" ("Face of the Dead"), a first-person narration memorializing a killed traitor. The majority of today's songs, however, are told from the position of the drug lord, a narrative of power and survival. This perspective does not moralize the dead but rather justifies the survivor's (i.e., the drug dealer's) success, which, in narcocorridos, often comes down to arguing for or presenting a superior masculinity—or, as in Rivera's song, a superior femininity. For instance, in the creepy "14 guerras" ("14 Wars"), Gerardo Ortiz declares:

I am the Taliban ghost of El Chapo . . .
I have tortured, decapitated, assaulted, and maimed
And if fear crosses my path I connect
With my intelligence
That's how I do my job, with heart, I am a killer . . .

Ortiz takes on the identity of an assassin and torturer who believes himself the ghostly presence of "El Chapo" Guzmán, the leader of the Sinaloa Cartel. The masculinity he presents is relatively complex, for it relies on intelligence to carry out the harshest violence on others. Yet this masculinity is unmistakably tied to masculine excess, for it is built to inflict pain and to do war.

Experiential codes are not only important because they connect the singer and the audience to violence. These codes also allow singers to be protagonists in the lives of excessive wealth depicted in the subset of narcocorridos that I refer to as "narco-lifestyle corridos." These performances engage with drug violence obliquely, as they tend to depict social interactions that are possible only as the aftermath of violent criminal activity. In these songs, such as Ortiz's "Culiacán vs. Mazatlán," the protagonist from Culiacán races his highly altered Camaro against the Viper of someone from Mazatlán. Though the Camaro loses, they race again; this time the Viper is up against a Corvette, and the Corvette wins. In the current imaginary of Mexican American youth, these displays of conspicuous consumption exist because of illegal actions related to drugs; the cars and the scantily clad women who always seem to circle the vehicles in related music videos stand for the spoils of violence, the economic and sexual rewards of joining the cartels. The song "A la moda," a huge hit for Ortiz, is full of expensive brands that define the hyperwealthy, including Ferrari, Dolce & Gabbana, Prada, and Rolex. In the music video that accompanies the song, Ortiz displays his wealth and fashion trendiness by changing outfits every few seconds; by entering the hall of an expensive hotel after driving his Ferrari; by being followed by several bodyguards; and by surrounding himself with beautiful women in a club with a table full of expensive liquor bottles. In short, Ortiz embodies the consumption and immoral frankness of the narco-lord. Moreover, he idolizes the lifestyle.

Violence and conspicuous consumption are two ways of exploiting an authenticity predicated on the experiential. What's more, the first-person narrative of violence and wealth allows fans to personally connect to violence and conspicuous consumption, even if this connection exists within a fantasy world. Narcocorridos tell the "pure truth," and fans can, however briefly, hold on to the notion that they are the ones who can inflict pain, not just receive it. They can imagine the experience of obscene wealth, even if after the dance club closes they must go back to their decrepit reality.

Authenticity is a powerful and demanding brand. As if to ratify that his colorful biography is evidence of his intimate knowledge of the violence he sings about, Ortiz barely survived an attack on him on March 20, 2011, in Villa de Álvarez, Mexico. His manager and promoter, Ramiro Caro, was not that fortunate. In a similar fashion, though Jenni Rivera died in a plane crash, news outlets in Mexico and the United States were quick to report that the DEA was investigating the owner of the plane, implying that Rivera's death was related to drugs. I somehow doubt it.

CONCLUSION

Leila Cobo is the executive director of Latin content and programming for *Billboard* and has written about Latin music for decades now, including a biography of Jenni Rivera in 2013. At the beginning of 2017, Cobo (2017) wrote an end-of-the-year report on the state of Latin music in the United States in 2016. Streaming of Latin music had grown by 13.6 percent, buoyed by the Latin consumer, the segment of the US audience most likely to use streaming and mobile-friendly devices like smartphones. One-quarter of Pandora's listeners, for instance, are Latino. The Latin music market is quite fragmented in more than one way. For instance, the Miami market and the New York market are quite different from the West Coast market. The yearly charts for best-selling albums were dominated by Regional Mexican artists, but the streaming charts for individual songs were dominated by urban music like reggaeton artists Nicky Jam or J. Balvin. Nicky Jam's collaboration with Daddy Yankee ("Hasta el amanecer" ["Until the Dawn"]) was streamed 121 million times, almost twice as many times as the highest representative of the Regional Mexican Music genre, Ariel Camacho and Los Plebes del Rancho's "Solo con verte," which had 72 million streams. Yet Ariel Camacho sold 50 percent more albums than J. Balvin. Albums, song purchases, and music streaming paint different pictures of the Latin market, and without a question, the importance of urban music is significant. Urban, which in the Latin segment includes Reggaetón and Cubatón, has a deep impact within and beyond Latino consumers, and the artists representing these soulful and danceable genres, like Shakira, Farruko, and Daddy Yankee, are the Latino artists most US Americans, whether Latino or non-Latino, recognize.

Yet Cobo follows the money and argues that Regional Mexican, led by banda and narcocorrido stars, is the foundation of the Latin music marketplace. This is so even though the crossover appeal of banda music is very small. Typically, my students at the University of Virginia have never heard of Gerardo Ortiz, the most successful Regional Mexican artist of the last five years, and they would not recognize banda music as one of the top genres of Latin music today. It is as if the rise of narcocorridos and banda in the United States were best-kept music secrets.

The reasons for the genre's appeal are unclear. It is difficult to explain Ortiz's relative invisibility outside Mexican American communities given that his Facebook page has more than 11 million likes. His Facebook fan clubs number in the dozens, with the largest, "Addiction," having more than 24,000 followers, and many of these fan clubs are initiated by women. His song "Dámaso" has more than 200 million views on Vevo and dominates the Regional Mexican charts. To some, including Elijah Wald, the writer of *Narcocorrido* (2001), and Shaul Shwarz, the director of the documentary *Narco cultura* (2013), the music appeals to listeners because people, in particular young men, tend to identify with the outcast and the criminal. Shwarz goes as far as claiming the music is just "entertainment," another example of fandom favoring bad-boy culture. Collapsing gender and hypermasculinity, Wald and Shwarz blame the popularity of narcocorridos on a "boys will be boys" logic that I believe avoids answering the question of why US-based Mexican American fans flock to concerts, investing time and hard-earned money in this specific type of violent culture, at this junctural moment in the history of Latinos in the United States. The "boys will be boys" hypothesis simply cannot help explain Ortiz's success, or female fandom, or female stars like Rivera. Fandom is much more complex than these thin explanations, and currently, to my knowledge, nobody has done a study of US narcocorrido fandom. This is a gap in our understanding that needs to be filled. Absent these studies, let me conclude this chapter with a few ideas that can be a starting point to understanding the success of the notorious genre. Some were discussed above, but some should be the starting point of future projects.

The music's success with audiences depends on the narcocorrido's ability to connote authenticity and to activate fantasies of place and of experience. The fantasy of place, which *Billboard*, Telemundo, and Univision profit from, reconnects music written, performed, produced, and consumed in the United States with Mexico's violent areas. Some Regional Mexican music is from Mexico, but the bulk of "authentic" narcocorridos are not. Fantasies of experience underscore the performances that define narco-stars like Rivera, Rios, and Ortiz, and this claim to the experiential lubricates the circulation of music among a population hungry for cultural experiences that can help them make sense of their place in society and push back against forces that keep this population marginalized. Deterritorialization may have ripped the genre away from its popular storytelling capacity, but reterritorialization has afforded new possibilities. Even if recorded or staged in the United States, norteño and banda music packs the feelings and values of religious and agrarian life alongside the complex power fantasies of the narco-imaginary. In so doing, the US narcocorrido becomes terrain fertile for the growth of new, if sometimes confounding, traditions of symbolic power and ethnic pride. These two types of subjective goods, power and pride, are in relative short supply for millions of Latinos due to the material and sociocultural effects of three historical phenomena: (1) the war on drugs in the United States, (2) the sense of vulnerability common among US Latinos due to the mainstreaming of anti-Latino nativism, and (3) the lasting effects of the economic crisis of 2008. Let me finish this chapter with a brief sketch of the effects of these phenomena on Latinos.

The war on drugs is a cancer demonstrating the symbiotic existence of Mexico and the United States. This cancer has different manifestations on the two sides of the border, but both are cruel, violent, and relentless, damaging countless lives and communities. Just as Mexico has become, according to some at least, a "narco-state," illicit drug consumption and trafficking have also challenged fundamental political and social values and goals in the United States. The US government has engaged in a war against its own population that has substantively damaged African American and Latino communities. This war has been the central reason for the increasing size and human and economic costs of the prison system, which now "houses" roughly 2.3 million inmates. The dramatic growth of this system correlates with the "tough on crime" policies of the Reagan administration, also credited with amplifying the war on drugs within and outside the United States. African Americans and Latinos have been the worst affected, and without a question, members of these communities have used art, music, and other types of expressive culture to meaningfully respond. In places like Compton, California, N.W.A.'s hometown, and East Los Angeles, where Chalino Sanchez first recorded his famous narcocorridos in 1987, these communities have lost a significant portion of the human, political, and economic potential embodied in Latino and African American youth to the perverse punishment of incarceration and the corresponding substandard postincarceration citizenship these "felons" forever have to suffer (Quinones 2009: 15). The easiest illustration of this type of citizenship is a former convict's reduced economic employment prospects and political power. Not only does prisoners' economic output fall to practically zero, but their employment rates and quality of employment after release too are significantly lower. According to the US Justice Department, one year after release, "as many as 60 percent of former inmates are not employed in the legitimate labor market." In states like California, former inmates are barred from whole industries like law, real estate, medicine, and education. As if these economic punishments were not enough, 13 percent of all African American men in 2000 did not have the right to vote because they were ex-felons (Petersilia 2001).

The effects of the war on drugs in these communities are multigenerational and help to explain the basis for Latino and African American marginalization, including the practical nullification of wealth-accumulation capacity, the lack of political representation, and the burden of being stereotyped in public culture as thugs and violent criminals. So many opportunities and lives have been destroyed by the war on drugs in these communities that the sentiment behind N.W.A.'s "Fuck tha Police," which parallels the antiorder and antilaw sentiment of most narcocorridos, seems a reasonable response. When placed in context, gangsta rap and narcocorridos are not simply reflections of social reality, but also rebuttals to the onslaught of damaging policies and law-and-order culture that take away both lives and the meaning of these lives. Gangsta rap and narcocorridos have helped members of these communities reimagine social agency as well as concrete and symbolic power. If the worst outcome of the rise of organized crime in Mexico has been corrupting the state to its core, the worst outcome of the US war on drugs is the mainstreaming of the corrupting ideology of racism and xenophobia that is still being used to justify the contemporary carceral state.

In addition to the damaging effects of the war on drugs among Latinos, the last couple of decades has seen the rise of mainstream anti-Latino nativism, which is currently at a high point with the election of President Trump and the legitimization of the alt-right, a far-right white supremacy political group that has gained traction in mainstream US politics. Anti-Latino and anti-immigrant hatred have been vindicated by these political processes, and Latino feelings of vulnerability are as high as ever. In another work, *Citizenship Excess* (2013), I detailed the cultural and historical mainstreaming of nativism after 9/11 and showed how nativism had become a pillar of right-wing politics under the banner of the Tea Party and how the mainstreaming of nativism had authorized damning policies against immigrants, especially undocumented people from Latin America.

The Great Recession of 2008 only exacerbated Latino vulnerability. As Rakesh Kochhar, Richard Fry, and Paul Taylor (2010) have demonstrated, the unemployment rate among Latinos in the second quarter of 2008 was 6.9 percent. One year later it had almost doubled, reaching 11.9 percent, with native-born Latinos suffering a higher rate of unemployment (12.9 percent) than foreign-born (11 percent). The same Pew Research team showed that one year later the recession had hit Latinos the hardest, erasing 66 percent of inflation-adjusted median wealth from 2005 to 2009 (Pew Social Trends 2011). In 2009, the median wealth accumulation among whites was $113,149, which was a whopping eighteen times larger than the median wealth accumulation among Latinos ($6,325) and almost twenty times that of African Americans ($5,677). Latinos experienced this huge degradation of wealth and a doubling of the unemployment rate at the same time that Arizona and other states were passing nativist legislation and mainstream media welcomed the nativist voices of Lou Dobbs, Glenn Beck, and Bill O'Reilly. From the fear of deportation to the economic fear of unemployment, Latino vulnerability has grown as fast as the popularity of narcocorridos.

Unlike in the previous chapter, in which narcoculture was defined partly by its relation to the censorial, here narcocorridos are shown as a culture thriving in the disjuncture between the political and legal, the economic, and the social. They are a testament to the creative labor of immigrant producers like Los Twiins; immigrant musicians like Alfredo Rios, Jenni Rivera, and Gerardo Ortiz; and US institutions like *Billboard*, Univision, and Telemundo, which, together, work at deciphering the riddle of how to sell these Mexican-based narratives of violence north of the border. Channeling Deleuze and Guattari, I showed that their decoding efforts have paid off. The result is a branding strategy that depends on first-person narration to claim firsthand experience of violence and wealth common among narco bosses. These first-person narratives also show the complex blurring of fictional fantasies with real events and people, their biographies and experiences. All of these aesthetic devices are found in the song "Dámaso," the example that began this chapter. This song, which honors a leader of the Sinaloa Cartel, is a first-person account of one of the most wanted criminals on earth and the enormous wealth and violence that surrounds him. Fiction blends with nonfiction and invites listeners to sing along, also in the first person, as if they too were the greatest kingpin of all, even while laboring in the overheated kitchen of a Chipotle.

5

Bloody Blogs

PUBLICITY AND OPACITY

There is a sphere of human agreement that is nonviolent to the extent that
it is wholly inaccessible to violence: the proper sphere of "understanding,"
language.
—Walter Benjamin, "The Critique of Violence"

Digital technologies, particularly the internet, the World Wide Web (WWW),
digital photography and video, have transformed the conditions for publicity. Thanks to these technologies, the conditions of "visibility" and
"access"—which index, among other things, the conditions for sharing
words, images, and videos with a large number of people—have radically
changed. There is a true democratizing effect inherent in these technologies as more and more people around the world have the capacity to share
information, culture, and ideas on a mass level. The benefits do not end
there. New types of mediation, which include the blogosphere and social
media, have reshaped the news sector and, in some instances and contexts,
have fortified it. In Mexico, for instance, this strengthening of the news
sector is necessary. Violence and coercion have weakened traditional journalistic organizations as killings, kidnappings, threats, and other types of
physical and emotional coercion against journalists have become routine,
particularly as the conflict with and within drug criminal organizations has
increased since 2007. The extraordinary affordances of digital technologies
have thus been an unquestionable blessing. They have provided avenues for
publicity, news creation, and news sharing that were not long ago unimagi-
nable. If Walter Benjamin's comment in the epigraph is correct—if shar-

ing ideas with each other through language has a peacemaking capacity—digital technologies could be central to Mexico's pacification and future. But things are not that simple, as this chapter shows through an analysis of one small but very visible subsector of this new Mexican informational environment, the anonymous blogosphere, and its connection to and structuring by violence.

This chapter is an analysis of the blogs *El Blog del Narco* (*EBDN*) and *Valor por Tamaulipas* (*VxT*) that centers on the uses and misuses of opacity by and around these popular sites and on the connections between opacity, space, technology, and publicity. This analysis is not meant to address all the publics that can and have converged in and around blogs and Facebook posts, only those that identify these blogs as praiseworthy types of citizen journalism. The chapter continues the conversation about the structural power of criminal drug violence in Mexico's publicity by examining the structural role of opacity, especially the uses of anonymity in Mexico's blogosphere. It examines the way anonymity is central to the blogs' mode of production and the particular discourses of authorship and citizenship energized by and around the makers of the blogs. These discourses display a notable connection between anonymity and displacement at the heart of violence, but first, before engaging with this anonymous blogosphere, the chapter explains the journalistic context that made these blogs necessary. The blogs, as I show in the following section, are a response to violence against traditional journalism, which has deeply affected Mexico's communicational environment.

SILENCING OF NEWS

Reporters Without Borders (RSF), one of the main international organizations trying to safeguard freedom of the press around the world, uses a "World Press Freedom Index" as a heuristic device that illustrates the challenges to journalism and public communication by country.[1] The latest rankings, for 2016 and 2017, were based on seven subcategories: (1) pluralism, (2) media independence, (3) media environment and self-censorship, (4) legislative framework, (5) transparency, (6) infrastructure, and (7) abuses. Finland had the best rank (8.59) and Eritrea the worst (83.92). Out of 180 nations evaluated, Mexico placed 149th, just below Russia and ahead of Tajikistan. The Mexican general rank, as bad as it was, did not tell the particular story of what it means to be a crime or political reporter in Mexico. This is better illustrated by the seventh subcategory, the "Abuse Score." This category measures instances of violence and threats against journalists, professional communicators, and citizen journalists. In that particular metric, Mexico was the eleventh worst, bested only by a totalitarian regime (China), eight nations in traditional and nontraditional wars (e.g., Syria, Iraq, and Libya), and Honduras, a victim of massive violence due to its own drug wars. Like Honduras, Mexico is burdened by the rise of drug criminal organizations, but Mexico's lowly ranking is only partly due to organized crime: insecurity that stems from government corruption and coercion is as important as the power of organized crime. According to RSF, Mexico is the worst country to practice journalism in the West, particularly for those communicators who specialize in crime or politics. From 2000 to April 2017, Artículo 19 (https://articulo19.org/) documented the killing of 103 journalists in Mexico, including 30 since President Enrique Peña Nieto took power; Oaxaca (8 killings) and Veracruz (7 killings) are the worst Mexican states in which to practice institutionalized or citizen journalism.[2]

RSF has compiled the World Press Freedom Index since 2002. It not only tracks the context for practicing institutionalized journalism but also includes and quantifies abuses against "netizens," individuals playing the role of journalists on the internet. The index is not a perfect snapshot of the journalistic environment. Compiling data on attacks on journalists is extremely difficult, as the data are messy. Rogelio Hernández López, the founder and executive director of the House of the Rights of Journalists (HRJ), has noted how different methodologies and ways of accounting for deaths and crimes against journalists can yield very different numbers.[3] Reports by local police can be misleading and can undercount violence that targets journalists. Without investigating each instance of violence or threats against the press, it is hard to fully understand the picture. Neither RSF nor HRJ has the resources to do that. However, because RSF has followed consistent methodologies, its index paints a decent snapshot of tendencies and trajectories.

According to the index, Mexico's lowly rank in 2016 was not particularly unusual. Figure 5.1 shows that this level of danger began roughly a decade ago. The chart traces the erosion of the journalistic environment, a decline that starts in 2004 with a twenty-two-place drop in rank and continues in 2005 with an additional thirty-four-place drop in rank. Since 2005, the decline has slowed down, but things have remained terrible: for six years (from 2011 to 2016) Mexico's rank hovered around 148. The worsening of Mexico's rank corresponds to an increase of news about narco-traffic. I showed and analyzed this increase in chapter 1, but it is worth mentioning here that, as

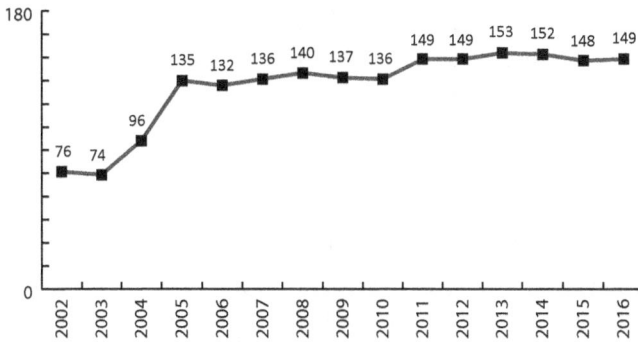

Figure 5.1. Mexico's World Press Freedom Index rank. Source: World Press Freedom Index 2017. Note: This figure is a compilation of the World Press Freedom Index since it began in 2002. Each number in the graph corresponds to Mexico's ranking against a field of 180 nations. The higher the number, the worse the ranking.

illustrated in figure 1.3, incidences of news on narco-traffic began increasing in 2004, with the biggest spike in 2005. General violence, on the other hand, increased until 2008 (see also chapter 1). This means that the environment for journalism eroded in 2004 before the spike on general violence in 2008 and was coterminous with an increase in journalistic attention on the dealings of organized crime. The different trajectories between the RSF index and the rise of violence point to the fact that DCO coercion of journalists is only one of the factors shaping their work environment. The other force is state coercion, which ranges from subtle economic and professional pressure on journalistic media to harsh aggressions including assault, homicide, and false imprisonment.

I spent the summer of 2012 interviewing journalists in danger in Mexico and the leaders of NGOs and state agencies trying to protect them. My trip was inspired by highly publicized cases of violence against journalists at the hands of DCOs, and, naively, I thought that cartel violence was the greatest threat. I quickly learned that to journalists and leaders of journalistic organizations (RSF Mexico, HRJ, and others), state coercion is as serious a danger to journalism as organized crime is. As the head of the Committee to Protect Journalists (CPJ) in Mexico put it when investigating the killing of reporter Jorge Ochoa Martínez on January 29, 2010, the likely culprits are "drug cartels or local political bosses, or the police. Sometimes they are all the same thing" (O'Connor 2010). On the *CPJ Blog,* Mike O'Connor points to the usual suspects and to the problem of the blurring boundaries between some state sectors and organized crime, a blurring that many in Mexico refer to as the rise of the "narco-state." While O'Connor is right when assessing who is likely to pull the trigger against journalists, the state of vulnerability of many journalists starts with the influence that the government has over the political economy of news in Mexico.

Historically, the vulnerabilities of journalists working in institutionalized media are rooted in economic reasons and the peculiar way the Mexican state influences news media. This economic influence is constant. State representatives use the assignation of official advertising as the most common tool to shape news. Given that state advertising is significant, often comprising the largest source of advertising revenue, media owners have no choice but to follow specific editorial guidelines and push for specific party agendas. Journalists and editors are pressured into doing the same, as detailed to me by Mexican author and journalist Marco Lara Sklar in 2012. Some media owners have long-term semi-formal arrangements with some politicians and parties; under these arrangements they offer their power to publish uncritical journalism in exchange for sustained advertising patronage. Using state advertising to enforce editorial guidelines and produce positive political profiles is illegal according to some laws and policies. Article 134 of the Mexican Constitution prohibits the use of "names, images, voices, and symbols related with the promotion of any public servant." Article 41 of the Constitution prohibits political parties from buying advertising on radio and television. The same article prohibits the use of official advertising during elections. But these constitutional boundaries do not seem to matter. More specific administrative policies, such as the "General Guidelines for Public Communication Campaigns of Dependencies and Entities of Federal Public Administration," tend to be vague and fail to require transparency. Patronage continues. Besides shaping editorial and journalistic behavior and reducing press freedom, this unusual system of public patronage also fosters a false pluralism, for it allows some media, which Mexicans call *pasquines* (lampoons), to exist only due to state advertising revenue. These media often have extremely low levels of readership, viewership, or listenership, but they target state resources to keep running while giving the impression that the Mexican media sector is more diverse and vital than it actually is.

The revenue provided by state coffers, which in 2014 amounted to almost $1 billion nationally, has become the lifeblood of a corrupt media system, but it is not the only economic source curtailing freedom of the press in

Mexico. A similarly severe problem is that the journalistic profession in Mexico is hugely underpaid and insecure. Although officially the minimum wage for journalists is roughly a very low *daily wage* of US$11 (Mex$224), it is now more common to be off payroll and do journalism as a freelancer, without health or life insurance.[4] In the provinces, this may mean being paid as few as US$11 per news item, regardless of the time it took to research and report it. Low-paid and insecure, the journalistic profession has split between a small group of very successful journalists at the top, who publish wonderful and fearless books—like Ricardo Ravelo's *El narco en México* (2011) and *Ejecuciones de periodistas* (2016), as well as Julio Scherer García's *La reina del Pacífico* (2008)—and a mass of journalists who live in precarious conditions, poor, without job security, without protection from police when they are under threat, and without economic or professional means to continue learning the best strategies to stay safe while doing their job.

This state of precariousness for journalists, and the state of dependency of media owners, form the basis of a political economy of journalism that punishes critical reporting and editorial ambition. It has also corrupted state officials, who feel entitled to positive reporting and, when the opposite happens, feel entitled to coerce or harm journalists, editors, or photographers that dare to break the implicit contract between the state and the press. Even though there are almost no structural incentives to criticize government officials, journalists continue testing the limits of criticism and cross the line in the sand, placing themselves in harm's way. For instance, photojournalist Rubén Espinosa Becerril dared to be critical of a state representative and backed off too late. Killed in 2015, Espinosa joined the many honorable reporters in Mexico who have died due to their professionalism.

If coercion by the state was not bad enough, the spike in criminal drug violence has placed news communicators in the crosshairs. These are typically reporters or photographers working the police beat who write or photograph something that seems to challenge the rights of a particular DCO to enact violence with impunity. Because they are dangerous, these beats require the highest level of professionalism, but they are some of the lowest-paid positions in a Mexican newsroom, and news organizations invest little money in the safety and training of their reporters. Placed in situations of great danger, reporters do their best to interpret the unwritten rules on how to report crime without making themselves into targets.

The list of journalists who have been threatened, beaten, tortured, kidnapped, disappeared, and assassinated is too long to reproduce here. Organizations like RSF, HRJ, Artículo 19, and the Committee to Protect Journalists

(CPJ) have been doing the crucial job of keeping track of all these crimes, the majority of which have gone unpunished. According to Mike O'Connor, a legendary reporter who headed the CPJ in Mexico and whom I had the pleasure of interviewing eighteen months before his passing in 2014, DCOs torture and kill reporters not simply as a side tactic to keep control in a plaza. Brutal violence against journalists, O'Connor believed, is a key strategy of DCOs and corrupt state elements in their efforts both to take over a new territory and to defend it. The same seems to apply to the threatening and killing of bloggers and other citizen journalists, which I will discuss in the next chapters.

The constant violence that news organizations and journalists have endured over the last decade has translated into systematic self-censorship and silence. In some cases, news organizations have published heart-wrenching statements in which they beg for mercy and editorial guidelines. After suffering several killings in a short period of time, the *Diario de Juárez* published such a letter on its website:

> Gentlemen of the different organizations disputing the plaza of Ciudad Juárez, the loss of two reporters affiliated with this newspaper in less than two years represents an irreparable affliction to all of us working here and, in particular, to the reporters' families.
>
> We are letting you know that we are communicators, not fortunetellers. For this reason, as information workers, we are asking you to explain to us what it is that you want from us, what it is that you want us to publish or stop publishing, so that we know what we must abide by.
>
> You are, at this moment, the de facto authorities of this city. (2010; translation mine)

Acknowledging the killing of two reporters, the editors recognize the need for editorial guidelines from the cartel(s), and they also admit that the cartels are the de facto sovereigns of Ciudad Juárez at that time. The killings here function as a type of communication between DCOs and the news media, a communication exchange that must take place for the newspaper to function.

Similar exchanges happen elsewhere. On March 7, 2013, several narcomantas appeared around the state of Coahuila making specific threats to a reporter writing for the newspaper *Zócalo* in Saltillo:

> Look, Juaristi, don't you remember me? I am "The 42," stop fucking and writing fucking shit in *Zócalo*. Continue following the governor's

style, who cannot revive his nephew, and who won't be able to revive you either. I have asked you already not to publish lies, just write what it is, continue with your behavior and I am going to fuck you up. . . . Even if you have protection, you are not made of steel and this is not a threat. Remember that you are a public figure and predictable, and I am not, I can fuck you up wherever. (EstadoMayor.mx 2013)

This specific warning was for a reporter working for *Zócalo*, but the threats on the newspaper were more general. Five days after the narcomantas, *Zócalo*'s editorial team decided to publish the following on their front page: "Because there are not guarantees nor security for the exercise of journalism, the Editorial Committee of the newspaper *Zócalo* has decided, starting on this date, to abstain from publishing information related to organized crime. . . . The decision to suspend the information related to organized crime is based on our responsibility to protect the integrity and security of our one thousand workers, their families, and our own" (*Zócalo* 2013). As with *Diario de Juárez*, the violence created a direct impact on *Zócalo*'s editorial direction.

The multiplication of cases like these have translated into an environment of silence and self-censorship. The tragedies have made necessary the notes imploring compassion, the systematic silences, the threats, the retreats, the bribes, and the reexamination of editorial policies that may assure survival. The structure of the set of institutions we have come to call the fourth estate has been coerced into change. In Mexico, today, the metaphor of the fourth estate, a metaphor rooted in an Arendtian notion of power, becomes resignified by a Hobbesian context. The power of the press, a power emanating from collectivity and from the ability to construct and activate publics, finds its match in the violent methods used by DCOs and state actors to turn the press into a puppet of organized crime and the corrupt state. The power of journalism may be real, but it is also negligible in the contest between words, laws, and bullets. There are many Mexicos: some are great, fair, and wonderful. But the Mexico of systemic violence against the press is the debris of modernity as it crashes against the rocklike endurance of coloniality.

THE RISE OF THE ANONYMOUS BLOGOSPHERE

The context of violence against institutionalized journalism has translated into a huge communicational gap in Mexico, particularly in regions dominated by cartels. Using the power of digital technologies, Mexican citizens have tried to fill at least some of this gap and use anonymizing techniques in public spaces—blogs, in particular—for debate and visibility. Despite their varied nature—including some blogs that have either brief publication runs or amateurish design—a few of these Mexican anonymous blogs have significantly impacted the Mexican and global public sphere. These include several versions of *El Blog del Narco* (elblogdelnarco.com, elblogdelnarco .net, elblogdelnarco.info), *Mundo Narco* (mundonarco.com), *Narco Violencia* (narcoviolencia.com), and several blogs and social media pages connected to *Valor por Tamaulipas* (*VxT*) (valorportamaulipas.com), including *Responsabilidad por Tamaulipas*, *Esperanza por Tamaulipas*, *Valor por Michoacán*, and *Valor por Veracruz*.

Each of these blogs and social media pages has its own identity, but they share several key characteristics: they are all trying to shed light on violent events happening in specific localities in Mexico, events that are often uncovered by traditional journalistic organizations; they are all anonymous; and they all participate in the publishing and sharing of some of the most grotesque and frightening images and videos known to humankind.[5] Visitors to these sites can read and share news and commentary on the violence, but they can also witness bodies displayed in horrific ways: in the midst of intense suffering; waiting in frightened expectation for death; and in the final moment, the very fraction of the second in which death mercifully arrives. If dying is a mystery, these blogs demystify it. There are videos of decapitations that are done with small cutting instruments that make the process long, the suffering incredible, and the blood gushing a dramatic event as bodies convulse through the agonic release of life. These blogs house, collect, distribute, and archive these images and videos, and they have become a true repository of the horrors of drug violence in Mexico.

Even though pain, shock, and even trauma cannot be avoided when interacting with the videos, news, and photographs often found on these blogs and on Facebook pages, they have been some of the most famous citizen journalism sites in and from Mexico.[6] At different times, *El Blog del Narco* (EBDN) has been the most important blog from Mexico in terms of visitors (I detail this below), and, at its most popular, *Valor por Tamaulipas* (*VxT*) had half a million followers on Facebook. Just as notably, the international community of observers of the violence in Mexico has embraced some of these blogs because of their importance, yet the reasons for their fame are unusual. They are not famous because the star power of those represented in and covered by the blogs. These blogs typically display the small-time dead and the small-time dying, the anonymous mass of blood and pain that defines Mexico's drug conflict. They are not famous because they were written by someone whose identity and biography symbolizes the future of a nation, like the blog *Generación Y* by Cuban human rights advocate Yoani Sánchez.[7] Instead, these blogs are the product of anonymous work, people who have embraced cryptic identities such as Historiador, Lucy, or El Administrador. These blogs are famous because they claim to intervene in Mexico's violence. Against the grain of a narcissistic blogging culture that, according to Zizi Papacharissi, "'interpellates' its citizens as consumers," these anonymous blogs seem set on contributing to a public sphere in the hope of "heightening civic engagement" (2010: 146). They do this through the unrelenting display and coverage of violence, and they do this anonymously.

In a sense, the blogs symbolize a type of devil's bargain that is the Mexican public sphere. Change cannot happen without intervention in the public sphere, without citizens being rallied to push back against the obscene power of the cartels and the ambiguous though equally deadly power of the Mexican state. Yet participating in the public sphere in the open, rallying the troops, is extremely dangerous, often resulting in the death of those calling for intervention. How to stay alive while being public? Opacity is an answer, though perhaps a bad one, to the likely contradictory needs for publicity and for staying alive. I use opacity to signal the ability to do things in secret, the capacity to have privacy from the powerful, and the power to share information in anonymity. In an age of violence and impunity, opacity marks Mexico's public sphere, which has become, among other things, a space for the faceless, the nameless, and the placeless.

What Are EBDN *and* VxT?

EBDN is not one but several blogs and websites that—according to Go-Daddy, their DNS provider—originated in May 2008. All of these domain names—elblogdelnarco.com, elblogdelnarco.net, elblogdelnarco.info, and the 2010 blogdelnarco.com—connect to Monterrey, Mexico, and to the same email address in Nuevo León, suggesting that all of them are owned by a single person or organization. It is, however, unclear who has managed or authored the blogs or even whether they have been managed or authored by the same person or people since 2008. The activity levels of all of the domains have changed throughout the years. The iconic *Blog del Narco* (blogdelnarco.com), created in March 2010 and one of the most important websites reporting on the drug war from 2010 to 2013, is inactive today. According to Alexa.com, the blog received between 2 and 5 million visits per

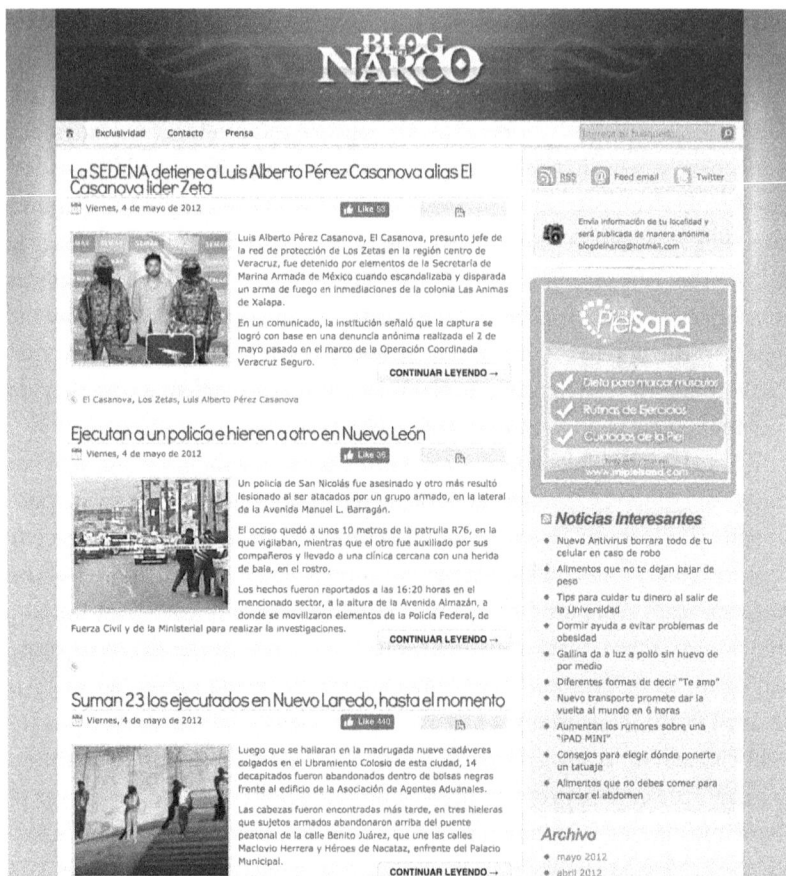

Figure 5.2. *El Blog del Narco* was highly active from 2010 to 2013.

week during times of intense traffic, and it was often in the top forty Mexican news sites. This site stopped publishing in 2013, shortly after its alleged author, "Lucy," published a book detailing his or her work and goals. Prior to March 2010 and after 2013, other domains were and have remained active. At present, *El Blog del Narco* exists under the domain elblogdelnarco .org, which at the moment of this writing ranks 1,172 in Mexico, according to Alexa.com, with two-thirds of its traffic coming from Mexico. It is a substantive site, with close to ten thousand articles archived, hundreds of videos, and thousands of photos. The iconic and inactive blogdelnarco .com still displays thousands of articles going back to January 2011; however, photos and videos are no longer available. For that reason, and because this chapter emphasizes photographic and videographic evidence, I have relied on the textual, videographic, photographic, and user data from elblogdel-narco.org to support my claims.

There are substantial differences between what EBDN does and what EBDN means to different publics. The site publishes daily news pieces and photos and videos not typically found in traditional news outlets. The news pieces are reports of violence or arrests or, less commonly, policy decisions or political scandals that may affect the way the state is fighting organized crime. There have been accusations that the site plagiarizes news pieces from traditional media. According to *Fronteras*, an internet news portal, EBDN has plagiarized news pieces from *Proceso*, *Reforma*, *El Norte*, and *Cambio*. *Proceso* has made similar claims, but the plagiarism has not gone in only one direction. Jorge Tirzo (2013), codirector of the *Revista Mexicana de Comunicación*, has shown that many traditional news organizations have also plagiarized from EBDN. In Tirzo's view, even with its weaknesses, the blog is a positive example of what is possible with the participatory potential of the web, including the ability to crowdsource content, publish at low costs, and perform collaborative curation of material. These positive characteristics are the most beneficial to society because EBDN publishes about narco-trafficking.

Even though EBDN has been controversial in journalistic circles, the manner in which Tirzo frames EBDN's role in society is echoed by others within and outside of Mexico. The reasons are complex, but they fit within a framework that values EBDN for the same reasons that we value the best of journalism; that is, the people have the right to know what is going on in their neighborhoods, cities, and states, and whoever does the job of disseminating truthful information to the people is playing a valuable role in society. Insofar as EBDN plays this role, even if this is not the only role it plays, it must be respected for the good it contributes to society. Yet these are not the only elements that have made EBDN unique among blogs publishing about the narco wars. EBDN's willingness to post graphic visual and video material submitted by users and its ongoing proximity to violence paved the way for its huge following from 2010 to 2013. This proximity to violence prompted the closing of the most popular of the EBDN sites in 2013.

Although the first of the sites associated with EBDN appeared in 2008, it wasn't until the site Blog del Narco (blogdelnarco.com) appeared in 2010 that EBDN began gaining users by the millions. The 2008 site was allegedly published by El Historiador, while the 2010 site was written and published by Lucy and an assistant or webmaster. The sites coexisted, but it was Lucy's site that created greater traffic and caught the imagination of many. At its highest points, in October 2011, Lucy's site—discussed at greater length in the next section—ranked forty-seventh as the most-visited site in Mexico and sixth among news websites, coming in behind only *El Universal, Milenio, El Norte, Reforma,* and CNN. Readership fluctuated greatly depending on the events published, but EBDN remained important in Mexico up until Lucy's site ceased publishing new material in 2013. Today EBDN is still active, but since 2013 the number of site visitors has dropped dramatically. Nonetheless, its relevance remains. Even in its diminished status, EBDN continues to fill a gap in the Mexican public sphere, inviting important conversations about the role of media, journalism, and the blogosphere in the struggle against violence and organized crime.

VxT has a dual presence on the World Wide Web. It has been a blog with several domains, including valorportamaulipas.com and valorportamaulipas.info. These blogs are relatively unpopular and spotty in their coverage. The majority of *VxT*'s appeal and presence is through a Facebook page that has been active since early 2012 and through a Twitter account. Created and maintained by an anonymous individual who is often referred to as El Administrador, *VxT*'s Facebook page has had up to half a million "likes," though its current instantiation has only around a quarter of a million "likes" and is likely not published by El Administrator. In 2015, the Twitter account had roughly twenty-four thousand followers. More localized than EBDN, *VxT* has from its inception used its blog and social media outlets as a way of alerting citizens in Tamaulipas of danger, violence, shootings, and the endless stream of *desaparecidos* (disappearances) that cannot possibly be covered by news outlets due to both the sheer number and the self-censorship that news institutions have had to embrace.[8]

VxT's history has been irregular since its Facebook page and El Administrador have closed and reopened sites, stopped and restarted contributions. The history of both sites, EBDN and *VxT*, has been similarly shaped by violence. This is neither because violence has shaped the reputation of the sites nor simply because the majority of the stories, images, and videos that make up the content of EBDN and *VxT* engage in violence. Instead, the specter of violence shapes EBDN and *VxT*'s modalities of production, and anonymity is, crucially, one of this modality's central characteristics. As such, acts of violence have marked like giant signposts these sites' popular standing.

On September 13, 2011, the bodies of a young woman and a man who had collaborated with EBDN and other social media platforms (Twitter, in particular) appeared hanging from a bridge in Nuevo Laredo, Tamaulipas. The woman was hung from her hands and feet, like a pig in a roast. She was tortured, seminude, and disemboweled. The man hung by his side, pierced through his hands and with a cut in his side so deep that his bones were visible. On the bridge and around their bodies were yellow posters, referred to as "narcomantas," which stated: "This is going to happen to all of those posting funny things on the Internet. You better fucking pay attention. I'm about to get you." These two victims had tweeted and blogged about drug violence and participated on sites like EBDN. The sign was signed by Los Zetas, a violent splinter cartel that has tried to control Nuevo Laredo for some time now. Eleven days later, the body of journalist and blogger María Elizabeth Macías Castro was found, decapitated, also in Nuevo Laredo, with the signature of Los Zetas. According to the narcomanta by her body, Macías was killed not simply because of her news reporting but also because of her comments on blogs and on Twitter. Lucy reports that on top of her body, the killers left "keyboards, a mouse, and other computer parts strewn across her body, as well as a sign that mentioned [EBDN] again" (*Blog del Narco* 2013, xi).

Similar events have been part of the history of *VxT*. Early in February 2013, narcomantas promising 600,000 pesos to whoever could give clues as to who administered *VxT* appeared in Tamaulipas and were widely photographed and shared on social media. A few days later, on February 20, someone shared a YouTube video of the execution of a *VxT* collaborator. The presumed collaborator speaks to the camera before being executed: "This message is directed to all the communities dedicated to publishing information, users of Facebook and Twitter on *Valor por Tamaulipas*. These persons now have the media technology and the localization technology, that they only need your IP address to track you down and find the precise location of the user. I am not the first one or the last one to be found. For your own safety, stop publishing any information or you will pay this same price." Then he dies. This victim goes further than stating the risks of participating in the public sphere: perhaps prodded by the killers, he details the technological capabilities of the cartels and the inadequacies of anonymity.

The threats continued. A few weeks later, on April 1, 2013, the Facebook and Twitter accounts of *VxT* were suspended, arguably to protect the makers. On April 7, the Facebook page was reactivated. Also on April 7, the administrator published a letter sharing his desire to close *VxT* on April 16. The administrator declared:

> Thanks to my experiences during this last year and months as administrator of the page, I have found that the social networks are a battlefield

in which all main users have some type of interest or role in the war, like users that belong to cartels that try to sell or exchange information, officers of the Attorney General's office that in some cities are the mediators of citizen collaboration. . . . I cannot remain in this trench for different reasons . . . I haven't given up. But I have given everything I can and by now my inability to administer the page is notorious . . . [9]

The administrator changed his mind, though, and the site continued. During those rough months of 2013, the administrator shared in other traditional media, including the famed magazine *Proceso* on April 30, 2013, about what it meant to manage *VxT*: "It meant the opportunity to live up to my duties and to confront those who damage the state. It was an opportunity to get off my chest the frustration to have fear and not do anything about it without risking my family. The irony is that after that stage, I returned to the same frustration." Forewarning of the risks taken by blogging, he added advice to those wishing to follow in his footsteps: "Be prudent; don't tell anybody, not even your own family. . . . Never share your identity with a user, it doesn't matter whether you fully trust them. Commit to work with the good people in the government and reject the criminals and collaborators. . . . Above all else, continue publishing about situations of risk and about the impunity of organized crime" (*Proceso* 2013b). Secrecy, caution, and survival, in other words, go hand in hand in these public practices.

More than a year later, on October 16, 2014, spectacular violence returned to haunt *VxT*. That day, María del Rosario Fuentes Rubio, a collaborator of *VxT* who used the nickname "Felina" ("Feline"), was kidnapped, and shortly thereafter she was killed. Before her kidnapping and murder, Fuentes Rubio, a physician, had used Twitter to share information about dangerous situations. Previously, on October 7, another user had threatened Fuentes Rubio for failing to criticize the Cartel de Guadalajara and for failing to point out the brutality of government forces. Shortly after the kidnapping of Fuentes Rubio, someone published two photos; in the first she was alive, facing the camera; in the second, she was bloody, lying down, and seemingly dead. There were also three messages published on the harasser's Twitter account: "#reynosafollow FRIENDS AND FAMILY, MY NAME IS MARIA DEL ROSARIO FUENTES RUBIO, I AM A PHYSICIAN, TODAY IS THE END OF MY LIFE." The second reads: "I HAVE NOTHING ELSE TO SAY [EXCEPT TO] TELL YOU NOT TO DO THE SAME MISTAKE, NOTHING IS WON, ON THE CONTRARY TODAY I LEARN THAT." The third one read: "I AM DYING IN EXCHANGE FOR NOTHING THEY ARE CLOSER TO US THAN YOU BELIEVE."

The same messages were forwarded to *VxT* and other social media. From the same account they shared a video of a young man decapitated with an axe and the text: "THIS IS GOING TO HAPPEN TO THOSE POINTING FINGERS ON *VXT*."

EBDN and *VxT* shared more than the desire to publish and distribute timely information about drug-related violence in northern Mexico. Both also depended on the capacity of digital technologies to shield identities and were produced anonymously while they lasted. Although it is easy to understand that anonymity was essential to the survival and safety of the producers of these sites, it is much harder to understand anonymity within the context of citizen journalism. So I ask: What does it mean that civic and political work needs to be carried out in secret? What does it mean that anonymity is accepted as part of civics? And what can the connection between anonymity and citizenship teach us about the national and transnational political cultures surrounding Mexico's violence? Answers to these questions require an engagement with the histories of modern political cultures, civics, and publicity. The next sections show that these histories are entwined at the onset of modernity and that contemporary understandings of publicity carry the imprint of contradictions unsolvable without recourse to a new historiography of publicity. This new historiography situates violence as a problem that publicity was meant to solve and anonymity as its communicational resolution.

SECRETS AND PUBLICITY

Contemporary uses of publicity, particularly in disciplines concerned with expressive culture such as media and communication studies, show a huge bias toward defining publicity in relation to openness. There is a general belief that publicity does what it does to our political lives because publicity exists in the open. It is common to confuse the public with being out in the open or to vehemently argue for this privileged connotation. If something is public, then it is meant to be seen, open, without walls, like a play performed in a Greek agora, which, not coincidentally, is the model many use to spatially "think" of the concept of publicness and the realm in which publicness is performed: the public sphere. It is certainly the way Hannah Arendt uses the term *public* in *The Human Condition*, and it is ultimately true in Jürgen Habermas's influential work *The Structural Transformation of the Public Sphere*. In both cases, that which is public is that which is in the open. In Arendt, openness is spatial and topological. In Habermas, openness is communicational—it implies self-disclosure—and spatial—it implies copresence.

This bias toward openness is more startling and more telling in Habermas, who starts his argument by clarifying terms and erasing the mistaken notion that "public" simply means "open." Yet when it comes to detailing the rise and fall of the public sphere, Habermas's examples hugely privilege a notion of publicity that depends on, and demands, openness and inclusivity, even if qualified by the type of people, like bourgeois men, who could participate in the public spheres he describes. Although later Habermas corrected this assumption of inclusivity and changed it to a recognition that multiple public spheres coexisted, including that of the illiterate poor, *The Structural Transformation*'s normative element is partly a universalizing potential conceivable only through openness (Hohendahl 2002: 20). The reason is perhaps predictable. As many have noted, Habermas's work is both a historical argument about the evolution of European polities in modernity and a normative text that holds on to the utopian potential of democracy. It is within the context of this normative ideal that openness remains key to those reading and embracing the imperfect history Habermas relates. From the salons and the coffeehouses to the public square, those following Habermas's first work embrace this bias, for the bias symbolizes the democratic ideal. This includes thinkers who criticize Habermas and who expand on his ideas to make them more inclusive and more attentive, and thus useful to contemporary settings and the new, mediated environments of contemporary Western nation-states, a group that includes Nancy Fraser, Peter Dahlgren, James Curran, and Manuel Castells, to name just a few. Even if publicity may mean a whole array of things, as Habermas notes and these authors sometimes rearticulate, public spheres are realms that should be open. At stake is the very possibility of democracy.

What does the normative element of openness imply in terms of publicness? If the public spheres are open, publicness, the way of being in the public realm, includes or implies the normative idea that to be public one must be willing to place oneself in the open. Publicness thus tends to be conceived as a spatially reflexive action, as a willingness and perhaps even a desire to make oneself visible, to move oneself away from opacity. In public one must be visible, yet this normative idea of publicness, like the biased notion of an open public sphere, assumes a number of theoretical and historical concessions that cannot and must not be taken for granted.

To begin to unpack some of the normative implications in the pairing of publicity and openness, we can start by noting that this pairing is a fair description of seminal views on publicity but also that it is limited. Jeff Weintraub reminds us of this in his analysis of the public/private distinction. This paired opposition is a complex binary that connects a number of rich, relational concepts that Weintraub tracks to two foundational orientations or metaphoric roots. One opposes private and public in terms of "what is hidden or withdrawn versus what is open, revealed, and accessible" (1997: 5). This is the foundational orientation that Arendt, Habermas, and most users of the concept of the public sphere take, and it is the one Weintraub refers to by the term *visibility*. Yet there is a second metaphorical root, one that opposes private and public in terms of "what is individual, or pertains only to an individual, versus what is collective, or affects the interests of a collectivity of individuals" (Weintraub 1997: 5). Weintraub refers to this second criterion as "collectivity." Only when publicness is defined exclusively by the visibility criterion does publicness need to be open. The collective criterion, Weintraub reminds us, can be achieved in the open or in secret, as when the collective good is carried out by the secret ballot. So there is such a thing as "secret publicity," or publicity that depends on normative ideas of publicness in which one must be willing to make oneself invisible. The pairing of invisibility and publicity is full of tensions that are very spatially instructive, tensions that help us see the blogger's case from quite unusual perspectives.

Anonymity and secrecy are part of a curious and important cluster of concepts that point to the difficulties and even risks of open communication in our political communities and legal cultures. Types of opacity, which include privacy and religious mysteries, tend to be social tactics aimed at constituting different spheres of communication and different spheres of impunity. As communicational tactics, they have been part of the human experience and legal practices from antiquity to the present. In the Judeo-Christian and Islamic traditions, for instance, the stoning prescribed by religious and legal frameworks as a result of illicit sexual encounters was typically performed in a public setting in which the identities of the stone-throwers were somewhat protected by the anonymity of the stoning crowd. Mysteries have often been associated with religious doctrine and are essential to the Judeo-Christian tradition. Of these, privacy is by comparison the newest of the concepts, for it implies a social contract that recognizes a space of impunity (Habermas 1989: 5). Starting with the absolutist state, these spaces have typically, though not always, included the home and the mind (Koselleck 1988) (see chapter 3).

In order to understand the meaning of the political and cultural work of *EBDN* and *VxT* vis-à-vis their anonymous standing and the discourse of civics, the next section places opacity in a historical context and examines the tension inherent between publicity as a space of communication and as a spatially reflexive action that depends on opacity to constitute the public sphere not as an agora but as a space of impunity. The historical context is essential, for this context shows that our current understandings of anonymity stem from the way it was used for political dissent in revolutionary nations like Mexico and the United States. Early uses of anonymity gave it a mythic veneer, and they are why we today overvalue anonymity in politics. This is a complex discussion that is made more difficult by the ways in which each of these communicational concepts overlap with the rest. So the first task is to disentangle these concepts.

Opacity and Publicness

Opacity is the property of objects to hide other objects and to make impossible the use of our senses to know what lies behind them. Opacity is a property that both refers to an object's essence, its molecular structure, and refers to the capacities and limitations of our senses or our mind. When confronted with opacity, we cannot see; we cannot know. Opacity is thus always a reference to the material world and to its knowability. It is fundamentally an epistemological and spatial concept, for it implies three locations: (1) the location of the looker; (2) the location of the object that is opaque and impedes the looking; and (3) the position of the actors and acts in front of and behind the opaque object. Opacity is richer in its metaphorical value than the metaphors of darkness and light that we use to periodize the premodern, the Dark Ages, and the age of Enlightenment, because opacity reminds us that light is not enough. Line of sight too, or visibility, is crucial to knowledge, and it should never be assumed, particularly in social and political inquiries. We know that people behave differently behind closed doors and that secrets are an aspect of social freedom. Our very political system is organized around the idea of opacity, as "chambers" (e.g., the Star Chamber, a judge's chambers) metaphorically call attention to interior and exterior spaces and the impossibility of being in both. Opacity is as complex as knowledge is.

Anonymity is displacement by another name. Like fear, anonymity is a narrative. It tells the story of a ghost, one who leaves behind a communicative trace like a pamphlet, a letter, a blog entry, a code, a manifesto, a mark within a place like a tree, a mailbox, a website, the blogosphere. The trace, meaningful both for what it tells and for whom it hides, is evidence of authorship but lacks an authorial claim (Gray and Gómez-Barris 2010: 6). Like a whisper, which skirts the audible region, the trace exists in an ambiguous state between fact and fiction, never quite capable of shaking off the uncertainty of its origins, the missing author, the runner. Not every element in the anonymous narrative rejects determination. The trace identifies, quite specifically, two interrelated places. One is a place of certitude, the communicative space, the media that was used to communicate: the tree, the letter, the social media site, the blog. The second is the space of an absence, the two square feet in front of the tree on which the person who nailed the letter once stood or the space in front of a keyboard, unidentified and perhaps unidentifiable, a keyboard on which the blog was once typed and posted. Anonymity is a story of abandoned spaces and can only be possible through displacement, through running away from the tree or hiding the digital location of the keyboard.

Like opacity, privacy is a spatial category that denotes three locations: (1) an outside, the position of the onlookers; (2) an opaque boundary that limits the possibility of looking in from the outside; and (3) the private space in which actions can be carried out without outside witnesses. So privacy is a concept describing activities that one keeps entirely to oneself, or to a limited group of people. In privacy, one's name may be public, but not a set of activities or facts about that name. By contrast, anonymity is when one wants people to see *what they do*, just not *that it is them* who are doing it. A typical example would be if one wanted to blow the whistle on abuse of power or other forms of crime in one's organization without risking career and social standing in that group, which is why we typically have strong laws to protect sources of the free press. In anonymity, what is hidden is someone's identity, not a specific set of facts about them.

Although privacy and anonymity produce secrets, they are actually the opposite. Anonymity, hiding your identity, is never full or meant to be total. Typically, when we talk about anonymity as a political good, we assume that someone, let's say a journalist, has corroborated the standing of the person sharing information. To trust a whistleblower, a journalist first has to verify that the person is indeed who she claims she is. When he got the request from Lucy to talk after she left Mexico, Rory Caroll, a reporter from the *Guardian,* asked her to prove that she was who she claimed by showing him that she was in control of the EBDN site. Lucy did. Thanks to the magic of digital communication, Lucy changed the site in the way Caroll requested, and by performing this technological gesture, Lucy acquired what lawyers may call "standing." With this gesture, mediated by keyboards, servers, optical fiber, and other technologies, Lucy proved that she had the authorial identity to make the claims she was making. In the embroidery of contracts that we call society, anonymity typically depends on standing. Even the most famously anonymous political act in Mexico and the United States, the secret ballot, depends on whether the anonymous voter has a valid ID or, in Mexico, *una cartilla electoral*. Your vote may be anonymous, but your standing cannot be. Standing is public and legal.

Opacity produces secrets, and all secrets require opacity. They are intertwined concepts, and, like opacity, secrets constitute social and political life. They are what happens backstage, to reference Ervin Goffman's dramaturgical notion of society. If we consider the many academic books written about public traditions, public expressions, public art, public rituals, and public norms, and the few written about conspiracies, corruption, and, in general, things that happen backstage, we must conclude that secrets are the least glamorous general category of social knowledge. However, the generous wellspring of secrets also provides other important categories of life and politics, including anonymity and privacy. Secrets are thus at the root of the promises and dangers of opacity in our public cultures. Secrets, Jodi Dean (2002) goes as far as to argue, are the very justification and legitimization of contemporary notions of publicity.

In *Publicity's Secret* (2002), Dean analyzes the way the idea of the secret is central to the value, and the very concept, of the public and, in parallel fashion, the value of the information age for humanity and for politics. "The people have a right to know" is the slogan of contemporary ideas on politics and on information, and it is thus in the uncovering of secrets that democracy and the information age connect. In Dean's work, the public sphere acts as a grantor of value for global technoculture, and it is in the capacity of information dissemination—to gather and organize publics—that digital technologies become an alibi for healthy communication culture (2002: 626). That the promise of full knowledge and disclosure can never be fulfilled makes the secret both a grantor of value and a permanent fixture in our political fantasies of democratic progress. So whistleblowers like Edward Snowden and, to a lesser degree, *EBDN*'s Lucy become both sources of secret information and emblems of the potential of open information to enlighten our democratic futures. Secrets are thus the thing that we want to avoid in public culture and the very reason for a public to exist.

As used by Dean, the secret is a broad communicational concept meant to cover over political backroom dealings; the informational logic of secret societies such as the Freemasons; unreachable information due to secret, often digital archives; and the secrets imagined or real at the heart of what she calls the "suspicious subject." Hence, the secret can be about actual information, as in the arcana of secret societies. It can also be a communication tactic, as in the need for keeping secret the membership of these societies. Or the secret can be a concept, as the one that signals a type of suspicious publicity, the very type of subjectivity that, Dean argues, defines post-Enlightenment political subjects. There are secrets; there is the need to keep secrets; and there is the powerful awareness that secrets surround us and we must try to uncover them.

As a tactic and as a concept at the heart of contemporary political subjects and structures, the secret validates the information age and the rise to prominence of journalism as a communicational practice that defines democracy. It is because of the secret and the need to unveil it that Thomas Carlyle talked in 1840 about the "Reporters' Gallery" as a "Fourth Estate," a space of power and influence as important to the running of democracy as the other three powers represented in the English Parliament: nobility, the Church, and the townspeople. Our suspicious political subjectivities are such that in times of crises we may trust only this Fourth Estate. In *The Soul of Man under Socialism*, satirist Oscar Wilde famously responded to the crises of capitalism: "Somebody—was it Burke?—called journalism the fourth estate. That was true at the time no doubt. But at the present moment it is the only estate. It has eaten up the other three. The Lords Temporal say nothing, the Lords Spiritual have nothing to say, and the House of Commons has nothing to say and says it. We are dominated by Journalism" ([1891] 1905: 57–58).

In an equally hyperbolic fashion, although much more optimistically phrased, Yochai Benkler starts his book *The Wealth of Networks* with a statement of faith, not scholarship: "Information, knowledge, and culture are central to human freedom and human development" (2006: 1). Jodi Dean's suspicious subject has different manifestations over time: it shows itself as political power in Carlyle; it becomes a type of Leviathan in Wilde; and it inspires mystic belief in Benkler.

The real and imaginary power of secrets—the metaphors it inspires, the slogans, manifestos, and statements of faith—acts as social boundaries and social glue. It constructs social relations and even communities, which exist not only because of the histories they share but also because of the secrets they maintain. Secrets are thus socially constitutive. They are the information depositories of the illegal, the immoral, the uncommon, and they hold the promise and the possibility of impunity from law and moral judgment. To the imperfect human, the sinner, the lawbreaker, the cheater, and the criminal—to us all—secrets constitute the very possibility of social standing.

Besides reminding us that our commitment to openness is a central part of the "suspicious subject" in today's society, Dean provides a useful historiography of the public sphere, which she builds by reference to the contrasting works of Reinhart Koselleck and Habermas. Both scholars trace the rise of publicness from feudalism to the present and emphasize how specific state formations gave way to specific forms of social organization that, from our vantage point, we recognize as the constitution of publics. Koselleck (1988) uses historical arguments to theorize the rise of society and of publicity. Unlike Habermas, Koselleck believes that secret societies in general hold clues as to how publicity and society emerged in most European states; after all, he implies that the absolutist state was a general feature of Europe. The absolutist state may have appeared at different times in different places; nonetheless, it was part of the historical transformation from feudalism to the modern nation-state in general. Hence, in Koselleck's argument the rise of publics tended to accompany the historical transformation from feudalism to modernity (see also chapter 3). Publics were not simply an epiphenomenon of the political transformations of the time: they were their essence.

In Koselleck, the move from feudalism to enlightened forms of state organization could not happen without new forms of social consent that could substitute religious and monarchic forms of legitimization. If to avoid religious wars the state had to be above religion, then state power could not be divine. And if kings and queens were not religious leaders, why follow them? In Thomas Hobbes's work, the answer is: one follows the king to be safe, protected, free from violence. That is the logic of absolutism. But peace is not a magical outcome. Koselleck writes: "Peace is guaranteed only if political morality, the quality that makes men cede their rights to the sovereign representing them, is transformed in the act of state-founding into a duty to obey" (1988: 32). Koselleck's core argument is thus the germination and growth of political morality, the notion that our moral compass ought to be at least partly attuned toward the state and government. Political morality is first public morality, and it is the coming together of these individuals as outraged or critical citizenry that marks the emergence of publics, the emergence of modern citizenship. The citizen in modernity is one who holds government to moral standards and is morally critical of the state.

These publics appeared in secret societies, which allowed for the forms of institutionalized political plurality, spaces where politics were held to moral standards and morality became a political good. These secret publics—the

Masons, the Illuminati, the Cosmopolitans, and others—appeared because of the same cultural and technological conditions that had fueled religious plurality in the sixteenth century: (1) the multiplication of discourse made easier by the printing press, (2) the rise of the mercantilist classes, and (3) the emergence of printing in vernacular forms. These cultural and technological forces were the conditions of possibility for political pluralism and moral criticism and the new postfeudal citizen. In absolutism, "the citizens, to be sure, lacked executive power, but they possessed and retained the mental power to pass moral judgments" (Koselleck 1988: 55). In this bourgeois sphere of dialogue, secret societies constituted communities without hierarchy that shared moral principles and techniques. These lodges attracted the new classes of people that were acquiring economic and social capital (e.g., mercantile classes, professionals, and even bureaucrats) but nonetheless had no power to shape politics. In the absolutist state, these groups needed spaces to come together, spaces that could allow them to share views about society and the state. These secret societies were thus places that fostered criticism and even political dissent. Secrecy was required, for in the absolutist state, dissent was dangerous to the dissenter. As historicized by Koselleck, these secret societies were responses to the absolutist state's tight grip on thought and association, so secrecy was central to (in Weintraub's terminology) care for the collective.

Unlike Habermas, who seems too reliant on the glimpses of open self-disclosure that he finds in coffeehouses and salons, Koselleck is highly attentive to the rules of survival in early modernity. Pluralism was dangerous. These societies had to have rules of behavior within and without. Secret memberships were the norm. Secret rituals that would help constitute leadership among these groups of men otherwise imagined as equals were also common. The Illuminati, which were initiated in 1776, the year of the American Revolution, also had rules of simulation. Koselleck comments: "The shedding of the 'camouflage' inside the order was accompanied by a relentless reminder to preserve it when facing the outside world, a technique which had to be learned with reversed symbols—for the good of the 'cause'" (1988: 91). Yet rules of secrecy were not reserved to secret societies. Some were born out of experiences in public, as in the case of le Club de l'Entresol, a French meeting place frequented by some Enlightenment leaders, including Montesquieu, Andrew Michael Ramsay, and Horace Walpole. King Louis XIV, after finding the club's political ideas threatening, "disbanded" it, but in reality, simply "compelled it to re-emigrate into the underground privacy of its origin" (Koselleck 1988: 69).

Unlike Koselleck, Habermas looks at the rise of secret societies as a pre-amble to an enlightened modernity that had the potential to deliver the democratic ideal. Unlike Habermas, Koselleck does not see secret societies as paving the way to a better community. In fact, he sees in secret societies the beginning of an Enlightenment characterized by hypocrisy. Just as the Illuminati claimed not to be political but secretly attempted to take over the state, the Enlightenment relied on deception. Sisko Haikala notes that in Koselleck's work, the utopian philosophies at the root of Enlightenment were promises about a future imagined not simply in temporal fashion, but a future as a resolution to the problems of the present and thus as the outcome of social techniques imagined outside the sphere of politics. Philosophers of history regarded themselves as "unpolitical and wanted to avoid all conflicts with the Absolutist system." Haikala continues: "This changed criticism into hypocrisy, drove the Enlightenment into Utopia" (1997: 74). These normal-ized deceiving practices eventually pave the way to the French Revolution and, later, fascism, which marked the early life of both Koselleck and Haber-mas. Peter Hohendahl clarifies the gap between the two thinkers: "Koselleck was the unacknowledged opponent, the neo-conservative who was more interested in the strength of the state than in democratic participation. . . . Of course, Habermas's theory reverses the evaluation of the development: where Koselleck saw an increased politicization leading to hypocrisy, Haber-mas observed the possibility of emancipation" (2002: 15).

Perhaps because Habermas embraced this normative ideal, his ideas on the public sphere have dominated contemporary research, yet from the perspective of the cases at hand—cases rooted in a nation born from colo-nialism, a Mexican state in which deception kept a single political party in power for more than seventy years in the name of democracy—Koselleck's ideas are appropriate reminders that whether social actions fit or fail to fit utopian ideals is not the only thing at stake in issues of publicness. Using publicness for inquiry should be about making sense of the manner in which contingent communicational and associational practices structure specific, not universal, forms of publicness and favor specific, not universal, forms of politics. Koselleck is again useful here. In his theoretical history of the Enlightenment, the failure of political philosophers was not, as Tocqueville had argued earlier, a lack of understanding of actual politics. The problem was that these philosophers lacked political consciousness and saw their ideas as independent from their desire to change political power and take over the absolutist state. The abstract nature of values such as justice and equality—or, in the context of publicity, truth, openness, and debate—hid the way these values were machinations about political power (Koselleck 1988: 132ff, 137). Habermas's work is, in this sense, nostalgic for spaces of apolitical utopianism even if his work is also useful for understanding the contingent political challenges that different forms of publicity aimed to shape.

Koselleck's work is also a useful reminder that the value of opacity, as well as of secrecy, anonymity, and privacy, in contemporary political cultures is rooted in these early experiences and organizations. When Thomas Paine anonymously published and distributed *Common Sense* in 1776, he was simply following the protocols of survival and political morality in an age of absolutism. The use of disguises by the Sons of Liberty in the American colonies or, in England, the Blacks, did the same. From early modernity to the present, anonymity remains a tool of dissent and revolution. Pen names and pseudonyms have been part of critical discourse; even the US Constitution was published anonymously early on. Michael Kimaid notes, "Many editorial pieces in the seventeenth- and eighteenth-century English Atlantic were written under the guise of pen names, and pen names were vital to the public discourse of the American Revolution" (2015: 76). Benjamin Franklin went so far as to suggest that the colonies ought to be narrated through anonymous and pseudonymous writings. Recognizing these practices in relation to moral and legal impunity, Franklin added that pseudonyms "enabled men of honor to behave dishonourably" (qtd. in Kimaid 2015: 76). They also enabled women to act in public, at a distance, under the guise of another. Since the eighteenth century, women like Mary Ann Evans and the Brontë sisters have routinely used pen names to be able to have a public or literary identity, and they have relied on deception to be able to participate in the public sphere. Anonymity, secrecy, and opacity were thus central not only to the play of politics in revolutionary nations but also to those wishing to push back against the patriarchy's absolutist power over women. Lucy's anonymous contribution as well as her pride to finally reveal herself as a woman in interviews in early 2013 connect back to these traditions against politics and patriarchy.

Similar practices of opacity were used in Mexico's War of Independence. In the important months preceding the armed rebellion of 1810, anonymous fliers, broadsides, graffiti, and cartoons were often found in important public spaces across New Spain, especially in the capital, Mexico City. Timothy Henderson notes: "The government did its best to assert its control . . . issuing harrowing decrees threatening harsh consequences for any who would 'alter the peace and fidelity of the Kingdom.' The Inquisition set up a force of detectives to chase down malefactors; hand-operated printing presses were outlawed; and rewards were offered for information leading to the arrest of dissidents" (2009: 50). The monarchy thus issued laws, harnessed the judicial power of the Inquisition, and tried to monopolize the technologies that were affording the very possibility of discursive and political pluralism, namely the printing press.

As in other nascent modern nation-states, opacity in Mexico was a tool of revolution, and the values of anonymity were grafted deep into the Mexican political imaginary. In nations like the United States and Mexico, nations born out of revolution and colonialism, anonymity also became entwined with heroic narratives, as anonymity was a communicational tool central to the birth of these nations. This is why we rarely face the fact that the rules of criticism in absolutism were the rules of the outlaw. Secrecy made impunity possible in a social context where the far-reaching fingers of the state could stop all public and open communication. Here secrecy is antithetical to law, yet, ironically, the political relevance of opacity today is clearest in the way that anonymity and privacy have become central to our legal preoccupations. We care about anonymity and privacy, and we wish to protect them, sometimes uncritically.

One of the most popular sections of the Mexican Constitution—one of the few that many Mexicans, including myself, could recite by heart since our childhood—is a sentence in Article 41. Concerned with the political structures necessary for democracy, including the constitution of political parties and the organization of elections, the article includes a famous sentence stipulating that parties are selected through "el sufragio universal, libre, secreto, y directo" (the universal, free, secret, and direct suffrage). In Mexico, this sentence is the thing of billboards and political slogans. Championed by Mexico's first revolutionary president, Francisco I. Madero, this sentence became part of the Mexican Constitution in 1911 and a symbol of the rebirth of Mexican democracy and its revolutionary origins. This article established not only that the vote ought to be secret but also that in this sentence, each of the four descriptors is understood as equally powerful, as if they existed in a horizontal semantic structure. That the vote should be universal, free, and direct is unquestionable. That it should be secret is a testament to the political imaginary of revolutionary nations like Mexico, nations that recognize that such political power, regardless of what it is called, has the imprint of absolutism. Although Mexico's democracy was rather imperfect for the better part of the twentieth century, the anonymous secret ballot became a visible and audible element of Mexican political culture, and the symbolic, anonymous gesture of voting was often equated to democracy itself. Jonathan Fox, a political theorist, articulates what most in Mexico regard as political common sense: "The right to a secret ballot is a necessary condition for political democracy" (2007: 112).

Yet anonymity is not intrinsically good or bad for politics. Indeed, even the standing of the secret ballot is debatable. John Stuart Mill, for instance, saw in the anonymous ballot a threat to democracy itself. Rather, the voter's choice "is strictly a matter of duty; he is bound to give it according to his best and most conscientious opinion of the public good." Thus, "the duty of voting, like any other public duty, should be performed under the eye and criticism of the public" (1977: 490). Perhaps it is unusual to hear Mill talk so positively about the public ballot, but his comments force us to think about how the secret ballot has been essential in the reproduction of unjust political systems. For almost a century and a half, the secret ballot has exempted white populations from having to publicly defend their unwillingness to vote for nonwhite candidates. Unsurprisingly, the value of the secret ballot for democratic processes is still debated. Sara Schatz argues that historically the secret ballot has been used by authoritarian incumbents facing reform and uncertainty (2000: 86). This is the case with the racialized political system in the United States; it is also the case in postrevolutionary Mexico, a historical point in which the secret ballot was used to make transition more calculable and electoral fraud more doable while simultaneously embracing the symbolic gesture most associated with democracy. It is significantly harder to rig an election based on open votes.

Anonymity is ensconced in our political imaginary because of our myths of origin. We are revolutionary nations, and even though we are no longer attempting to overthrow the state, we imagine ourselves as the great dissenters and hugely overvalue anonymity. When listening to the defenders of anonymity, it is easy to forget that most political ideas and political theories make publicity and self-disclosure, as predicted by Mill, central elements of politics. James Gardner (2011) would further note that most democratic theories—such as liberal, aggregative and/or republican, deliberative—depend on ideas of citizen behavior that can only be carried out openly and publicly (936–39).

Anonymity is a communicational technique. It does not have an inherent value. Neither does openness. Yet the myth of origin tells us otherwise. This myth has helped people characterize the anonymous work of EBDN and VxT as an example of civics, citizenship, a courageous communicational act, and a type of citizen journalism. The myth of our revolutionary past regards anonymity as evidence that a public action has a collective goal.

Civic Communication

Weintraub (1997) reminds us that one of the metaphorical roots of public-ness connects it to collectivity. Using this criterion, anonymous publicity is not an oxymoron, but a type of publicity with a specific history that connects it to absolutism and the political cultures of revolutionary nations like Mexico. But digital communication such as EBDN and *VxT* presents further complications for analysis. Did the blogs have collective effects on their users? Were these blogs civic-minded?

These are not easy questions, as the blogs engaged different users, some of whom used the blogs as civics texts, while others used them as spaces they could visit to engage with documents and audiovisual materials from different and often disturbing perspectives. As referenced above, some users in and outside Mexico saw the blogs as citizen journalism and civics, but these uses were not the only common ones. Echoing the findings by Sue Tait (2011) regarding body horror, the comments sections of both blogs show a wider range of spectactorial and ideological positions available to the users of the blogs. First, EBDN and *VxT* existed as elements of the complex network of publicity used by cartels, and many of the commentators see in the garish audiovisual material evidence of a specific cartel's superiority. These commentators understood the videos and killings as a type of spectacular communication between cartels. Others, international users in particular, use the material as evidence of Mexico's inferiority, which is often cast in racial terms. The video of the execution of a woman published on EBDN on December 5, 2014, for instance, is followed by comments that include those by a *nonadado* (someone from South America) who states: "A esos hijos de su puta madre asi les va a ir en [M]exico tambien hay asesinos entrenados esos perros hijos de mierda son solo unos indios aborigenes por como hablan" (Those motherfuckers are going to lose Mexico as there are also trained assassins. Based on how they talk, those sons of bitches are only aboriginal Indians). A commenter named Carlos adds: "Tipico [*sic*] de estos aztecas primitivos que gustan de las telenovelas, programas paranormal y [L]aura" (This is typical of those primitive Aztecs who love their telenovelas, shows about the paranormal, and *Laura* [a popular Peruvian talk show that moved to Mexico's Azteca network in 2009]). There are others that simply take pleasure in the graphic material and want to continue engaging with it, who ask for more and more graphic videos and photos.

Although practically every post that I analyzed includes comments by those siding with specific cartels, those who use the posts to put down Mexicans, and those who claim to take pleasure in the audiovisual material, every comment section also includes viewers who take complex ethical perspectives, empathize with the victims, and express their sorrows about what Mexico is experiencing. Muller M., for example, writes: "Pero que tienen en la cabeza!!!!!! POR DIOS! Asquerosos de mierda pobre mujer! ESO NO TIENE PERDÓN DE DIOS !!! EL INFIERNO LOS ESPERA MAL NACIDOS!!!!!" (But what do you have in your heads!!!!! FOR GOD'S SAKE! You are disgusting[,] poor woman! THAT ACTION WON'T BE FORGIVEN BY GOD!!! HELL IS WAITING FOR YOU, ILL BRED!!!). Others take a complex civic perspective and use the comments section to talk about government corruption. Aquiles Esquivel Madrazo writes, apparently without hiding who he is: "LA FISCALIA DE DURANGO ES UN CARTEL. . . . . AHI ESTA EL COMANDANTE DIEGO MONCADA QUE LEVANTO A MUCHOS ZETAS Y LOS ENTREGO A MI2 EL LENTES Y ASI SE HICIERON LAS FOSAS, CUANDO USTEDES ZETAS VAN A MATAR AL COMANDANTE MONCADA GARCIA DE LA D.E.I.?? ESE CABRON HASTA SE BURLA DE USTEDES YO QUE USTEDES LO MATABA" (DURANGO'S DISTRICT ATTORNEY OFFICE IS A CARTEL . . . THERE YOU WILL FIND THE COMMANDER DIEGO MONCADA WHO GRABBED MANY ZETAS AND DELIVERED THEM TO MI2 EL LENTOS AND IN THAT WAY THEY FILLED THE MASS GRAVES. WHEN ARE YOU ZETAS GOING TO KILL THE COMMANDER MONCADA GARCIA OF LA D.E.I.?? HE IS LAUGHING AT YOU, I WOULD KILL HIM) (my translation).

These comments are evidence of complex ethical engagements. The first shows how religious morality helps this user express sorrow for the victim. The second shows how the video serves as a makeshift platform from which the user can criticize a corrupt Mexican official and even incite Los Zetas Cartel to kill him. These examples show that at least a portion of EBDN users utilize the collective criterion as part of their engagement with the blog.

The writers and publishers of the blogs also saw their work through the lens of the collective criterion. In 2013, in response to the threats and intimidation that began shortly after VxT was created, El Administrador wrote for the magazine Proceso:

> Creen que todos los ciudadanos nos tenemos que rendir ante ustedes y eso no es así. . . . En nuestro estado son incontables los casos de quienes se han resistido a ustedes, en la mayoría de los casos los buenos son los que terminan perdiendo. Pero por lo menos esa gente tiene más dignidad que aquellos que deciden agachar la cabeza y aceptar la tiranía y el esclavismo a que nos tienen sometidos.

(They believe that all the citizens have to surrender to you and that is not the case. . . . In our state, the cases of people who have resisted you are countless, in the majority of these cases the good ones end up losing. But at least those people have more dignity than those who decide to lower their heads and accept the tyranny and slavery you have submitted us to). (*Proceso* 2013c, my translation)

El Administrador clearly believes his blog and Facebook page are acts of citizen resistance against oppression, hence aligning his work with the good of the collective. Similarly, on July 8, 2013, in one of her last posts Lucy, the writer of EBDN, writes, full of desperation and insight: "Inicié Blog del Narco y mi suerte cambió. ¿Si no hubiera hecho nada? ¿Si hubiera sido una mexicana indiferente con la realidad? ¿Si me hubiera quedado callada? ¿Si hubiera decidido dejarme la venda en los ojos?" (I initiated the Blog del Narco and my luck changed. What if I had done nothing? What if I had been a Mexican indifferent to reality? What if I had remained quiet? What if I had decided to keep my eyes covered?).[10] She saw the digital realm as a space where secrets needed to be revealed, shown to all, and where revealing these secrets would help those endangered by violence, where her words and activities would make a difference in society. Later she states that does not tolerate lies or secrets: "Quería que la gente conociera la realidad de lo que estaba ocurriendo en México" (I wanted people to learn the reality of what was going on in Mexico). She saw her blog as a way of participating in civil society, a way of doing politics with a small *p*. This perspective was shared by a segment of the international community that complimented EBDN's work and admired the style of civics the blogs represented.

Even if it is contested, there is enough evidence to argue that these bloody blogs were indeed doing some civic, collective work and thus that they performed politico-cultural work fitting the term *public*. They corroborate Weintraub's arguments about the complex roots of publicness and challenge the notion that publicity is simply about openness. They also reintroduce spatial and topological concerns, albeit in new and instructive ways. Instead of privileging topological metaphors of openness, the collective mission of these digital platforms has to be explained in relation to opacity, a more pertinent and perhaps richer spatial category than openness. Opacity is essential to publicity in violent and corrupt environments because, in contexts like Mexico, civics can often be pursued only from the shadows, a space defined not by privacy, but by bounded publicity.

This is not historically new. As noted above, according to Koselleck and Habermas, secret societies were seminal examples of bounded publicity in the seventeenth and eighteenth centuries. Seeing publicity as openness is perhaps altogether a predilection based on biased perspectives. Wasn't Athens, the original archetype for the public sphere, also bounded? The agora was anonymous to most people in Athens, hidden by the city walls that kept slaves and foreigners, 70 percent of the urban settlement we call Athens, out of sight (Benhabib 1996: 75). One person's utopia is another's nightmare. One person's front stage, to recall Goffman's terminology, is another person's back stage. We prefer not to think about the agora in relation to the city walls. But as Seyla Benhabib suggests, the agora also included the walls that kept the majority outside, and publicness also included the rules constituting the gendered private sphere and the Athenian soldiers that secured the walls (1996: 75). From this expanded spatial definition, the communicational tactics within the agora were more in line with secret societies than we acknowledge. The fact is that in complex societies—and Athens was a microcosm of complexity—violence lurks and openness is a risk. Then as today, trust was spatial, so the deterritorialized digital sphere invites complications and ambiguities particular to that realm.

Let me illustrate these complications. In traditional physical space, the topological is organized mostly using materials that can be quickly evaluated in terms of their capacity for opacity. A wall made of brick and mortar is opaque, and users of a space surrounded by brick walls can behave accordingly. A dramaturgical theory of social interaction, including theories of publicness, depends on this reflexive awareness. Before we behave, we make a material assessment of the space in which the interaction may take place. The most important preconditions of publicity are spatial and material, and they affect the way place and particular materials connect to mediation. This is essential to bounded, secret publicity. In Edgar Allan Poe's famous short story "The Purloined Letter" (1844), C. Auguste Dupin's challenge is to physically find an incriminating document that needs to remain hidden. Royal secrets are at stake if he does not. The short story is an exercise on how secrets written in a letter made of paper can remain secret. The conceit of the story notwithstanding (the letter was on display in a card rack), secrecy in this media context has a material meaning, for the opacity of matter was assumed to be knowable. The tactics to find it, detailed by Poe in the actions taken by the Parisian police, are also based on assumptions about materials. It is impossible to transpose this short story to the current

digital media context. With the electrons, circuits, and binary ones and ze-
roes that are the basis of digital communication, true opacity does not exist.

Yet we describe the digital realm with metaphors borrowed from the
past, terms like *firewall*, *ePurse*, *key*, *Trojan*, and *domain*. We talk of breaches,
viruses, and worms, and it is easy to forget that our spatially reflexive digital actions, including those by EBDN and *VxT*, are confusedly determined
by the ambiguity of digital immateriality. From abstract digital space to
abstract digital security systems to abstract digital identities, the whole
of the digital ecology is a space where day-to-day opacity is experienced
as a hope, not as the real possibility of fully controlling who we are communicating with. The digital spaces we use to collectively communicate
with each other about civic issues and politics—our email, social media
platforms like Facebook or Twitter, our blogs—are protected by weak digital walls that quickly crumble when the right algorithmic tool is deployed
against them. The result is that the digital realm is also a place of lurkers,
criminals, and bullies who do in the open what others will do only under
the cover of darkness.

In Mexico, violent agents are more than lurkers. In the context of these
blogs' work, in the states of Monterrey and Tamaulipas, the places from which
the blogs were likely published, violence has been rapidly restructuring
publicity. But building-based metaphors involving walls, chambers, secret
passages, and agoras cannot capture the fundamental issues of opacity
and publicness in the digital world. Instead, we can imagine this contingent Mexican digital agora as a space defined by trenches, at once open and
closed spaces, from which combatants troll, threaten, and throw the oc-
casional punch or bullet to whomever dares to stand up and speak. EBDN
was a subsection of that lumpy, uneven, agoric space, never fully bounded,
walled, or secret. From the trenches, anonymous people spoke, and from
other nearby trenches, they were threatened, taunted, and promised death.
The comments sections are vicious places. These bloggers received hundreds of threats on their lives. When EBDN and *VxT* published content that
somehow threatened other anonymous combatants, members of the state
or members of DCOs, the combatants would simply move toward the voices,
raise their weapons, and shoot. Digital anonymity of the type was normal
on EBDN. Creating a fake email, using a VPN or a proxy server, was hardly
effective; it was relatively easy for DCOs and corrupt state agents to track
down contributors, as those hanging from Nuevo Laredo's bridge in September 2011 tragically found. These digital trenches were simply not deep
enough.

I continue exploring the case of Lucy in the next chapter. Here let me conclude my arguments about anonymity and civic participation. One of the main reasons many believe digital media is reanimating the public sphere is that it allows for low-cost communication and participation in public debates without the burden of temporal and/or spatial presence. One can participate in civic communication across time and distance, hence expanding the civic power and potential of each statement. From this perspective, digital media magnifies the agora effect, and, perhaps predictably, digital media have energized the citizen journalism sector. However, the facts that the most successful *EBDN* URL, Lucy's site, is today silent and that El Administrador is no longer in charge of *VxT* are clear reminders that these agoric effects are always at risk of disintegrating, especially in the presence of violence. In Mexico today, violence has restructured the rules of participating in the public sphere, making anonymity a necessary tactic for those wishing to speak directly about DCOs and the dangers their activities bring to neighborhoods and cities. In many cases, including the ones documented here, anonymity simply allows for a window of opportunity to behave civically. DCOs interested in silencing a blogger will go to great lengths to acquire and deploy the technological tools to find those wishing and needing to remain anonymous, and they will close that window with relentless force.

Opacity has its limits, and the limits of opacity mark the limits of publicity in violent contexts. Anonymity is imperfect, as imperfect and imprecise as most other spatially reflexive actions taken within the digital realm. Informed by misplaced metaphors of the materials meant to constitute opacity, we believe, like Lucy and El Administrador, in the walls that give us the courage to speak to power. In Mexico, as in most of the world, this trust is foolish.

6

Trust

To be a journalist in Veracruz is an act of courage, but this does not make
us heroes. We are persons. We are journalists.
—Oscar Martinez, Nuestra Aparente Rendición, my translation

Speaking to power may be foolish, but people speak nonetheless. The rise of
massive violence due to organized crime that Mexico has experienced since
the beginning of the presidency of Felipe Calderón in 2007 has brought
powerful challenges to Mexicans wishing to participate in the public sphere,
but public participation has not stopped. Yes, traditional journalism has
been under siege, with journalists routinely killed, kidnapped, beaten, and
threatened due to their reporting of drug violence (see chapter 5). And yes,
as a result self-censorship in journalism has risen, and it has become increasingly common for violent crime to go unreported by news organizations.
Yes, investigative reporting in the most affected regions has all but disappeared. And yes, these gaps to public knowledge created by the violence
on traditional journalism cannot be filled by anybody or anything, but this
does not mean that some people have not tried to do something about it.
Journalists continue to be killed because they seem to always be testing how
far they can go in their reporting, but there are also citizens who, protected
by the mantle of anonymity, try to fill the informational gap. As noted in
the last chapter, anonymous bloggers see themselves as partly addressing
the need to create spaces for public knowledge about the violence, and although their ability to do so is limited, they have tried, even at great risk.

Anonymity here is needed, just as it is in the many instances in which soldiers and police officers, who are directly fighting drug cartel violence, have to wear masks to hide their faces in order to protect themselves and their families. Blogging, however, is different from policing and soldiering. The meaning and value of anonymity changes when it is embodied in a person meant to participate in the public sphere, one not protected by powerful state institutions, one meant to convey trustworthiness individually as opposed to institutionally.

This chapter continues the analysis of the anonymous Mexican blogosphere, with particular attention to *El Blog del Narco* (EBDN), run by an anonymous administrator under the pen name "Lucy," one of the two most famous of these anonymous blogs.[1] This is a highly visited blog that is controversial for at least three reasons: (1) EBDN routinely publishes some of the most gruesome depictions of violence, including decapitations, dismemberments, and all sorts of vile executions that leave viewers wondering about the very humanity of the perpetrators. (2) The blog has been accused of being a mouthpiece for the cartels because the brutal visual content is provided by users, many of whom undoubtedly belong to the very drug cartels EBDN claims to be fighting against. (3) The blog has repeatedly been accused of plagiarism from mainstream Mexican news sources such as *Proceso* magazine. This means that every element of the blog—the disturbing nature of its content, its photos and videos, and its news pieces—have been criticized by many.

These controversies notwithstanding, as noted in the previous chapter, EBDN has often received high volumes of traffic, and its fame has extended to international observers, who have lauded EBDN's public role, painting it as nothing short of heroic. Diverse commentators in 2013, such as Melissa del Bosque, writing for the *Texas Observer* (April 3, 2013); Bernardo Loyola, writing for *Vice* (May 13, 2013); Sonja Peteranderl, writing for the journal *Digital Development Debates* (October 2013); and Rory Carroll, writing for the *Guardian* (repeatedly during 2013), shared this heroic view of EBDN's creators. They all believed that the bloggers deserved heroic treatment because they are placing themselves in danger in the hopes of helping fight the power of the drug criminal organizations (DCOs) and corrupt elements of the Mexican state.

In the case of EBDN, anonymity, violence, and mistrust converge in the figure of the anonymous hero, the bloggers' public personas. This convergence is the clearest in the public understanding of Lucy, the most famous of these bloggers and the one who is most commonly singled out as the creator of *EBDN*. Using public discourse about Lucy, this chapter investigates the gaps and paradoxes inherent in Lucy's heroicness. I argue that these gaps and paradoxes illuminate foundational ideas about publicity in modernity. In particular, they help me expand Seyla Benhabib's (1992, 1993, 1996) classic interrogations of Hannah Arendt's notions of publicity, recuperating some key insights found in the work of both Arendt and Benhabib. The combination of new media technologies in violent contexts puts these foundational ideas through the harshest test and highlights the need to retheorize publicity in the resulting new political and communicational contexts.

The first section examines the particular discourses of heroicness and civics attached to Lucy. The second section places these discourses within theories of publicity, highlighting the connection between identity and the public hero. The third section examines the discursive and theoretical connections between anonymity, publicity, trust, and digital technologies, foregrounding the paradoxical type of publicness and heroicness that digital anonymity constitutes.

THE ORIGINS OF LUCY

Given the violence against journalists had already achieved staggering levels by 2010 (see chapter 5), the year *EBDN* began, why would anyone try to do a journalist's job? The answer, both simple and complex, is that they felt it was their civic duty. This feeling is the affective signature of a new modern citizenship shaped by a democratic opening that in Mexico coincided with the rise and mainstreaming of digital technologies. Michael Schudson (1999) would call this style of citizenship "rights-bearing" citizenship, a particular modality of being civic characterized by the ongoing monitoring of society and government to identify things, events, and policies that may impinge on people's rights. Although with these ideas Schudson was trying to make sense of the evolution of citizenship in the United States, particularly during and after the 1960s, similar changes were happening in many other nations around the world, including Mexico.

The modality of rights-bearing citizenship was also common in Mexico during and after the 1960s, even if the political climate was different. The Institutional Revolutionary Party (PRI) ruled consistently and sometimes harshly against political mobilizations, yet since the 1960s, in urban Mexican centers, youth and other groups including teachers and union members have been highly politicized, with a clearly normalized expectation of substantive rights and political mobilization. I remember arriving in Mexico

City in the 1980s to do my undergraduate work at the Instituto Politécnico Nacional (the National Polytechnic Institute), and within days I was participating in my first gigantic political march. The group of perhaps ten thousand protested against violence against students at the hands of government forces, or at least that was what the leaders believed. Our campus was far from the Zócalo (the main square), the National Palace, and the Mexican Congress, so we hijacked public buses and, surrounded by police helicopters, rode to the Zócalo. It felt powerful to be seventeen and experience the feeling of thousands marching together. It was also clear at the time that I had decided to attend university in Mexico City and move far from my little city in Sonora in order to experience that very feeling of political unity. That is, even in Navojoa, a small city far away from Mexico City, I knew that the identity of a university student included the expectation of political participation and mobilization. While our portfolio of rights looked quite different from the portfolio available to most US Americans, political rights and, eventually, democracy were the unquestionable goal of those generations of Mexicans.

The ending of Mexico's authoritarian phase in 2000, thanks in part to the ongoing mobilization of Mexicans all over the nation, opened more spaces for political action at the same time that digital technologies and the internet gave a growing portion of Mexicans new, easy, fast, and far-reaching possibilities for social influence and speech. It is no surprise that journalists during these violent times felt compelled to continue their job, even if danger was always around the corner, and it is also no surprise that when journalism ceased to be effective in some regions, people like Lucy, and the thousands that collaborated on her blog, felt that their duty was to monitor their neighborhoods and use digital technologies to report what was happening.

Schudson's rights-bearing citizen, who monitors constantly, does not describe everybody in the United States, just as my comments above are not meant to universalize that peculiar feeling of being politically desirous and active in Mexico. Yet for some Mexicans, this type of modern citizenship was normal, and embracing one's civic duties included the willingness to be critical of the state, to try to do something about it, and to feel this duty as an obligation. The affective side of these civic obligations has evolved alongside publicity, which Reinhart Koselleck (1988) and Jürgen Habermas (1989) understand first as a willingness and desire to criticize absolutism in secret societies, and, later, as a similar expression of civics in literary societies, cafes, and salons, locations in which publicity *was* civic life. These two thinkers may disagree on some important things, as I showed in the last chapter, but they agree on this: one's willingness to criticize the state, to understand this speaking as a duty, and, increasingly, to wrap this duty in feelings of obligation toward others is the communicative side of modern citizenship. If Benedict Anderson (1991) successfully argued that willingness to die for one's nation is the central affective power of the modern nation-state, I say that willingness to speak on behalf of others is the civilian equivalent in today's context. Schudson here echoes Jodi Dean's (2001: 639) "suspicious subject" in that both types of civic subjectivity are engaged in systematic surveillance, but in Schudson's rights-bearing citizenship, the individual's goal is to speak to power and to hold the state accountable.

Speaking to power and understanding speaking as a duty, particularly in dangerous times, is what propels the modern emphasis on expressive freedoms and what helps us understand expression as the most modern of all rights (Starr 2004). In the information age in particular, this civic duty is at the heart of Schudson's rights-bearing citizen and Jodi Dean's (2001) "suspicious subject" (see chapter 5), both of which embrace the impersonal yet powerfully felt notion that "the people have a right to know." Democracy is at stake, but so is the soul of the citizen. Dr. Martin Luther King Jr., who to many epitomizes the character and values of the rights-bearing citizen, succinctly brought together this view of civics when in his first speech in Selma, Alabama, on February 12, 1965, he argued: "Our lives begin to end the day we become silent about things that matter." In this quite modern metaphor, silence is equal to death just as speech is equal to life. Dangerously, ontology and publicity become one, and this unnerving fusion explains why even in the midst of persecution and death threats, Rubén Espinosa (see chapter 5) was able to succinctly summarize his duty as a journalist as the duty to "give voice to the voiceless," even if doing so would bring him death. From what we know about Lucy, she was no different from these men.

Lucy repeatedly couched her actions in the language of duty. In her book and blog posts she describes herself as a young woman in her midtwenties who created EBDN as a way of filling the information gap in cities like Monterrey, where violence had ramped up and reporting was scarce. Single, without children, and a patriot, Lucy repeatedly noted that her actions also had the goal of correcting the global perception of Mexicans as corrupt, uneducated, and violent. Lucy describes herself sometimes as a journalist and, in other instances, simply as someone with "experience gathering information" (*Blog del Narco* 2013: 3). It is unclear whether she ever was trained as a journalist or worked as one in a news organization. Regardless, she has framed her blogging practices as "citizen journalism." Besides Lucy herself, others like David Sasaki (2010) and Andrés Monroy-Hernández and Luis Daniel Palacios (2014) also call EBDN citizen journalism. Citizen journalism is used to designate the reporting and civic work of individuals not associated with news institutions. The work of citizen journalists is thus "free" in the sense that it is unpaid and also in the sense that it is voluntary: bloggers feel that their work is akin to their civic duty.

Like all duties, the duty to speak up is also a burden, and one has the choice to embrace it or reject it. There are rewards for both, and there are also likely punishments. Risk is a calculation, and in the mediatic context in which Lucy existed, the duty to speak up was filtered through the affordances of digital media, which likely changed the risk equation. Digital anonymity greatly reduced the likeliness of punishment, or at least that is what most of the anonymous bloggers believed during the first few years of the massive increase in violence in Mexico. Lucy's thinking was no different. Her goal was to use anonymity to bypass the forces of censorship that were silencing traditional journalistic sources. These forces, she argued, included government and organized crime efforts to stop news organizations from reporting and to encourage them to report the bare minimum. In her view, the government was censoring by underreporting or hiding the chaos that regions in Mexico were experiencing.

The risks were immediately evident. The blog was under attack from the beginning; often, Lucy states, these attacks were cyberattacks from the Mexican government. In the *Guardian*, Carroll quotes Lucy: "We change where we live every month. We've been in basements. It's very difficult. We hide our equipment in different places. If the authorities get close we run" (2013). As the killing of bloggers in 2011 and the ongoing threat and attacks demonstrate, Lucy's concerns were not just paranoid. Clearly, the DCOs and some members of the Mexican state were going to great lengths to control the public sphere and to force, through the most brutal coercion, silence over clamor. In that interview in 2013, Lucy spoke about being highly traumatized by these events, as they dramatically reminded her of the precariousness of her situation.[2] In the introduction of her 2013 book *Dying for the Truth: Undercover inside the Mexican Drug War*, published in Spanish and English, in which he or she narrates a year in the life of the blog, Lucy recalls how in the four days before writing the book's introduction, she and her partner had received nine different photos of killings with messages written on top of the photo: "You are next, *EBDN*." Violence seemed to always be near, even if anonymity kept it at arm's length.

In the last chapter I showed that anonymity is part of our political imaginaries because of our origin myths, particularly the myth that nations like Mexico and the US are revolutionary nations that require extreme rules for public engagement. Thanks to this myth, anonymity is both normalized and made heroic, but heroicness has a second and equally important historical trajectory within publicity theory. Why is Lucy's anonymity portrayed as heroic? To begin answering this question, the next section examines classic theorizations of publicity connecting publicness to heroicness. Then I examine the conditions of publicity and anonymity in Lucy's case.

THE PUBLIC HERO

In *The Human Condition* (1958), Arendt develops seminal ideas about publicity in modernity that she anchors in an analysis of classical Greek life. She argues that in Athens, publicity was possible only through the coming together enabled by language and human communication, which made possible social arrangements free of violence (1958: 26). She explains that the Greeks, like our contemporaries, were very concerned with avoiding violence and finding methods of social interaction that would eliminate it. Violence existed, but not in the sphere of politics, which was ruled by talk, rhetoric, and the ideal of shared understanding.

Benhabib (1993) has noted that Arendt's ideas about publicity are not without complications. She uses not one, but two models of publicity. In the Greek city, the public realm "was permeated by a fiercely agonal spirit, where everybody had constantly to distinguish himself from all others, to show through unique deeds or achievements that he was the best of all" (Arendt 1958: 41). This "agonistic space," to use Benhabib's term, is a textured and competitive space in which moral and political greatness is "revealed, displayed, and shared with others" (1993: 102). It is eminently dramaturgical, the space of heroes, as this space is meant to be not homogeneous, but a stage full of different values that allow some actors and their voices to headline debates and some persons—and personas—to gain and continue gaining public stature. This topological thinking is also theatrical, meant to foster passion, thought, and action.

There is a second type of publicness—an "associational view of public space," Benhabib (1993) calls it—that in Arendt's case is more conducive to positive political outcomes (102). This associational type of publicity, which manifests anytime "men act together in concert," is part of Arendt's conceptualization of power, force, strength, and violence (1958). Benhabib notes that this associational space represents "the kind of democratic or associative politics that can be engaged in by ordinary citizens who may or may not possess great moral prowess but who acquire the capacities of political judgment and initiative in the process of self-organization" (1996: 125). Power is acting together—the power of the *polis*, the seminal meaning of politics, one of the normative notions that Arendt relies on in *The Human Condition* and in *On Violence*. For Benhabib, "these diverse topographical locations become public spaces in that they become the sites of power, of common action coordinated through speech and persuasion" (1996: 125, referring to Arendt 1958: 78).

The notion of a public hero, the type of heroism that some have tried to cast on Lucy, is at home in Arendt's first model, the topological and agonistic conception of publicity. Lucy claims that she attempts to reveal the dark, bloody secrets of Mexico's drug conflict, and in the process she must attempt to conquer a style of preeminence, a high point, a stature, from which she can share with others her visions of a better Mexico. In this agonistic space, the textured drama of life necessitates actors who use loud and perhaps even spectacular forms of personal display and action in order to command attention. Without attention, the message is lost.

Benhabib (1993) finds fissures in Arendt's ideas, in particular in Arendt's separation of the private and public realms. However, this is not the only fissure in Arendt's argument. Benhabib's classical feminist analysis of Arendt's work questions Arendt's phenomenological essentialism, or the notion that different human activities have their own place and, thus, that the different boundaries that define the public—including the public and private *and* the public/political and violence/prepolitical—neatly separate human activities (1993: 104). Benhabib's concern is not violence, but the separation between the private and the public, an argument that has stood the test of time. Yet violence is not simply the fulcrum that allows the public to exist and that should be dismissed once the public is established; violence is also an activity that should be phenomenologically de-essentialized. For instance, even though Benhabib questions the domestication of the Homeric warrior who, in Arendt, ceases using violence and instead uses deliberation and rhetoric, Benhabib never interrogates the fact that the social landscape inhabited by Homer's heroes is one of deadly violence and conflict. As such, Benhabib's critique of Arendt's weaknesses simply falls short. There is a dismissal of violence as an object of theory in both Arendt and Benhabib, one that needs correcting.

This dismissal of violence reveals a particular perspective in both theories: the dangerous notion that theories of publicity naturally belong to a political ecology in which the state has a monopoly of power. This is true even though Arendt's own ideas were drawn against the context of totalitarianism, a type of political organization in which violence is indeed monopolized, and even though Benhabib's ideas were sketched in the context of women's struggle against the patriarchy. The issue is not simply whether or not Homer is read properly. The issue is that Arendt's and Benhabib's notions of politics do not match the history of Western nations and are simply inapplicable to nations in which the state does not have a monopoly on power, in which corruption of state actors weakens the state of law. What are heroes in these contexts? What is publicity in the bloody modernity that Mexico is experiencing? What can Lucy's case teach us about the missing parts in these theories of publicity?

The Hero's Odyssey

Lucy's story does not end with her promotion to civic hero by the international community. On May 5, 2013, only weeks after Lucy's series of interviews in March and April revealed her work to the public, her colleague, the webmaster who helped with the technical side of the website, called her one last time and simply uttered the word *run* (Carroll 2013). No one has heard from Lucy's colleague again.

After hiding for a few days, Lucy fled, first to the United States and then to Spain. A few days later, she contacted Carroll, the writer who had previously interviewed her for the *Guardian* via Skype, and revealed her state of panic and loneliness. Her last post on EBDN was dated May 3, 2013, and claimed that she did not intend to resume control of the site. She was staying in a boardinghouse with enough money to last a few months, but was otherwise without contacts and almost without identity in a country not her own. Carroll writes: "Her biggest fear is she will see her colleague appear on a video of the type that frequently appeared on their blog: battered, interrogated, gazing into the camera, knowing a terrible fate awaits" (2013).

In the meantime, her stay in Spain did not improve. On June 5, 2013, Lucy started a personal blog, blogdelucy.com, in which she wrote about her race to survive. She writes: "Sí, ha sido un gran error venir a España. Yo sé, España es un gran país, pero lamentablemente no me había percatado de las buenas relaciones que tiene con Felipe Calderón Hinojosa. Acepto que ha sido un error" (Yes, it was a big mistake to come to Spain. I know, Spain is a great country, but sadly I wasn't aware of the great relationships it has with Felipe Calderón Hinojosa. I accept that it was a mistake).

This short-lived blog was available on Internet Archive, but no longer. The only traces are in Twitter (#elblogdelucy) and in my own archive. Her first entry is about the publication of the book *Dying for the Truth* (*Blog del Narco* 2013). Her second one, on June 6, 2013, is about her race to survive away from Mexico. Sometimes thankful to all who had reached out and spoken to her encouragingly through email and Twitter—using the hashtags #blogdelnarco and later #elblogdelucy—sometimes morose, Lucy spoke of her struggles, hungers, the sense of betrayal she had to live with, and her pessimistic opinions about the Mexican political system, in particular the executive power led by President Calderón.

In July 2013, she published an angry letter asking the international community to help her leave Spain. She seemed aware that her journalistic quest was understood through a different register than the work of other famous new-media political stars, and she argued that she had not received any help because "I am Mexican, and not Cuban like Yoani Sánchez, or US American like Edward Snowden." Sánchez, the creator of the famous human rights blog *Generación Y*, has dedicated her life to shedding light on Cuba's internal dissonances, including its poor human rights record, the challenges to freedom that Cubans routinely experience on the island, and the small corruptions involved in having to spend every day waiting for basic necessities, from electricity to bread. Her blog is a trusted source of political commentary and criticism, and she is broadly recognized and respected around the world, particularly after *Time* magazine's international version placed her on the cover in 2008 and named her one of the year's most influential people. Her fame has allowed her to go on fund-raising trips to different locations, including Mexico in October 2013, where she has received strong monetary support to continue her work. Lucy herself declared her support for Sánchez's work, yet their experiences as female Latin American bloggers could not be more different (Corsa 2008). The year after Lucy disappeared, Sánchez's blog became an independent digital newspaper called *14ymedio* .com in Cuba, further adding weight to her words and views on Cuban society and politics.

Unlike bloggers Lucy and Sánchez, Edward Snowden came to fame as a whistleblower, a computer professional who leaked classified information from the US National Security Agency (NSA) in 2013. Among other things, his leaks revealed the illicit manner in which the NSA spied on other nations, including allies like Germany and Brazil. Although these leaks were highly controversial, Snowden has become a hero to many for his willingness to break US law, arguably for the well-being of others and for the principles of good government and just international relations. His life after the leaks in 2013, like Lucy's, has required ongoing hiding and relative isolation (Burrough, Ellison, and Andrews 2014). The key difference is that while he might fear jail, Lucy fears death.

On July 22, 2013, a request for funds to get Lucy out of Spain was issued by her or on her behalf on the crowdfunding site Kapipal. According to the site, she only collected around 500 euros, a mere pittance. Was Lucy correct? Was the international community's apathy a type of racism or anti-Mexicanism? I do not think so, and to help me explain this I want to again turn to Arendt's work, which I argue is better at explaining the most likely reason for Lucy's failure to raise the type of sympathy and support that other acts of internet courage have.

When Arendt discusses what Benhabib refers to as the agonistic public realm, she centers her argument on the nature and pairing of action and speech. The actions that distinguish those who deserve to be in public, those that single out an individual and that make them worthwhile of admiration and respect, are actions always followed by or explained by speech. It is through action and speech that individuals reveal their uniqueness and their identity, their difference, vis-à-vis the world. Actions without words lose their subject: "The action he begins is humanly disclosed by the word, and though his deed can be perceived in its brute physical appearance without verbal accompaniment, it becomes relevant only through the spoken word in which he identifies himself as the actor, announcing what he does, has done, and intends to do" (Arendt 1958: 179). The spoken word is what characterizes the action's entrance into the public realm, and only through words can actors leave behind a lasting influence on social relationships. Through speech, actors reveal their "life stories," and through self-disclosure, social actors can become protagonists on the web of social stories, the monuments and histories that surround the hero and propel the hero to memory. In Arendt's agonistic realm, anonymous publicity is an oxymoron.

Arendt (1958) acknowledges that in war situations, anonymity is often required to act in public, but anonymous speech in warring contexts is, for her, "mere talk," incapable of revealing the "who," and hence incapable of transcending the moment. This "mere talk," as she would label Lucy's public intervention, cannot be memorialized because a public act becomes story only through the courageous act of self-disclosure (1958: 180). The case at hand reveals the prescience of Arendt's words. Lucy's actions, her blogging, her writing, her willingness to publish others' work, are quickly being erased from memory and were already insufficient in 2013 to incite significant response. This lack of response to Lucy is rooted in the type of mediation she used and in her anonymity, which became the production tactic and emblem of the danger in which she existed. Her heroic persona was linked to her need for anonymity, and digital technologies provided the techniques to establish this anonymity. Because she embraced anonymity, however, her actions lost the ability to transcend and are bound to be forgotten.

Casting her profile against the politicized heroic identities of Sánchez and Snowden, Lucy's anonymous efforts against cartels and corrupt Mexican politicians gave her no platform from which to springboard herself into international stardom. Even though the threats on her life have been more certain and terrifying than the risks for Sánchez or Snowden, Lucy's quest never fitted the parameters of heroic stardom that have become the norm in internet celebrity culture. The reasons include self-disclosure. Sánchez herself has reflected that the fame of her blog gave her relative protection from Cuba's government. It is likely that Snowden felt the same. In a sense, they have both been relatively protected by fame and by their willingness to openly reveal their identities alongside their deeds. Lucy, who feared the impunity typically enjoyed by the DCOs, did not have the luxury to reveal herself to others.

Arendt can explain some features of Lucy's case, but Lucy's case also clarifies some features of Arendt's thoughts. In particular, Lucy's need for anonymity reveals what is missing in Benhabib's and Arendt's ideas on publicity: *the a priori of publicity is trust, and trust is concretized by sharing one's identity in and through media technologies.* These missing elements are central to understanding publicity in the West and essential for evaluating publicity in violent contexts.

ANONYMITY, TRUST, AND (NEW) MEDIA TECHNOLOGIES

Arendt's heroes existed in the age of orality, when stories told about the past depended on faithful learning and repetition of each story in each generation. Homer's heroes—Ulysses, Achilles, Paris, and Hector, to name a few—come to us through the web of sociality made possible by oral stories. As I noted above, Benhabib shows us that these heroes became domesticated in Arendt's work, distinctive not because of their capacity to act and survive violence but because of their memorialization in speech and stories. The agonistic realm that she sketches for us is also indebted to Arendt's ideas on orality. The act of self-disclosure central to publicity was courageous not because, as with Hector's faith, showing oneself in public would mean certain death. In Arendt's work, "courage and even boldness are already present in leaving one's private hiding place and showing who one is, in disclosing and exposing one's self" (1958: 186). But not to worry, the opponent waiting in this case is not Achilles, only a stronger debater who will bring reason and leave the sword behind. In the political imaginary constructed by Arendt and reproduced in many theories of publicity, orality underscores most principles of publicity, including the nature of the courage one must embrace when entering the public realm (Benhabib 1993, 1996). This is a courage that assumes the basic safety of those in public. The public realm is a contest of speakers, not killers; its heroes engage in a war of ideas and rhetoric, not bullets.

Orality implies self-disclosure, but once we leave behind orality, things quickly grow complicated. Violence may loom. These complications are not simply the result of the heterogeneous nature of modern societies, which is Benhabib's argument, but also the result of the very affordances of technology and media. Mistrust is not simply the result of different views on life, politics, and values. To de-essentialize the phenomenology of mistrust (borrowing from Benhabib's insightful criticism), we must recognize the materiality and spatiality of trust and the manner in which technologies of space complicate, muddle, and even negate trust. For things changed after orality. Can trust exist without self-disclosure? Can self-disclosure exist without copresence?

Communication technologies stand between individuals and mediate in a way that is fundamentally paradoxical. Because of the latter, from the origins of writing to today, all communication technologies have been tools of anonymity or, at the very least, for making self-disclosure ambiguous. Because they don't require copresence, post-oral communication technologies constitute types of mediation between a person and, potentially, an unknown. All media technologies insert opacity into social relations. To address the otherwise inevitable insecurity of technology, people have developed "trusted systems" to assure secure communication and reduce or bypass opacity. Although today we associate the term *trusted systems* with computer-mediated technologies and communication, trusted systems have always been part of mediation. In writing and later printing, we have used seals, signatures, and rules of authorship that are meant to assure readers that they indeed know who is communicating with them, even if they cannot see them or touch them (Illich and Sanders 1988: 34–51). I trust I know who wrote *El laberinto de la soledad* because Fondo de Cultura Económica printed the name Octavio Páz on the cover of their 1991 reprint, and I trust that I know what Páz wrote in that book because Fondo is a highly respected Mexican publishing house. In other words, trusted systems are indexical of opacity and point to the secrets at the heart of mediation communication.

The development of trusted systems in computer-based environments is very complex, but here I want to highlight a way of making sense of these systems in relation to the particular challenges to publicness in digital environments that Lucy had to face. The challenges are connected to the ability or inability of computerized media technologies to replicate open, trusted, face-to-face, civic (or polite) interactions in violent contexts. These challenges can be organized into two categories summarized in the idea of "open civic communication": (1) The term *open communication* refers to the topological challenges of publicity in a violent context, or the challenges brought about by space, identity, and trust. (2) The term *civic communication* highlights both the goal of the specific communication and the type of content it includes.

Open Communication
Trusted systems in writing were meant to connect writer and reader and were about establishing identity and authorship. Adam Seligman puts forth a useful definition of trust that serves our purposes well: he calls trust an "institutionalized model of generalized exchange" (1997: 106). In writing, trusted systems were not about agreement but about recognition. I don't have to agree with what Páz wrote, but I trust I know with whom I am disagreeing. In fact, the most evident examples of mutual trust in communication come in the context of unmediated, copresent debate.

In face-to-face debate, we need to have two types of trust. First, we must trust we know who the other speaker is, even if we disagree with her or him, and second, we must trust the other's behavior during the disagreement. In debate, trust translates into safety, which, not coincidently, has the Old Norse etymological origin of *treysta,* which means "to make safe" (Garmonsway 1928: 144). Trust is thus not simply the faith resulting from an institutionalized way of communicating, but the outcome of that faith or the feeling it provides, the confidence that allows us to disagree without fear. In Spanish, which did not benefit from the Old Norse precedent, trust translates simply as *confianza*: the belief that everything will be fine, particularly if we exchange words in very specific, predetermined, and recognizable ways. Trust during disagreement is an outcome that cannot be taken for granted but that can more or less be predicted in certain institutionalized contexts, when it belongs to a social system, a habitus. In particular, feeling safe even in disagreement is part of the modern habitus, and this element of sociality has a particular history that can be traced as the rise of "civility" and "politeness" in public settings (Bourdieu 1990; Seligman 1997: 65).[3] We trust we can disagree with each other without needing violence if we feel we are in a "civilized" context and with people who are civil, who are polite. The relation to publicity is not coincidental, but foundational. The term *civility* itself and the behaviors it implies are rooted in the Latin *civitas*, the same root as *citizen*, which in turn comes from the Greek *polites*, which refers to a member of the *polis* (Smith 2003: 106). Civility and politeness thus mean more than good manners; they refer to the personal characteristics needed to be part of a democracy, which includes debating without violence. Civility and politeness are trusting systems in copresent debate. They refer to predetermined protocols of interaction that allow us to communicate without fear of reprisal.

Trusting systems are needed in publicness, for debate, and they are even more necessary when face-to-face open communication is impossible and the trusting effects of openness are needed. This is especially true in contemporary societies, which tend to be complex social arrangements that bring together dissimilar populations. More than ever, today's democracies depend on systems of cohesion, which can only be the result of debating about our differences. Yet mediated communication is a general model of exchange that seems to privilege intellectual harmony, not debate. Readers, listeners, or viewers who find something that they disagree with do not have an ethical duty, which is part of face-to-face interaction, to engage with the other's ideas or argument. They can simply stop reading, listening, or viewing. The echo-chamber effect that many have written about regarding US media is partly a technological problem and partly a problem of socialization, a way of avoiding intellectual disagreement by sticking to the easy exchange of ideas with those who agree with you. Face-to-face conversation is great for sustaining community, but it can be more socially meaningful in debates and thus in pluralistic societies.

This is partly why Habermas's *Structural Transformation* (1989) tracks the rise and decline of the public sphere, from publicness to what he calls the "re-feudalization" of the public sphere—in terms of an erosion of face-to-face sociability, the rise of the power of public opinion and the eventual substitution of public opinion for public relations, a market-driven way of being social and political (135). In this case, trust is not gone, but depleted or difficult to attain. The trust needed to hold a system of agreement together is a minor thing compared to the robust trust needed to hold a system of disagreement together (Putnam 1995). In this system of exchange, impoliteness and a lack of civility can quickly become violent. Absent the power of copresence to invoke an ethical relation of trust between the self and the other, the self may quickly normalize impoliteness and incivility (Dahlgren 1995; Peters 1999).

The echo-chamber effect is not the predetermined result of mediating techniques. Not every aspect of technologically mediated communication reduces trust. Live television, for instance, reignited the possibility of immediate trust by allowing some aspects of copresence to be part of technological communication (Auslander 1999: 12; Peters 2001). Mexicans trusted Jacobo Zabludovsky, who anchored Televisa's news for almost three decades, as much as US Americans trusted Walter Cronkite, who for almost two decades anchored CBS. We may not have agreed with them, but we trusted that we knew with whom we were agreeing or disagreeing. Our trust was needed, as both anchors represented institutions wielding huge cultural and political power. Liveness is not openness or face-to-face communication. It is an institutionalized form of communication understood as performative. It is a replica of openness, a copy that represents some core elements of openness and leaves off others. On live television news, we can see the faces of the anchors, their serious demeanors, their emotional outbursts, and we can hear their words at roughly the same time they utter them. The replica is socially and dramaturgically powerful.

Critics have argued that replicas of liveness seem to constitute weak communities, which are less likely to be civically engaged. This is true in general, but not because mediation automatically produces disengagement. In times of violent crises, the replica can be powerful and elicit the strongest sense of trust. Sometimes the liveness of broadcast seems to dissolve the technological structures that separate anchor and audience and elicit more than a thin agreement. When on November 22, 1963, Cronkite announced the death of President John F. Kennedy, and we heard his voice breaking and saw his hand reaching up for his glasses and saw him barely able to contain his tears, we trusted the information, and we trusted the person; we knew how he felt about the event, and we became one with him.

On September 19, 1985, immediately after the catastrophic earthquake that killed between fourteen thousand and forty thousand people (depending on the source) in Mexico City, Zabludovsky had his Cronkite moment. The 8.0-magnitude earthquake happened at 7:19 a.m., and Zabludovsky was still at home. He raced out to his car, which had one of the first car phones in the world, and transmitted reports while driving toward the Televisa News Building in Chapultepec. From that car phone, his voice reached a frightened regional and national television audience. He was the only reporter giving testimony of what was going on in one of the most devastated areas of the city. His report tells us much about how liveness can activate the most powerful ethical connection between anchor and viewer. In this report, Zabludovsky is driving and walking through the devastation in downtown Mexico City, and though he has made a career as an anchor unfazed by events, we trust his words the most when we hear his feeling of uncertainty and fear, as when he is temporarily in danger because gas tanks are being moved just feet from him, or when he is moving by a building so tilted that he knows it may fall at any moment. Trust is liveness, the feeling of the body, not cold objectivity. He keeps going, describing what he can see. Even though audiences cannot see what he sees, he describes it the best he can, naming the buildings that are up, the ones that are down. Zabludovsky is walking through an unrecognizable downtown. He helps viewers recognize by pointing out the landmarks still visible, even the billboards. The report famously ends when he arrives at the main building of Televisa News, his network, and finds it destroyed. He has been narrating all this time with tragic emotion, but he is the most powerful then, when in tragic sadness he can no longer talk. His coworkers are trapped or dead in the crumbled building. At that moment, liveness was at its most effective. At that moment, audiences not only felt the sense of bodily risk that Zabludovsky shared with them throughout his difficult trajectory. They felt they were with him, face to face, sharing his pain (Peters 2001).[4]

These replicas of open, oral communication all bypass an important element of face-to-face communication, one central to publicness. In the copresent debate and sharing that we associate with idealized forms of publicness, openness is possible because of reciprocity of trust (Papacharissi 2010: 122). So idealized forms of publicness, such as Arendt's, rely on the trust of two, the speaker and the listener, the writer and the reader, the singer and the audience, the anchorperson and the viewer. Zabludovsky and Cronkite were live and trusted, but not present. Almost always their bodies were hidden from those who in rage may have listened and wanted to respond, those who wished to disagree with them, or even harm them in anger. We trusted them, but they didn't need to trust us. Reciprocity of trust was not required. Therefore, the replica cannot fully reconstruct publicness. We call them public persons, but these anchors benefit greatly from the opacity permitted by media technologies.

Like Zabludovsky and Cronkite, Lucy wanted to be trusted but could not fully trust some of the users of EBDN; she actually feared them, as she repeatedly stated when referring to the threats by state forces and DCOs. Unlike Zabludovsky and Cronkite, she did not have a powerful news institution shielding her from danger nor cops ready on speed dial to protect her in case of need. Instead, she relied on the peculiar affordances of new media technologies to generate trust through liveness and anonymity through digital opacity. These two affordances, however, are complexly intertwined, which raises the possibility that certain types of publicity in digital realms will never fully work in contexts of violence.

From the blog creator's perspective, from Lucy's perspective, the key elements that generate trust are liveness and/or authorial identity. Liveness replicates copresence just as authorial identity stands in for self-disclosure. Both mechanisms allow users and readers to understand whose work they are using or reading or viewing. The feeling of liveness is relatively easily achieved through new media technologies, which are good at replicating a sense of embodied copresence and thus at generating this aspect of trust. Chatting through the web allows you to almost see how a finger on the other side of the world, perhaps one in a customer support station in India or Brazil, has just pressed the letter q, giving you a feeling of their embodied presence. Temporal immediacy replicates copresent, face-to-face communication. It was therefore easy for Lucy to convey trust while she updated her blog daily, and her ongoing, embodied labor could be felt. Authorial identity was assumed. Users no doubt felt that only Lucy (or whichever anonymous entity they imagined as author) could be in charge of the changes. This assumption about authorship is partly the result of the ubiquity of trusted systems and the users' awareness of their existence.

Trusted systems are key at establishing authorial identity in the digital realm, and most users of digital media have to interact with at least some of these systems on a regular basis. To use the World Wide Web, for instance, requires emblems, logos, signatures, secret codes, URLs, key chains, and passwords to give and receive assurances about identity. In fact, to attest to the staggering number of unknown elements in digital communication environments, most computer communication uses multiple trusted systems simultaneously. For instance, I wrote this chapter at a coffee shop using a computer that is accessible only to me because it requires a password to log in. My computer relies on security software to identify new malware, Trojans, and computer viruses that could harm it. I store my files on "the cloud," so I have to use a password to access the coffee's shop wireless system, which uses my URL as part of the trusted systems it depends on. The cloud system I use requires a "digital certificate," a high-tech identity marker that assures the cloud that I am who I say I am or, if you prefer, that my computer is "who" my computer says it is. These trusted systems use security protocols, cryptography, and hardware security systems to assure that the chapter you are reading is written by me, that it is safe and backed up, and that nobody can steal my ideas, so that you can eventually read them. Digital identities and communication cannot exist without these security mechanisms. Trust would otherwise be as impossible as proving authorial identity.

While retaining their individual anonymity, Lucy and her partner used these systems of trust too. They were part of the risk equation. They registered and bought space for their website from a legitimate internet service provider (ISP) using a "signature," in this case a real email address originating in Monterrey, Mexico. They used a series of pertinent passwords to enter their domain name system (DNS) provider's website and modify the EBDN website. In fact, these basic trust systems allowed Lucy to prove to Carroll (the Guardian's journalist) that she was indeed who she claimed to be. Significantly, this proof was modifying the website, and thus Lucy's proof was at the level of the embodied labor of the publisher. But because these trusted systems are partly assurances about the embodied location of the author, they create a paradox for bloggers like Lucy.

The paradox of digital trusted systems is that the mechanisms that establish authorial identity (i.e., IP addresses, ISPs, and the passwords connecting these two) are also some of the systems used to construct anonymity. Lucy and her partner used these trusted systems to protect themselves from dangerous users, but the digital walls proved to be insufficient. While a physical barrier often hid and protected Zabludovsky and Cronkite, the digital walls meant to protect Lucy's identity and location were much easier to circumvent, as the disappearance of Lucy and her partner proved.

Can an anonymous public hero exist in the digital realm? Not if the hero needs something back from people or from institutions. Members of

Anonymous, the famous organization of hackers that uses digital snooping as a way of performing activism, can expect to be treated as heroes only while they inhabit the masked persona they are known for. Their anonymity has not stopped their vulnerability, as members of Anonymous Veracruz experienced after launching OpCartel in 2011, an operation that targeted Los Zetas. The operation was quickly stopped when one of Anonymous's members was kidnapped by the cartel and Los Zetas threatened the family of the kidnapped person and promised to kill ten members of Anonymous if they dared to reveal the information the hackers had gathered about the criminal organization (Naone 2011). When the heroic act cannot even be performed and police cannot or prefer not to protect, "hacktivists" cannot be called digital heroes. Similarly, Lucy's public role could not be truly open; her heroicness, if that is what we need to call it, could not be attached to her identity as in the case of Snowden or Sánchez; she could not trust some of the visitors to EBDN, and as she has powerfully narrated, her day-to-day activities were carried out in hiding, in fear, by tricking the trusted systems, by moving from location to location, and by never revealing who she was or where she was.

Lucy's anonymity did not work forever, as tricking digital trusted systems is much harder than most realize. While it did work, though, her anonymity allowed thousands of contributors and commentators to share their experiences and views about and with drug violence in Mexico. She was trusted, even if this trust was not universal, but whatever trust she gathered through her role as citizen journalist withered away once her reporting stopped. Trust in her necessitated a different type of maintenance than trust in other public persons, other heroes, whose identities are entwined with their heroic actions. Unless Snowden or Sánchez betray the spirit of their extraordinary acts of publicity, our admiration for them will remain attached to their life stories and their bodies, the very emblems of the risk they took for their communities. Without ongoing activity, without exposing her life to danger—that is, the elements of liveness that Lucy could deliver—Lucy's pleas quickly became alienating, those of an unknown other, one who will likely be forgotten.

CONCLUSION

Violence forces us to look deeply into social and media theories, including theories of publicity, which, I argue, are tested to the limit by the case at hand, a case involving violence and the digital realm. The case shows the significant limits of digital publicness that individuals experience during times of violence, and also reveals often-unexplored assumptions central to publicity theory. Publicness demands bilateral trust and spaces in which this trust can be presumed, yet not every public endeavor can fulfill this demand. At the very least, in violent contexts and in cases of digital communication, spaces of trust are muddled businesses. Secrets are often necessary, as in the case of journalists being able to hide their sources, in the case of whistleblowers like Snowden, or in the case of hacktivists like Anonymous. These secrets are meant to protect the identities of those who stand up to power and who, contradictorily, wish to reveal secrets and illuminate what is hidden. Lucy falls in this muddled category of public actors wishing to control the level of self-disclosure, and her case reveals the limits and even dangers of anonymity. The space of trust was not for Lucy. This space depended on the hero treatment, and this treatment necessitated a face, a body, and an identity. Lucy could not occupy the space of hero, rebel, and fighter that was embodied by and identified with Sánchez or Snowden. She was both openness and secrets, a hero and a fugitive, words without a face. But even in this state of ambiguity and contradiction, she taught us all a lesson: anonymity is not anathema to publicity.

Secrets do have uses in the public sphere, and not only when administered by and within legitimate institutions like the press or the state security apparatus. In a world besieged by pluriform violence, one in which corruption has yielded useless claims that distinguish between the state and criminals, the a priori of politics can no longer be the Hobbesian maxim that the state should have a monopoly on violence or that the state should have a monopoly over secrets. The base of politics should be—as Lucy foresaw in her darkest hour and enacted through her stubborn, unadvisable, and dangerous reporting of violent events—a collective, imagined society that exists street by street, not on the scale of the state or nation.

Conclusion

I began this book at a time when the violence in northern Mexico had escalated to a point where I could not ignore it, even from the United States.
I began devouring articles, books, and media from and about Mexico, particularly those that were reporting, narrating, dramatizing, and explaining
the rise in violence in 2007. Most of the cities in crisis were in the region
where I grew up. I was born and raised in Navojoa, the southernmost city of
Sonora, and Sinaloa, the cradle of some of the most powerful drug cartels,
was just miles from my town. I had relatives all over the region, which made
the news about the violence something that I could not simply experience
as spectacle; the news felt personal, and the pain and horror of learning
about my region's descent into violence was rooted in biography, not some
sort of cosmopolitanism. Let me be clear here. My desire to write on the
subject began as a desire to intervene in the violence, through my craft as
an intellectual. I imagined that if I could think something, anything, to help
ameliorate the horror, then my work would be worthwhile. I imagined that
at the very least what I wrote could inform people in the US and in global
academies of events that were often discussed only in newspapers. Great
books were being written by policy experts, political scientists, and journalists, but the perspective from a humanist, a culturalist, and a local were, and
still are, quite rare.

I had a few challenges ahead of me. As I dove into the literature on
violence, particularly from a humanist perspective, I learned that much
of the literature engaged with political, not criminal, violence. This was
a particular epistemological dissonance that bothered me early on, but I

could neither describe nor explain the reason for this troubled feeling. Was there room to critically engage the study of violence and culture from a perspective focused on massive criminal violence that did not simply lump violence into a political category? Could the massive effects of violence be theorized through a framework different from "political violence"? Was this necessary?

The literature in media studies offered little guidance. The intellectual categories typically used to understand culture and violence, such as deviance, politics, crime, means and ends, media effects, desensitization theory, cultivation, theories of excess (often in humanist approaches), and even evil, were of limited use in the case of the cultural and social effects of violence in Mexico. Was culture an epiphenomenon of the violence, or was violence an epiphenomenon of the culture? Were the worn-down Mexican political cultures of limited liberalism, democracy, populism, and corruption the logical place to start an investigation on criminal violence and culture? Was the maddening force with which neoliberalism was redefining Mexican subjectivity behind the ease with which cartels captured the imagination of citizens? Was the problem of violence, transnational drug cartels, trendy drug consumption, and the complicity of nation-states the new dark face of globalization? How could I contextualize any of these problems within history without trimming away fundamental aspects of reality?

Each of these questions had its merits, and the theoretical assumptions they called upon—notions of hegemony, power, cultures of corruption, and theories of globalization, to name a few—had some but, in my view, insufficient explanatory power. Seriously confronting these very different questions meant understanding that their differing yet partial strengths were related to their epistemological shortcomings, to the fact that violence tended to fixate our gaze only on the bleeding wound and on our desire to stop it.

Most scholarship on violence, to put it simply, tends to be normative at heart. I understand the reason well, for that was my own impulse. I had to make a decision, and the resulting book was the outcome of that decision. I decided that to make the most of the diverse set of theories that propose how to stop the bleeding, I had to withhold my own normative impulse, my desire to intervene, and make that desire itself an object of reflection.

So this book is indebted to two intellectual goals acquired through this process of thinking through the literature and the events. The first goal was to abandon the attempt to write a clean narrative that would position my work as giving answers to the question of how to fix the culture of violence Mexicans and US Americans have experienced as a result of the drug wars.

The stories I have written, thus, are not able to lend solutions, and I confess that even years after I began writing on this subject, I still cannot comprehend much of the cruelty that I have witnessed in my research, nor the impulse to record this cruelty and share it for the world to see. On this, I am no wiser today than when I began. I can also share that my heart physically aches *because* I cannot explain things. I so wish I could. It would give meaning to my life and my craft, but I haven't found that solace yet, which brings me to my second goal.

Early on I committed myself to trying to explain my own normative impulse, my own desire, and even my hope that my research would ameliorate the culture of violence. Where did my normative impulse come from? I hypothesized that it was, first, an intellectual habit rooted in the very craft of thinking about culture, politics, and violence. To support this hypothesis with the research at hand, I needed to connect today's massive violence in Mexico and the culture it inspires to foundational, normative ideas about the modern nation-state in general, and culture in particular.

The vehicle for this query was publicity theory, a theory crafted as a way of explaining the birth of modernity in politics, and the way cultural and media technologies are central to the project of Western liberalism and deliberative politics today. Publicity theory seemed also the place from which many, if not most, normative feelings come. Those writing from a lens of political science, criminology, policy, and journalism tended to share a deep faith in the state as a perfectible institution that could deliver peace and safety to its populations. We like to think of modernity and current liberal democratic principles in, for instance, Lockean terms, but my research showed that when confronted with violence, we are all deeply Hobbesian.

My normative impulse was not only shared by social scientists. It was also common among many humanists—from Hannah Arendt to Aihwa Ong—even if radical criticisms of the state form (e.g., Saskia Sassen) were more common among them. It seemed to me that many of us were for the most part tinkering with the nation form, and that the only difference between policy and humanistic research was perspectival. One carried out normative research at the ground level; the other did so while attending to the macrotheoretical, historical, and philosophical. I am not even sure at this moment that we would have the contemporary academy without the normative impulses that glue together whole disciplines (e.g., theories of publicity or ideology or order or dialogue or community) and that serve as a common language across the social sciences and the humanities. What is clear to me, though, is that it is in our interest to at least once in a while ask, "Where does our intellectual habit of thinking through normative categories come from?"

This book has shown publicness through time as a complex technology that we use to craft populations. From Classical Athens and Rome, jumping ahead to the absolutist state, the bourgeois public sphere, and today, publicity has been at times a tool of outright exclusion (Amaya 2013), but it has also been a tool for modulating the core of our citizenship experiences and the best of our civic values. Yet insofar as publicity theory assumes the absence of violence, it has recognized only structures that are missing in most places in the world, which lack the foundational media, political, and legal infrastructures to constitute the conditions of safe debate that publicity presupposes.

For most people around the world, publicity is not a normative theory; it is a unicorn, a magical political entity that one may as well reserve for children's books and fairy tales. While it is noble to dream the impossible, we are not better off dreaming what is totally unassailable. The academy has a duty to the general populace not to live by utopianisms, but to build a bridge toward them. The work of demystification is thus a work of displacement and movement that attempts to relocate the object of our desires to a more reachable distance. Although demystification alone cannot assure that the distance can be bridged, the work of demystification is necessary if we ever hope to get closer to our utopian object.

Many of us Western scholars do not slow down and ponder these issues because we, well, cheat. We often start from the assumption that, because some people in a few societies at one point in their history used and embraced deliberation, debate, and publicness, the principle is available to people at other locations and other moments in history. In a sense, this is due to scholars like Habermas, who found fault in publicness not because the principles and the realities of its deliberation were contingent and its successes were insular (in a few societies in the world and for some time only) but because they interpreted the contingency of publicness in terms related to the advance of capitalism, transformations due to media technologies, and the changing nature of Western political cultures. That is what Habermas's *The Structural Transformation of the Public Sphere* ultimately argues, and what those trying to recuperate these theories from their contingent insularity also believe.

The interpretation linking the success of publicness to the economy, media technologies, and politics has profound consequences. Let me reflect briefly on these consequences by referring to the work of Craig Calhoun, one of the most respected scholars on the subject. In his introduction to the quite famous *Habermas and the Public Sphere* collection, Calhoun notes that publicness is only one possible way of coordinating human life and warns that power and the economy are two other nondiscursive ways of organizing life (1992). There is no guarantee, he astutely warns us, that discourse will be the primary source of coordination. I like this simple use of metaphors because it succinctly illustrates the theory of publicity, the adversaries of publicity in any society, and the difficulties of bringing the promise of discursive deliberation to most places. Calhoun has no problem showing that nondiscursive ways of organizing life—power and the economy—tend to be the primary principles organizing life just about everywhere. Like me, he is in the business of demystifying, yet his work on demystification is based on the metaphor of these three different ways of organizing life competing constantly against each other. As he shows us, discourse often loses.

But there is a potential logical fallacy at the heart of Calhoun's illustration. Calhoun does not recognize the disturbing possibility that discourse, in the way that he and Habermas imagine discourse to be able to coordinate life in a society, may be a by-product of power, coercion, and economic exploitation. This means that the metaphor Calhoun uses may be substantively fraught. This book has shown that this is more than a possibility. It shows enough clues to make this a likely theory, one that needs to be further analyzed, and one that can explain publicness's contingent insularity. If my clues hold, they would mean that publicness is not deserving of our love and admiration. Perhaps we should dispose of it and put in the box of broken tools created by the West, which already contains social technologies such as "civilization" and "development."

PUBLICITY'S CONTINGENT INSULARITY

Before pronouncing that publicness is a broken tool, let me first show how the chapters in this book sketch a theory of publicity's contingent insularity. This theory argues that publicness is a by-product of coercion and exploitation; it is a theoretical tool and framework that has to be retheorized if it is to be useful to anyone outside the tiny confines of its ideal milieu. The theory I am presenting here is not fully formed, but it can be glimpsed through a process of suturing together the different historiographic and conceptual arguments found in the previous chapters. In particular, I am interested in repositioning the arguments in chapter 3 not simply as arguments about state failure and state success, but also as arguments about publicness. This process of reorienting my own arguments in chapter 3 provides the historiographic basis for understanding the normative impulses underlying publicity theory as dependent on conditions of possibility that include coercion and exploitation.

Although this book began as a project to make sense of current cultural events in Mexico and the United States, the arguments I present here depended on historicizing different elements and ideas central to publicity. Most arguments originated in, or at least connected with, early modernity and even antiquity. My engagement with antiquity and early modernity is not only an implicit argument about the need to historicize the present. That should be obvious. My engagement with the past is also tactical and epistemological. It is meant to show publicness as a normative value with a beginning, or, perhaps better, two beginnings: one in early Athens, the second in European and American (i.e., US and Mexican) early modernities. It is also meant to show publicness's beginnings as two moments in which the normative principles of talk, debate, and peaceful communication depended on conditions of safety and trust, the outcome of efficient modalities of coercion and exploitation. In these arguments that were meant to foster a retheorization of publicness, publicity is complexly linked to violence.

In classical antiquity, publicness, or at least publicness's early precursor, is found in the Athenian context, a place and a time in which the principle of talk among citizens constituted a political culture of ideas, debate, and communication. This is the world that inspires Arendt's work on the subject, which has the virtue of making publicity a remedy for violence and thus of connecting them in alterity: "To be political, to live in a *polis*, meant that everything was decided through words and persuasion and not through force and violence" (1958: 26). In a few words, Arendt sketches a theory of politics, one in tension not with monarchies and feuds but with violence and outsiders. This polis imagines itself through the eradication of violence, as Hobbes would have it, even if the eradication has meant simply its rather imperfect monopoly. These words are also a glimpse into a theory of citizenship constructed in alterity to a prepolitical other, those outside the walls and outside the polis. Also implied is a theory of intersubjectivity based on space, mediation, and materiality (the agora and the walls), which constitute the psychical bases of peaceful debate. Those who exist by and for the rules of nonviolent argumentation, the male citizens of Athens, are protected by the wall from those outside who, Arendt proposes, may settle disputes with violence. Women and metics—foreign residents without citizenship rights—may have existed within the walls, but they did not have political rights and hence could not participate in the assembly, the space of legislation. As I noted in chapter 6, Athens was bounded, a city-state dependent on the walls, the soldiers, and the exclusionary power of citizenship rules (Benhabib 1996: 75).

While Arendt's work is widely respected in contemporary academic circles, her arguments on the connections of publicity to violence are far from hegemonic. In fact, they are relatively marginalized. Those interested in exploring contemporary public spheres often ignore her work or treat it as a precursor to other, more pertinent arguments, particularly those by Habermas, who rejects Arendt's insights. In his 1962 classic, *The Structural Transformation of the Public Sphere*, Habermas repeatedly notes that Greek publicity, the site of inquiry in Arendt's work, and modern liberal publicity are dramatically different. He argues that, in the Athenian context, the connection between publicity and the state was robust and the participation of citizens in the agora was reliant on oppression, not equality.

I agree. In this context, Habermas argues, civil society did not properly exist. The household, ruled by male citizens, and the agora were in relative harmony. By contrast, the bourgeois public sphere of the seventeenth and eighteenth centuries was the space for the regulation of a transforming civil society independent from the state, a space constituted around criticism. Habermas's work implies that Arendt's writing does not address the new formation of the public sphere after European feudalism and thus should not be the basis for modern theories of publicity. The question then becomes whether Habermas's work is any better.

In Habermasian historiography, the conditions of possibility for publicness in early modernity include the rise of the bourgeoisie and the changing economic relations in cities, which allowed for new classes of people to disturb the mostly vertical process of ruling in European monarchies, even those with parliamentary systems. The bourgeoisie claimed independence from above, the state, the monarch, to engage in a debate over the general rules of governing relations in the basically privatized but publicly relevant sphere of commodity exchange and social labor (1989: 27). This marked a different structure of power. Since the thirteenth century, monarchs had used the landed aristocracy as a mediating force between the sovereign and the people. This was possible because the economy was chiefly an economy of basic goods, agriculture, cattle, and mineral extraction. This economy was organized around land, and whoever controlled land controlled the economy. A lord did that; workers were under his tutelage. Working the land or the products of the land was based not on the principle of free labor, as Marx would later note in regard to capitalism, but on the principle of rent. A worker rented a lord's land to work it, and what she or he produced was taxed by the lord, the legal owner of the land. This is why Marx used the term *alienation* from the means for production to describe the relationship between peasant and the land. Here alienation means separation; the worker did not own the land and thus could not control his or her economic future. The aristocracy was wealthy because of the taxes they charged, and the lord had a sort of political power because he was also given the right, for centuries, to demand from his workers, his peasants, military service. So, in his worker, the lord also had an army, which gave him the right to rule over the life of the worker and power in their relationships to the monarch. The lords were useful and necessary to the monarch because the aristocracy provided the monarch with taxation revenue and with the means to defend the territory.

The feudal world changed for many reasons, some intrinsic to this world, such as the slow but steady growth of agricultural productivity due to technological innovation and the multiplication of enclosures (see chapter 3) which translated into rural unemployment and sizable and steady migrations to cities and ports. In the year 1500 London had roughly 50,000 people. It had quadrupled in size by 1600, reaching 200,000. Around 1675, when John Locke was composing *The Two Treatises on Civil Government*, London had reached half a million inhabitants.

So it was in the sweltering capital city of an empire being transformed by mercantilism, colonialism, and migration that Locke famously argued for a state constituted through the will of the people, and a state invested in the protection of the human rights of life, liberty, and property (2nd Tr., §6). While life and liberty may be assumed to operate at a different ontological register than property, in Locke we find property as the genesis of other rights, including liberty: "Every Man has a Property in his Person. This nobody has any Right to but himself. The Labour of his Body, and the Work of his Hands, we may say, are properly his" (2nd Tr., §5, 26). In this theory of property, common property becomes private property when individuals use their labor to transform it, and governments are established simply to protect private property. Someone like Jean-Jacques Rousseau may have rejected the property regime, but on this point his ideas became marginal. The property regime won (see chapter 3). This regime, Carol Rose (1994) argues, is at the root of modern narratives of justice and self-ownership and has its origin in these Lockean arguments, which later influenced the revolutionary intellectuals of the eighteenth century. James Madison's powerful belief that "government is instituted to protect property of every sort" is just a modest extension of Locke's arguments, as is his argument that every right is rooted on the value of property and that everything that is of value hints to the pervasiveness of property in human life. Expansive rights here are coterminous with expansive ideas of property. This is the Western liberal vision of the modern world.

This vision is not only about law and economics. It is also about the constitution of a Western liberal subject, one structured around the rules of behavior required for coexistence in the complex political milieus that would serve as its backdrop. To behave with propriety, Rose would note, was expected "to keep the good order in the commonwealth or body politic" (1994: 58). Habermas repeatedly notes how courtly polite behavior served as the basis for the bourgeois public sphere, and he acknowledges that courtly modes of intersubjectivity paved the way to "sociable discussions that quickly developed into public criticism" (1989: 30). That these were also peaceful debates and forms of interaction is only implied in Habermas, but social debates and disagreements needed the expectation of safety that "proper" behavior guaranteed. The history of the property regime thus is also the history of "civility" and "politeness" in public. All of these terms point toward a web of norms for those wanting to participate in the public sphere. Today, though publicness can be defined in different ways, the definitions share the expectation of civility, which is at the heart and at the root of publicity.

The condition of possibility for publicness in early modernity, what permitted the rise of the bourgeoisie, was a changing economic landscape transformed by mercantilism and colonialism. The geometry of equality, the horizontal imaginary that allowed an increasing number of individuals to imagine themselves as somehow coequal to others, was available to a class of urbanites with increasing educational and economic means. Unsurprisingly, criticisms of the Habermasian model often refer to the exclusionary nature of the bourgeois public sphere—the fact that women and the poor, for instance, could not participate. Habermas's criticism of Arendt and of the model of Athenian publicness is based not on exclusion but on the fact that publicness in Athens was part of the state and hence did not exist independent of it. But this procedural criticism of Athens, which Habermas uses to signal a sort of modern exceptionalism that separates the Enlightenment from antiquity, fails to see that from the perspective of the slave, women, and the noncitizen, the differences between Athens and modernity are minimal and that the citizen in both periods props himself high atop the shoulders of those he exploits. With this in mind, Habermas's criticism of Arendt is not substantive. It is the simple recognition that the size and complexity of modern nations could not sustain the system of Athenian direct democracy and that the constitution of modern civil society pertains to the complex nature of today's nation-states and the relative expansion of citizenship rights. But as I have argued before, citizenship is still dependent on exclusionary methods of participation and economic systems of exploitation (Amaya 2013). The scale of modern nations has necessitated a different structure of ruling, and this new structure includes a civil society that uses and controls the media systems central to contemporary processes of consensus.

From the perspective of the disenfranchised, the power of the citizen is always a power rooted in an excess of wealth, of cultural capital, of social capital, of political influence, and this excess is possible only because of exploitation. The feminist critique of Habermas starts from the unambiguous exclusion of women from the Athenian and bourgeois public spheres. There were also other visible or audible markers of identity that precluded participation in these spaces, including race, ethnicity, and nationality. To these clear markers of exclusion, one must add the ambiguous but equally effective thresholds of wealth and education that had to be met by those who wanted to enter the cafes and the salons where publicity was enacted, the places where equality was part of the menu and where criticism of art or the state was normal and normalized. These thresholds could not exist without the excesses of wealth and political power due to patriarchy, early industrialization, and mercantilism.

This book points toward a new critique of publicness, one from the perspective of coloniality. I recognize and use the substantive critiques of publicness due to exclusionary systems that existed from the perspective of the city, the street, and the household, those critiques from the standpoint of gender inequality, racial inequality, and class inequality, but I believe it is necessary to expand our engagement with publicity by further exploring the conditions that produced publicness's contingent insularity.

A critique of publicness rooted in coloniality is partly scalar in nature. This critique starts with the recognition that the bourgeois public sphere, and indeed all models of publicness, are based on an ideal of politics and communication that has been shown to exist mostly in conditions of an excess of power. I argued in chapter 3 that the property regime that furnished the ideology of order at the heart of normative ideas of politics and the state was funded by the processes of colonial extraction of early modernity.

(Others, I hope, may argue that more contemporary forms of publicness were also furnished by the wealth generated through neocolonialism.) In that chapter I showed that the political economy of order, which includes the concretion of spaces of orderly deliberation for the constitution of consensus, was sustained by the growth of the Atlantic trade due to colonialism (Acemoglu, Johnson, and Robinson 2005). The merchant groups that were strengthened by this trade are the groups that constrained the power of monarchies and helped construct institutions that would protect property rights. The Western forms of government that followed monarchic arrangements, based on liberal and republican values, strengthened the institutions of order and expanded the property regime.

In the field of media studies, my field, much has been made of the disrupting force of the printing press from the fifteenth century onward, and the corresponding role this new media technology played in the unsettling of hegemonic Catholicism and absolutism, and the rise of the modern nation-state. The press was the necessary precondition for newspapers, journalism, mass popular culture, popular literature, and public opinion, and its influence on society corresponded to its relative cost efficiency. The cheaper it became to print, the greater the social and political effects of the press. These effects were not always positive, but they were always substantive.

Gutenberg invented the printing press in 1440; Columbus "discovered" the Americas in 1492. Perhaps because of this sequence of events, media studies and other disciplines traditionally tell the story of European pluralism in the sixteenth century as a history of technology and/or a history of the diffusion of ideas. Mexico's own type of modernity challenges this view, as the history of its pluralism cannot be told without acknowledging the role the Inquisition played in the New Spain. Other national histories would likely offer similar challenges. It is possible to account for these challenges by acknowledging that modernity was not one process but many, as Shmuel Eisenstadt (2002) and others have noted. But this book sketches a new site for future research and a different type of answer, one that explains the normative at the heart of publicity theory as rooted in and dependent on the formation of institutions that were imaginable and feasible thanks to colonialism. The hypothesis can be summarized as follows: publicity's contingent insularity is not an accident of history. It is precisely due to its history.

It is tempting to imagine the arguments in this book as approaching sufficiency, particularly after I represent them in this conclusion. That is not the case. To say that publicity's contingent insularity results from its history is not the same as to show that colonialism provides the best explanatory framework for the reactivation of publicity as a normative construct starting in the seventeenth century. Others may do this work, and depending on their success or failure, we shall welcome publicity back among the normative tools that can help us craft a better future, or we shall discard it in the recycling bin of history. Discarding publicity's normative ideal would not mean discarding the value of dialogue or communication to democracy. It would simply recognize that conditions for communication are rarely ideal and that presuming ideality can endanger those citizens whose understanding of civics is indebted to the principles of publicness. I am referring here to citizens like all the journalists who have been killed in Mexico because of their craft, citizens like Lucy, El Administrador, and all of those who have needed to use anonymity to participate in the public sphere. Most of the time, in most places around the world, violence is more than a specter haunting those wishing to speak to power. Violence is a structural force of the talking field, and we must recognize it as such.

Notes

INTRODUCTION

1 Throughout the book I use the word *we* to designate my different communities. Hence, these indexical shifts correspond to the intersectionality of my authorial identity. Sometimes *we* refers to the academy; other times it refers to Mexicans; other times it refers to US Americans; and at times it refers to Mexican Americans and Latinas/os.

2 Josh Kun (2005b) points out the tension inherent in the musical personas of Los Tigres del Norte and the band members' actual civic experiences, documented in their song "Mis dos patrias" ("My Two Nations") and throughout their lives as immigrants.

3 Kant's original formulation of publicness was articulated in *To Perpetual Peace: A Philosophical Sketch* (1795). For an argument about Kant's particular notions of publicness, see Luban 1996.

4 Publicity is the central cog of Kant's political philosophy and of the Enlightenment (*Aufklärung*), a political notion that proposes that only the united will of the people can legitimate authority. See, for instance, Marey 2017.

5 *Quality television* is a term used to refer to the postcable surge of television networks like HBO seeking a niche market through the use of complex narratives and branding that distinguishes them from mainstream broadcast fare (C. Anderson 2008; Jaramillo 2005).

6 I do not take for granted that all publicity theorists would accept mediated discourse as part of the public sphere. Famously, Habermas (1989) has stated that the demise of the public sphere is related to the increasing salience of mass media. However, for the purposes of this book, I side with those who believe that meaningful political consensus in contemporary societies depends, practically always, on media, media access, and media participation.

7 This dramaturgical approach is part of most theories of the public sphere even if some, like Habermas, have failed to note the dramaturgical character of their proposals.

8 *Displacement* and *cultures of displacement* are terms today associated with "displaced" populations such as exiles and refugees. Violence is often part of the past of these populations and even their present, but the relationship between violence and displacement is epiphenomenal, not discursive. One appears when the other one exists. Displacement may in some cases be treated as an epiphenomenon of violence. The way I use the term here instead makes displacement the root of the metaphoric tree of violence.

9 Others have noted the "violence of non-places," the manner in which the spaces in between transit become symbolically and really connected to violence (Roberts 2014: 17). Nonplaces are the locus of the displaced, the traveler, the refugee, the immigrant. Although for Les Roberts (2014), for instance, nonplaces are specific zones of transit, stasis, and lack of agency, from the perspective of immigrants, refugees, and exiles, all new places are nonplaces, characterized by violence, insecurity, and fear.

10 In the 1980s, in the midst of two forms of drug crises, one crisis of consumption and crime in the United States and another crisis of trafficking and violence in South America, the governments of the United States, Colombia, Bolivia, and Peru attempted to collaborate in reducing the amount of coca leaf available to the drug cartels and implemented a crop substitution program aimed at convincing coca farmers to stop growing the raw material for cocaine. It did not work, for in a hurry to produce solutions, the US government, the program's instigator, failed to make time to develop and implement the research needed for the program to have a chance. Though in this case these governments seemed to be tackling transnational economic issues, they did so with significant limitations. Whatever poverty farmers in Bolivia, Peru, and Colombia have to endure, it is poverty caused by the lasting cultural and economic legacy of global capitalism and asymmetrical economic relations between center and periphery. Even back in the 1980s, USAID had already warned the US government that crop substitution would not work, for no other crop could take coca's place in the global agricultural trade system. No one listened (Marcy 2010: 18–20).

11 Scrutinizing the drug trade through politics, not economics, is misguided. In politicizing drug violence we confuse the dramatic social effects of trade with political effects and produce solutions based on politics, not economics. Immanuel Wallerstein, commenting on the confusion between political and economic analysis, writes: "The distinctive feature of a capitalist world-economy is that economic decisions are oriented primarily to the arena of the world-economy, while political decisions are oriented primarily to the smaller structures that have legal control, the states . . . within the world-economy" (1974: 67). Can we address the global trade of drugs by regulating politics alone? No.

12 Jorge A. Sánchez Godoy notes that narcoculture is not simply about drug mafias; rather, it is about the mixing of licit and illicit sectors, the multiple

actors that "reconstitute, reproduce, and legitimate, every day, this construction of the imaginary that has roots eminently rural" (2009: 99, my translation). However, as Tony Cella (2014) notes, as the business of drug production and distribution becomes a global phenomenon, these rural elements lose ground and some relevance.

13 As Reinhart Koselleck (1988) would note, my project, like his own, uses some of the Enlightenment tools it means to criticize, including the pervading sense of crises that gave rise to the hegemonic standing of the philosophy of history.

14 For a detailed account of the rise of societal thinking, see Koselleck 1988 and Strydom 2000.

CHAPTER 1. PRELUDE TO TWO WARS

1 President Zedillo also carried out the arrest of Raúl Salinas de Gortari, the brother of Carlos Salinas de Gortari, the man that Zedillo succeeded and a central member of the PRI. Although the official charge against Salinas was homicide, his alleged involvement with DCOs is quite famous.

2 *El Universal* has another advantage. It is based in Mexico City, a city that has seen little drug-related violence. This data thus gives us a glimpse into how the theme of organized crime violence circulated in nonviolent areas, which, at 70 percent, is the majority of the Mexican territory.

3 *El Universal* does not tell the whole truth. The paper targets the urban (upper) middle classes, which are its powerful main readership. In areas directly affected by the violence, and from rural perspectives, things are more complex. For instance, as Pavel Shlossberg (2015) notes, those living in rural areas affected by drug violence in Michoacán would often draw negative and critical comparisons between what they observed as their local reality and what was reported in the press.

4 I use the term *narcotráfico* because it is the term most often used to refer to the violence and the problems generated by DCOs. I tested my searches by randomly reading one hundred entries from 2000 to 2014 and found that every time the term was mentioned, the news item did indeed refer to DCOs. I did the same with other terms including *drogas*, *narcos*, and *cartel*. These terms were also good indicators but had their weaknesses. For instance, using *drogas* retrieved many items related to health. Using *narcos* was too selective, as the term was not used every time the issue of DCOs was discussed. The same happened with the term *cartel*.

5 Embassy Mexico, "Ambassador's Meeting with Presumed President Elect Calderon," WikiLeaks Cable: 06MEXICO4310, dated August 4, 2006, http://wikileaks.org/cable/2006/08/06MEXICO4310.html.

6 Embassy Mexico, "Mexico's Government, Media Process Ambassador's Message on Violence," WikiLeaks Cable: 06MEXICO5312, dated September 19, 2006, http://wikileaks.org/cable/2006/08/06MEXICO5312.html.

7 Embassy Mexico, "Calderon's Security Cabinet," WikiLeaks Cable: 06MEX-ICO6871, dated December 11, 2006, http://wikileaks.org/cable/2006/08/06MEXICO6871.html; Embassy Mexico, "Calderon Debuts with a Deft Hand," WikiLeaks Cable: 06MEXICO7033, dated December 21, 2006, http://wikileaks.org/cable/2006/08/06MEXICO7033.html.
8 Embassy Mexico, "Calderon Debuts with a Deft Hand."
9 Embassy Mexico, "Calderon Debuts with a Deft Hand."

CHAPTER 2. ALMOST FAILING

1 The evidence is not exhaustive, as I used LexisNexis Academic to digitally retrieve these reports; however, given the importance of these three newspapers, and the fact that international political news is typically part of this digital database, it is very likely that these results are indicative of the manner in which the mainstream print and digital press has used the term *failed state* in relation to Mexico.

2 In *The Archaeology of Knowledge* (1972), Foucault proposes that one can effectively analyze discourse by analyzing how objects of inquiry are constructed, by looking at what links all different statements together, by referring to how specific concepts are used in rhetorical schemata, and by investigating how specific discourses are distributed through history. Although Foucault's is not the only way of performing the analysis of discourse, it is particularly apt for the discourse here and will serve as a methodological guide in this section.

3 The relevance of Hobbes to contemporary political thinking is undisputed, yet his relevance is partly the result of the way Hobbes has been read and studied. That is, his relevance is not in orthogonal relation to the depth or innovation of his thought. Like any other scholar, he reappropriated old ideas; he repurposed political ideas of the time; and in the process he made them his own. As important, others after Hobbes used his ideas to construct political theories. Many of the arguments used in this chapter, for instance, were reanimated in contemporary political philosophy with the publication of C. B. Macpherson's *The Political Theory of Possessive Individualism: Hobbes to Locke* in 1962. For decades this book was highly influential, making McPherson's ideas relevant, but also pointing others toward Hobbes and Locke for inspiration.

4 Some of Hobbes's basic ideas are found in the allegory *Argenis* (1621) by John Barclay, a narrative that argues that the monarch should assume responsibility for bringing peace, and in exchange its subject would recognize the monarch's sovereign standing (Koselleck 1988: 17–19).

5 Although the elimination of violence to justify ruling had been a constant in natural law political theory since Aristotle, Hobbes, continuing a British legal tradition connecting back to Henry de Bracton, envisioned that the best way to reduce violence was through contracts, as a form of social glue. Other theories of natural law prior to Hobbes's, such as Thomas Aquinas's, had strong religious imprints and typically theorized reducing violence based on a legal system

legitimized by God's words, making religious documents (the Bible or the Qur'an, for instance) the true arbiters of laws and sovereigns. Though also using God as his source of legitimacy, Bracton believed differently and, anticipating state secularism, wrote in the thirteenth century: "The king must not be under man, but under God and under the law, because law makes the king" (Bracton quoted in Bobbio 1993: 55). The radical thought of placing the law above the sovereign signaled a modern style of juridical thinking. Like Bracton, Hobbes placed the law at the center of his argument, but he disagreed with Bracton on the issue of the sovereign and proposed instead that nothing should supersede the sovereign, not even the law.

6 James Tully (1993: 28–29) reminds us also of the influence of Hugo Grotius, who, in 1625, introduced these arguments about the state and violence.

7 As John H. Jackson (2003: 786) notes, the Treaty of Westphalia (1648)—a set of recipes to reallocate land claims in the embroidery of feuds that was Europe—took its contemporary meaning over time. The concept of sovereignty is currently challenged in many significant ways, but this discussion is beyond the scope of this chapter. For a quick sense of the nature of these criticisms, I recommend Jackson's succinct review of critical views of the concept and Robert Jackson's 2007 book, *Sovereignty*. The notion of weak states or failed states exists as a critical response to the concept of sovereignty, for a weak state recognizes the need for the international community, or sometimes a superpower, to intervene.

8 Jurisdiction, which has many meanings and uses in legal cultures, is largely dependent on territory. It refers to the power to exercise authority over a geographical location. It is, at its most fundamental, ensconced in Westphalian international law as the fundamental principle guaranteeing sovereignty. Most nation-states, including Mexico and the United States, are further divided in terms of geography; from counties (the United States) or municipalities (Mexico) all the way to federal territories, jurisdiction is often connected to space. There are exceptions including those that divide populations by age (minors, for instance, may have a different court system) or those that divide authority by type of juridical process (tax violations as opposed to traffic violations) (see the "Jurisdiction" entry in the Legal Information Institute, www.law.cornell.edu/wex/jurisdiction).

9 For a more detailed look at the economic outcome of enclosures, see Inikori 2002: 49–52.

10 There is nothing transparent about whether land can be owned. For a critical examination from an ontological perspective, see Mei 2011.

11 Another popular legal argument was forwarded by Francisco de Vitoria, the most influential Spanish jurist of the time, the founder of the School of Salamanca and of international law. Vitoria used an argument by the Scottish philosopher John Major from 1510 that suggested that the natives were the "natural slaves" that Aristotle discussed in his *Politics* and, as slaves, could not have rights of ownership (Pagden 1990).

12 Wallerstein (1974: 70–76) also notes the way in which colonialism participated in the increase in economic activity of Western Europe, helping stabilize and eventually lower prices across Europe, thus connecting the world system at the level of commodity trade, commodity ownership, and labor cost.

CHAPTER 3. CENSORING NARCOCULTURE

1 This is particularly true in dramaturgic theories of publicity like Arendt's (1958), which rely on metaphors of space such as the "agora" or, as in Habermas (1989), the public sphere. It is worth noting that Arendt's publicity is different than Habermas's. Arendt is concerned with antiquity and with the types of interaction that characterized the political sphere. Habermas, as he reminds us, is concerned with interactions outside the political sphere, in the realm of the social, in the salon rather than the agora. Arguably his most important contribution is the identification of the rise of social criticism and the liberal value of making politics accountable to society. This significant difference notwithstanding, Arendt and Habermas construct theories of publicity that rely on notions of space.

2 In February 2013, Mexico's Supreme Court Justice declared Governor López Valdez's tactic of taking away liquor licenses illegal. In the ruling, which avoided using the language of free speech and/or censorship, Mexico's highest court found that the governor's office did not have the right to take away liquor licenses for reasons other than public health and that the governor had not cited health-related issues as the primary reason for this new policy (Sánchez Barbosa 2013).

3 Vincent Mosco (2009: 3) defines political economy as "*the study of control and survival in social life*" (italics original), and this definition helps us see the banning of narcocorridos, which are cultural and economic forms, as a classic political economy problem. Censorship is a clash between the state's political efforts to control and individuals' efforts to communicate and profit while being controlled.

4 All translations are mine.

5 Drug and criminal organizations do the most to censure Mexican journalism and social media. These topics are covered in chapter 6 and the conclusion.

6 It is important to note that critics of these ideas, such as Fernando Escalante Gonzalbo (1992), argue that applying these political theories to the Mexican context presupposes the existence of citizens. The relevant actors, Escalante argues, were the corporations, the army, the Church, and Indian communities. However, others, like Charles Hale (1968), observe a strong liberal and republican political movement within, for instance, constitutionalist processes.

7 For a compelling historiography of Mexico's political life, including republicanism, see Van Young (2012).

8 This marks a departure from Greek principles of politics. In her discussion of the Greek understanding of politics, Arendt (1958) reminds us that in this context

politics were precisely antithetical to economics and that the very notion of "political economy" would have been oxymoronic. That said, even in Greek life the fixity provided by private ownership of land constituted part of the citizenship franchise: "[Without] owning a house a man could not participate in the affairs of the world because he had no location in it which was properly his own" (Arendt 1958: 29–30).

9 In Roman times, the connection between symbolic order (morality) and economics grew thicker. Salazar goes so far as to state that "from that point, 'censorship' strides the republic. Censor[ship] is, in other words, not about private morality, but about money and how money relates, in symbolical or material terms, to power" (2004: 8). On a relevant note, in the tasks assigned to the censor, the figure on which Roman republican values intersected, private wealth and private morality become public measures of worth that determine an individual's ethical and civic value. Echoing my argument in the last chapter, here are, connected again, the political economy of order and a property regime, echoes of which are found in the republicanism of the Enlightenment, which unapologetically used landownership as a marker of political worth. Similar processes connecting republican order to landownership are part of Mexico's history, as Shelton (2010) and Schaefer (2014), among others, have argued.

10 Interview with Deputy Jorge Zermeño Infante, published by the Cámara de Diputados on March 7, 2007, pp. 4–5.

11 Comments by Deputy Irineo Mendoza Mendoza, Gaceta Parlamentaria of the Cámara de Diputados, March 6, 2008, pp. 68–69.

12 See Diario de los Debates (2001) of the Cámara de Diputados, April 24.

13 Comments by Deputy Irineo Mendoza Mendoza, Gaceta Parlamentaria of the Cámara de Diputados, March 6, 2008, p. 68.

14 Comments by Deputy Boone Salmón (PRI), Diario de los Debates, 2011, p. 991.

15 Comments by Deputy Boone Salmón (PRI), Diario de los Debates, LXIII Legislatura III(57), April 7, 2001, p. 8.

16 Comments by Deputy Arce Paniagua, Diario de los Debates, LXI Legislatura 1(5), January 20, 2010, p. 102.

17 Comments by Deputy Irineo Mendoza Mendoza, Gaceta Parlamentaria 2460(I), March 6, 2008, p. 68.

18 This is not so different from US law of the period—up through World War I, it was common to censor speech that had a "bad tendency" to harm morals or order.

19 My translation.

20 Summary of legislators' comments in front of the Federal Legislative Assembly. They can be found in the Diario de los Debates 2 (36), December 7, 2001, p. 9.

21 Comments of Arce Paniagua, Diario de los Debates, LXI Legislatura 1(5), January 20, 2010, p. 103.

22 Comments of Arce Paniagua, Diario de los Debates, LXI Legislatura 1(5), January 20, 2010, p. 104.

1　According to Roque Planas (2016), at the time of this writing the actual successor to El Chapo seems to be Ismael "El Mayo" Zambada García.

2　EMA includes the following musical groups or artists: Alfredo Rios, "El Komander"; Los Bukanas de Culiacán; El R. M.; Los Buchones de Culiacán; La Edición de Culiacán; Los Dos Primos; Los Mayitos de Sinaloa; El Junior de Culiacán; Los Favoritos de Sinaloa; La Fuerza de Tijuana; Grupo Ondeando, and Saul Loya, "El Mazzivo." EMA's members have independent recording careers, but they also record numbered compilations issued as *El Movimiento Alterado Vol. 1* and so on. So, they have a recording identity that is both individual and communal.

3　Víctor Cordero was inducted into the Fonoteca Nacional de México in 2014. See his biographical note on the Fonoteca's website: www.fonotecanacional.gob .mx/index.php/noticias/505-ingresara-a-la-fonoteca-nacional-acervo-sonoro-de -victor-cordero-compositor-posrevolucionario (accessed June 25, 2017).

4　The oldest and perhaps most central narrative trope in the narcocorridos is trafficking, not drugs. According to Juan Carlos Ramírez-Pimienta (2011), the oldest precedent to narcocorridos is a song about Mariano Reséndez, a wealthy trafficker of textiles who moved Mexican clothes to the United States in the last decade of the nineteenth century. Paredes (1976) and others also note that memorializing traffickers continued during Prohibition with several famous corridos about tequila bootleggers in Texas, including "El Contrabando del Paso," "El Corrido de los Bootleggers," "El Contrabando de San Antonio," and others (101–4). These *corridos tequileros* showed several characteristics that would be part of the narcocorridos today: they are warnings about engaging in trafficking; they justify trafficking due to poverty; and they preach the value and reality of impunity.

5　Video cameras are now so common that you can find some videos of these emotional performances during funerals on YouTube.

6　As of 2015, mun2 is called NBC UNIVERSO. See NBCUniversal 2015.

7　"Los Tigres del Norte—El Niño y la Boda," YouTube, posted July 5, 2007, www .youtube.com/watch?v=9z77wdm3I1M.

8　I collected this data on January 12, 2017, using YouTube, Vevo, and Vimeo.

9　This is not the case everywhere or for every target group. In the United States, undocumented immigrants have shown a reluctance to use the web to buy music, and this has hindered distribution to that group (Cobo 2007).

CHAPTER 5. BLOODY BLOGS

1　The anagram RSF comes from the French (Reporters Sans Frontières).

2　See Artículo 19's website, https://articulo19.org/.

3　Based on interview by the author in July 2012, in Mexico City, Mexico.

4　See the 2016 report by the National Commission of Minimum Wage: Secretaría de Gobernación, December 19, www.dof.gob.mx/nota_detalle.php?codigo =5466000&fecha=19/12/2016.

5 Facebook restrictions on violent photos and videos limit the ability of *VxT*'s Facebook page to share violent content.

6 As I explain below, several websites have carried the mantle of *El Blog del Narco* since 2008, and several domains redirect to the same website in the current instantiation of EBDN. For simplicity's sake, I will refer to these domains and blogs using the singular descriptor of *El Blog del Narco* or EBDN.

7 See Yoani Sánchez, *Generación Y*, accessed October 12, 2015, http://generacionyen.wordpress.com/.

8 *El Blog del Narco* had a Facebook page, too, but its use was quite limited, due in part, as Edith Beltran argues, to the inability to remain anonymous on Facebook. This page operated for only six months and was taken down in March 2011 (Beltrán 2015: 84).

9 The letter was published by the magazine *Proceso*. See *Proceso* 2013a.

10 She published this in *El Blog de Lucy*, the blog started while she was on the run. See chapter 6 for a more detailed description and analysis of this specific blog.

CHAPTER 6. TRUST

1 *El Blog del Narco* has been arguably as famous as *Valor por Tamaulipas* (*VxT*), another anonymous blog with similar production techniques. Unlike EBDN, *VxT* has become famous through a notoriously popular Facebook page, which has more than 250,000 followers.

2 Rory Carroll, writing for the *Guardian* on April 3, 2013, was able to corroborate that the person he interviewed was indeed in control of EBDN, but some of the rest of the information in this and other interviews have not been corroborated due to Lucy's anonymity.

3 In Spanish, we still prefer the word *cortés*, or "courteous," a word that reminds us that this aspect of trust developed first in modernity in the courts of the aristocracy.

4 Data for this paragraph come from the following: *El Universal* published an interview with Jacobo Zabludovsky by José Luis Ruíz-Barba on the anniversary of the earthquake in 2010. In 1995, on the tenth anniversary of the earthquake, Televisa also transmitted a special that included Zabludovsky's famous narration in abbreviated form. I was also in Mexico City that terrible day and remember that broadcast as if it were yesterday.

References

Acemoglu, Daron, Simon Johnson, and James Robinson. 2005. "The Rise of Europe: Atlantic Trade, Institutional Change, and Economic Growth." *American Economic Review* 95 (3): 546–79.

Águila, Justino. 2012. "Questions with Angel del Villar." *Billboard*, January 7–21, 8.

Aguilar Camín, Héctor. 2012. "On Mexican Violence." In *Rethinking the "War on Drugs" through the US-Mexico Prism*, edited by E. Zedillo and H. Wheeler, 47–56. New Haven, CT: Yale Center for the Study of Globalization.

Alatorre, Felipe, et al. 2009. *Diagnóstico sobre la realidad social, económica y cultural de los entornos locales para el diseño de intervenciones en materia de prevención y erradicación de la violencia en la región centro: El caso de la zona metropolitana de Guadalajara, Jalisco.* Edited by Dra. Guadalupe Rodríguez Gómez. Mexico City: CIESAS-Occidente.

Alexander, Gregory S. 1997. *Commodity and Propriety: Competing Visions of Property in American Legal Thought, 1776–1970.* Chicago: University of Chicago Press.

Amaya, Hector. 2013. *Citizenship Excess: Latinas/os, Media, and the Nation.* New York: New York University Press.

Anderson, Benedict. 1991. *Imagined Communities: Reflections on the Origin and Spread of Nationalism.* New York: Verso.

Anderson, Christopher. 2008. "Overview: Producing an Aristocracy of Culture in American Television." In *The Essential HBO Reader*, edited by Gary R. Edgerton and Jeffrey P. Jones, 23–41. Lexington: University Press of Kentucky.

Anguiano, Arturo. 2012. "La guerra que no dice su nombre." *El Cotidiano*, no. 173: 15–20.

Appadurai, Arjun. 1996. *Modernity at Large: Cultural Dimensions of Globalization.* Minneapolis: University of Minnesota Press.

Arendt, Hannah. 1958. *The Human Condition.* Chicago: University of Chicago Press.

Arendt, Hannah. 1973. *The Origins of Totalitarianism*. New York: Harcourt Brace Jovanovich.

Armitage, David. 2000. *The Ideological Origins of the British Empire*. Cambridge: Cambridge University Press.

Astorga, Luis A. 1996. *El siglo de las drogas*. Mexico City: Espasa-Calpe Mexicana.

Astorga, Luis A. 1999. "Drug Trafficking in Mexico: A First General Assessment." Presented as Discussion Paper 36 of the United Nations Educational, Scientific, and Cultural Organization (UNESCO)'s Management of Social Transformations (MOST) Program.

Astorga, Luis A. 2001. "The Limits of Anti-drug Policy in Mexico." *International Social Science Journal* 53 (169): 427–34.

Astorga, Luis A. 2005. *El siglo de las drogas: El narcotráfico, del Porfiriato al nuevo milenio*. Mexico City: Plaza y Janés.

Auslander, Philip. 1999. *Liveness: Performance in a Mediatized Culture*. New York: Routledge.

Bagdikian, Ben H. 2004. *The New Media Monopoly*. 20th ed. Boston: Beacon.

Banet-Weiser, Sarah. 2012. *Authentic™: The Politics of Ambivalence in a Brand Culture*. New York: New York University Press.

Baranowski, Michael. 2013. *Navigating the News: A Political Media User's Guide*. Santa Barbara, CA: Praeger.

Bauman, Zygmunt. 2000. *Liquid Modernity*. Malden, MA.

Beittel, June S. 2013. "Mexico's Drug Trafficking Organizations: Source and Scope of the Violence." Congressional Research Service (CRS) Report for Congress, Washington, DC, April 15, 2013.

Beltrán, Edith. 2015. "Mexico's Fearscapes: Where Fantasy Personas Engage in Citizenship." In *Fear and Fantasy in a Global World*, edited by Susana Araújo, Marta Pacheco Pinto, and Sandra Bettencourt, 75–98. Amsterdam: Brill Rodopi.

Beltrán del Rio, Pascal. 2011. "De nazis y buchones." *Excelsior*, May 22. https://www .excelsior.com.mx/opinion/2011/05/22/pascal-beltran-del-rio/738742.

Benhabib, Seyla. 1992. "Models of Public Space: Hannah Arendt, the Liberal Tradition, and Jürgen Habermas." In *Habermas and the Public Sphere*, edited by Craig Calhoun, 73–98. Cambridge, MA: MIT Press.

Benhabib, Seyla. 1993. "Feminist Theory and Hannah Arendt's Concept of Public Space." *History of the Human Sciences* 6 (2): 97–114.

Benhabib, Seyla. 1996. *The Reluctant Modernism of Hannah Arendt*. Vol. 10, *Modernity and Political Thought*. Thousand Oaks, CA: Sage.

Benjamin, Walter. (1921) 1996. "Critique of Violence." In *Walter Benjamin: Selected Writings*, vol. 1, *1913–1926*, edited by Marcus Bullock and Michael W. Jennings, 236–52. Cambridge, MA: Harvard University Press.

Benkler, Yochai. 2006. *The Wealth of Networks: How Social Production Transforms Markets and Freedom*. New Haven, CT: Yale University Press.

Benveniste, Émile. (1939) 1973. *Indo-European Language and Society*. Translated by Elizabeth Palmer. Study in General Linguistics. London: Faber and Faber.

Ben-Yehuda, Ayala. 2008. "Orchard Inks Key Regional Mexican Labels." *Billboard*, October 8. https://www.billboard.com/articles/business/1302787/orchard-inks-key-regional-mexican-labels.

Bilgin, Pinar, and Adam David Morton. 2002. "Historicising Representations of 'Failed States': Beyond the Cold-War Annexation of the Social Sciences?" *Third World Quarterly* 23 (1): 55–80.

Blog del Narco. 2013. *Dying for the Truth: Undercover inside the Mexican Drug War by the Fugitive Reporters of "Blog del Narco."* Port Townsend, WA: Feral House.

Blomley, Nicholas. 2003. "Law, Property, and the Geography of Violence: The Frontier, the Survey, and the Grid." *Annals of the Association of American Geographers* 93 (1): 121–41.

Bobbio, Norberto. 1993. *Thomas Hobbes and the Natural Law Tradition*. Translated by Daniela Gobetti. Chicago: University of Chicago Press.

Bourdieu, Pierre. 1990. *The Logic of Practice*. Translated by Richard Nice. Stanford, CA: Stanford University Press.

Bunck, Julie Marie, and Michael Ross Fowler. 2012. *Bribes, Bullets, and Intimidation: Drug Trafficking and the Law in Central America*. University Park: Pennsylvania State University Press.

Burgos Dávila, César Jesús. 2011. "Música y narcotráfico en México: Una aproximación a los narcocorridos desde la noción de mediador." *Athenea Digital* 11 (1): 97–110.

Burrough, Bryan, Sarah Ellison, and Suzanna Andrews. 2014. "The Snowden Saga: A Shadowland of Secrets and Light." *Vanity Fair*, May. www.vanityfair.com/news/politics/2014/05/edward-snowden-politics-interview.

Calhoun, Craig. 1992. "Introduction: Habermas and the Public Sphere." In *Habermas and the Public Sphere*, edited by Craig Calhoun, 1–48. Cambridge, MA: MIT Press.

Call, Charles T. 2008. "The Fallacy of the 'Failed State.'" *Third World Quarterly* 29 (8): 1491–1507.

Campos, Isaac. 2012. *Home Grown: Marijuana and the Origins of Mexico's War on Drugs*. Chapel Hill: University of North Carolina Press.

Cañeque, Alejandro. 2004. *The King's Living Image: The Culture and Politics of Viceregal Power in Colonial Mexico*. Vol. 5, *New World in the Atlantic World*. New York: Routledge.

Carpenter, Ted Galen. 2009. "Troubled Neighbor: Mexico's Drug Violence Poses a Threat to the United States." *Policy Analysis*, no. 631: 1–16.

Carroll, Rory. 2013. "'They Stole Our Dreams': Blogger Reveals Cost of Reporting Mexico's Drug Wars." *Guardian*, April 3. www.theguardian.com/world/2013/apr/03/mexico-blogdel-narco-drug-wars.

Castells, Manuel. 2008. "The New Public Sphere: Global Civil Society, Communication Networks, and Global Governance." *Annals of the American Academy of Political and Social Science* 616 (1): 78–93.

Cella, Tony. 2014. "Un análisis sociocrítico de algunas narconarrativas mexicanas." PhD diss., University of Virginia.

CESOP (Social Studies and Public Opinion Research Center). 2011. *Tendencias predominantes en estudios de opinión*. Mexico City: LXI Legislatura Cámara de

Diputados. http://www5.diputados.gob.mx/index.php/camara/Centros-de
-Estudio/CESOP/Historico-2002-2018/Tendencias-predominantes-en-estudios
-de-opinion.

Ciaramitaro, Fernando, and José Luis Souto. 2012. "Censura y opinión pública en la
Nueva España." *Histórica* 36 (1): 183–94.

Cobo, Leila. 2007. "The Latin Lag: Genre Sales Plummet in First Half of 2007."
Billboard, July 21, 16.

Cobo, Leila. 2008. "Regional Mexican Revival." *Billboard*, October 7. www.billboard
.biz/bbbiz/genre/latin/regional-mexican-revival-1003871249.story.

Cobo, Leila. 2011. "Inaugural Billboard Mexican Music Awards Deliver Strong
Ratings on Telemundo." *Billboard*, October 31. www.billboard.biz/bbbiz/genre
/latin/inaugural-billboard-mexican-music-awards-1005454952.story.

Cobo, Leila. 2013. *Jenni Rivera: The Incredible Story of a Warrior Butterfly*. New York:
C. A. Press.

Cobo, Leila. 2016. "*Billboard*'s Latin Power Players List Revealed." *Billboard*, November 3.
www.billboard.com/articles/columns/latin/7564703/billboard-latin-music
-power-players-list-2016.

Cobo, Leila. 2017. "What Happened in Latin Music in 2016? Consumption Up, Market Divided." *Billboard*, January 6. www.billboard.com/articles/columns/latin
/7647617/latin-music-2016-consumption-sales-trends-analysis.

Contreras, Claudia. 2008. "Dice no a narcocorridos." *El Universal*, February 29. www
.eluniversal.com.mx/espectaculos/81871.html.

Corsa, L. 2008. "Notes from the Underground." *Hispanic*, September, 32–34.

Coscia, Michele, and Viridiana Rios Contreras. 2012. "Knowing Where and How
Criminal Organizations Operate Using Web Content." Paper presented
at the proceedings of the Twenty-First ACM International Conference
on Information and Knowledge Management (CIKM), Maui, Hawaii,
October 29–November 2.

Cresswell, Tim. 2006. *On the Move: Mobility in the Modern Western World*. New York:
Routledge.

Cuéllar, Mariano-Florentino. 2008. "The Political Economy of Criminal Justice."
University of Chicago Law Review 75: 941–83.

Curran, James. 2000. "Mass Media and Democracy: A Reappraisal." In *Mass Media
and Society*, edited by James Curran and Michael Gurevitch, 82–117. London:
Edward Arnold.

Dahlgren, Peter. 1995. *Television and the Public Sphere: Citizenship, Democracy, and the
Media*. London: Sage.

Dahlgren, Peter, and Colin Sparks, eds. 1991. *Communication and Citizenship: Journalism and the Public Sphere in the New Media Age*. London: Routledge.

Day, Patrick. 1997. "Jean-Jacques Rousseau's *Lettre à d'Alembert sur les spectacles*: A
Philosophical Aberration or a Moral Imperative?" In *Rousseau on Arts and Politics*,
vol. 6, *Pensée libre*, edited by M. Butler, 141–50. Ottawa: North American
Association for the Study of Jean-Jacques Rousseau.

Dean, Jodi. 2001. "Publicity's Secret." *Political Theory* 29 (5): 624–50.

Dean, Jodi. 2002. *Publicity's Secret: How Technoculture Capitalizes on Democracy*. Ithaca, NY: Cornell University Press.

Dearing, James W., and Everett M. Rogers. 1996. *Agenda-Setting. Communication Concepts*. Thousand Oaks, CA: Sage.

Decker, Scott H., and Margaret Townsend Chapman. 2008. *Drug Smugglers on Drug Smuggling: Lessons from the Inside*. Philadelphia: Temple University Press.

Deleuze, Gilles, and Félix Guattari. 1983. *Anti-Oedipus: Capitalism and Schizophrenia*. Minneapolis: University of Minnesota Press.

Domínguez, Jorge I., Chappell Lawson, and Alejandro Moreno, eds. 2009. *Consolidating Mexico's Democracy: The 2006 Presidential Campaign in Comparative Perspective*. Baltimore: Johns Hopkins University Press.

Eisenstadt, Shmuel N. 2002. *Multiple Modernities*. New Brunswick, NJ: Transaction.

Ely, James W., Jr. 1992. *The Guardian of Every Other Right: A Constitutional History of Property Rights, Bicentennial Essays on the Bill of Rights*. New York: Oxford University Press.

Escalante Gonzalbo, Fernando. 1992. *Ciudadanos imaginarios: Memorial de los afanes y desventuras de la virtud, y apología del vicio triunfante en la República Mexicana: Tratado de moral pública*. Mexico City: Centro de Estudios Sociológicos, El Colegio de México.

Escobar, Cristina. 2004. "Dual Citizenship and Political Participation: Migrants in the Interplay of United States and Colombian Politics." *Latino Studies* 2 (1): 45–69.

EstadoMayor.mx. 2013. "Amenazan en 'narcomantas' a propietario del periódico 'Zócalo.'" *Blog de Información Militar y Seguradidad National*, March 8. www.estadomayor.mx/22279.

Fairclough, Norman. 1992. *Discourse and Social Change*. Cambridge: Polity.

Farmer, Paul. 2004. "An Anthropology of Structural Violence." *Current Anthropology* 45 (3): 305–25.

Fazio, Carlos. 1997. "México: The Narco-General Case." Transnational Institute: A Worldwide Fellowship of Scholar Activists, December 1. www.tni.org/en/article/mexico-narco-general-case.

Fineman, Mark. 1998. "Zedillo Vows to Fight for Dignity in War on Drugs." *Los Angeles Times*, March 8.

Flannery, Nathaniel Parish. 2013. "Calderón's War." *Journal of International Affairs* 66 (2): 181–98.

Foucault, Michel. 1972. *The Archaeology of Knowledge and the Discourse on Language*. Translated by A. M. Sheridan Smith. New York: Pantheon.

Fox, Jonathan. 2005. "Unpacking 'Transnational Citizenship.'" *Annual Review of Political Sciences* 8: 171–201.

Fox, Jonathan. 2007. *Accountability Politics: Power and Voice in Rural Mexico*. New York: Oxford University Press.

Fraser, Nancy. 1990. "Rethinking the Public Sphere: A Contribution to the Critique of Actually Existing Democracy." *Social Text* 25/26: 56–80.

Friedman, Thomas. 1995. "Foreign Affairs: 14 Big Macs later . . ." *New York Times*, December 31, 9.

Gadamer, Hans-Georg. 1975. *Truth and Method*. Translated by G. Barden and J. Cumming. New York: Seabury.

Galeano, Eduardo. 1997. *Open Veins of Latin America: Five Centuries of the Pillage of a Continent*. New York: Monthly Review Press.

Galeano, Eduardo. 1998. *Patas arriba: La escuela del mundo al revés*. Madrid: Siglo XXI Editores.

García Canclini, Néstor. 2001. *Culturas híbridas: Estrategias para entrar y salir de la modernidad*. Buenos Aires: Paidós.

Gardner, James. 2011. "Anonymity and Democratic Citizenship." *William & Mary Bill of Rights Journal* 19 (4): 927–57.

Garmonsway, George Norman, ed. 1928. *An Early Norse Reader*. Cambridge: Cambridge University Press.

Goffman, Erving. 1971. *The Presentation of Self in Everyday Life*. Garden City, NY: Doubleday Anchor.

Gray, Herman, and Macarena Gómez-Barris, eds. 2010. *Toward a Sociology of the Trace*. Minneapolis: University of Minnesota Press.

Grayson, George W. 2010. *Mexico: Narco-Violence and a Failed State?* New Brunswick, NJ: Transaction.

Greer, Allan. 2012. "Commons and Enclosures in the Colonization of North America." *American Historical Review* 117 (2): 365–86.

Grillo, Ioan. 2012. *El Narco: Inside Mexico's Criminal Insurgency*. New York: Bloomsbury.

Guerra, François-Xavier. 1992. *Modernidad e independencias: Ensayos sobre las revoluciones hispánas*. Madrid: Editorial Mapfre.

Gutierrez, Michel Estefan. 2011. "Violence, in Mexico? Homicide in a Democratizing Society." MA thesis, University of California, Berkeley.

Habermas, Jürgen. 1989. *The Structural Transformation of the Public Sphere: An Inquiry into a Category of Bourgeois Society*. Translated by Thomas Burger and Frederick Lawrence. Studies in Contemporary German Social Thought. Cambridge, MA: MIT Press.

Haikala, Sisko. 1997. "Criticism in the Enlightenment: Perspectives on Koselleck's *Kritik und Krise* Study." *Finnish Yearbook of Political Thought* 1: 70–86.

Hale, Charles A. 1968. *Mexican Liberalism in the Age of Mora, 1821–1853*. Vol. 11, Caribbean Series. New Haven, CT: Yale University Press.

Harris, Cheryl I. 1997. "Whiteness as Property." In *The Judicial Isolation of the "Racially" Oppressed*, edited by E. Nathaniel Gates, 1–84. New York: Garland.

Harvey, David. 1990. "Introduction." *Sociological Perspectives* 33 (1): 1–10.

Haughton, Suzette. 2011. *Drugged Out: Globalization and Jamaica's Resilience to Drug Trafficking*. Lanham, MD: University Press of America.

Havercroft, Jonathan. 2012. "Was Westphalia 'All That'? Hobbes, Bellarmine, and the Norm of Non-intervention." *Global Constitutionalism* 1 (1): 120–40.

Hay, James. 2004. "Toward a Spatial Materialism of the 'Moving Image': Locating Screen Media within Changing Regimes of Transport." *Cinema & Cie* 5: 43–51.

Hay, James, and Mark Andrejevic. 2006. "Toward an Analytic of Governmental Experiments in These Times: Homeland Security as the New Social Security." *Cultural Studies* 20 (4): 331–48.

Henderson, Timothy J. 2009. *The Mexican Wars for Independence.* New York: Hill and Wang.

Herlinghaus, Hermann. 2009. *Violence without Guilt: Ethical Narratives from the Global South.* New Directions in Latino American Cultures. New York: Palgrave Macmillan.

Hernández, Guillermo. 1992. "El corrido ayer y hoy." In *Entre la magia y la historia: Tradiciones, mitos y leyendas de la frontera,* edited by José Manuel Valenzuela Arce. 319–37. Tijuana: Programa Cultural de las Fronteras, El Colegio de la Frontera Norte.

Hill, Jonathan. 2005. "Beyond the Other? A Postcolonial Critique of the Failed State Thesis." *African Identities* 3 (2): 139–54.

Hobbes, Thomas. (1651) 1965. *Leviathan or the Matter, Forme, & Power of a Common-Wealth Ecclesiastical and Civil.* Oxford: Oxford University Press.

Hohendahl, Peter Uwe. 2002. "The Theory of the Public Sphere Revisited." In *Sites of Discourse, Public and Private Spheres, Legal Culture,* edited by Uwe Böker and Julie A. Hibbard, 13–23. Amsterdam: Rodopi.

Hsueh, Vicki. 2006. "Cultivating and Challenging the Common: Lockean Property, Indigenous Traditionalisms, and the Problem of Exclusion." *Contemporary Political Theory* 5 (2): 193–214.

Human Rights Watch. 2014. "World Report 2014: Mexico." Accessed October 20, 2018. www.hrw.org/world-report/2014/country-chapters/mexico.

Husserl, Edmund. 1990. *Ideas Pertaining to a Pure Phenomenology and to a Phenomeno-logical Philosophy: Second Book Studies in the Phenomenology of Constitution.* Vol. 3, *Husserliana: Edmund Husserl—Collected Works.* Dordrecht, Netherlands: Kluwer Academic.

Hutchinson, W. T., and William M. E. Rachal, eds. 1962. *The Papers of James Madison.* Chicago: University of Chicago Press.

Ignatieff, Michael. 2002. "Intervention and State Failure." *Dissent* 49 (1): 114–23.

Illich, Ivan, and Barry Sanders. 1988. *ABC: The Alphabetization of the Popular Mind.* San Francisco: North Point.

Índigo. 2011. "El sonido de la violencia." *Zócalo Saltillo,* September 4. www.zocalo .com.mx/seccion/articulo/el-sonido-de-la-violencia.

Inikori, Joseph E. 2002. *Africans and the Industrial Revolution in England: A Study in International Trade and Development.* Cambridge: Cambridge University Press.

Jackson, John H. 2003. "Sovereignty-Modern: A New Approach to an Outdated Concept." *American Journal of International Law* 97 (4): 782–802.

Jackson, Robert H. 2007. *Sovereignty: Evolution of an Idea. Key Concepts.* Malden, MA: Polity.

Jaramillo, Deborah. 2005. "The Family Racket: AOL Time Warner, HBO, *The Sopranos,* and the Construction of a Quality Brand." *Journal of Communication Inquiry* 26 (1): 59–75.

Jay, Martin. 2010. "Liquidity Crisis: Zygmunt Bauman and the Incredible Lightness of Modernity." *Theory, Culture, and Society* 27 (6): 95–106.

Jones, Branwen Gruffydd. 2008. "The Global Political Economy of Social Crisis: Towards a Critique of the 'Failed State' Ideology." *Review of International Political Economy* 15 (2): 180–205.

Justice in Mexico. 2011. "Pending Amendments would Criminalize Inciting Crime through Music, Media." November 17. https://justiceinmexico.org/pending -amendments-would-criminalize-inciting-crime-through-music-media/.

Kaplan, Abraham. 1964. *The Conduct of Inquiry: Methodology for Behavioral Science*. San Francisco: Chandler.

Kemper, Robert, and Anya Royce. 1979. "Mexican Urbanization since 1821: A Macro-historical Approach." *Urban Anthropology* 8 (3/4): 267–89.

Kimaid, Michael. 2015. *Modernity, Metatheory, and the Temporal-Spatial Divide: From Mythos to Techne*. New York: Routledge.

Kochhar, Rakesh, Richard Fry, and Paul Taylor. 2010. "Employment and Unemployment in the Recession and Recovery." Pew Research Center. Accessed March 12, 2017. www.pewhispanic.org/2010/10/29/ii-employment-and-unemployment-in -the-recession-and-recovery/.

Koeninger, Frieda. 2014. "*El negro y la blanca*: La censura de una obra abolicionista en Madrid y México." *Dieciocho* 37 (1): 123–38.

Koselleck, Reinhart. 1988. *Critique and Crisis: Enlightenment and the Pathogenesis of Modern Society*. Studies in Contemporary German Social Thought. Cambridge, MA: MIT Press.

Kössler, Reinhart. 2003. "The Modern Nation State and Regimes of Violence: Reflections on the Current Situation." *Ritsumeikan Annual Review of International Studies* 2: 15–36.

Kraidy, Marwan. 2005. *Hybridity, or the Cultural Logic of Globalization*. Philadelphia: Temple University Press.

Kun, Josh. 2005a. *Audiotopia: Music, Race, and America, American Crossroads*. Berkeley: University of California Press.

Kun, Josh. 2005b. "Listening to the Line: Notes on Music, Globalization, and the US-Mexico Border." *Iberoamericana* 5 (17): 143–52.

Kun, Josh. 2007. "Jorge Hernandez." *Bomb*, January 1. https://bombmagazine.org /articles/jorge-hernandez/.

Lacoste, Véronique, Jakob R. E. Leimgruber, and Thiemo Breyer. 2014. *Indexing Authenticity: Sociolinguistic Perspectives*. Vol. 39, *Linguae & Litterae*. Berlin: Walter de Gruyter.

La Jornada. 2002. "Prohiben los Narcocorridos." December 14.

La Jornada. 2014. "La Banda y su Punzante Ritmo, el Sonido del México Moderno." July 3. https://www.jornada.com.mx/2014/07/03/espectaculos/a14n1esp.

Lakoff, George, and Mark Johnson. 1980. *Metaphors We Live By*. Chicago: University of Chicago Press.

Lasorsa, Dominic, et al. 1998. "Television Visual Violence in Reality Programs: Differences across Genres." In *Television Violence and Public Policy*, edited by James T. Hamilton, 163–79. Ann Arbor: University of Michigan Press.

Leal Valenzuela, Luis Alfonso. 2012. "La música como elemento del derecho humano a la recreación, la creatividad artística y la cultura." *HumanarES* 3 (17): 26–28.

Lefebvre, Henri. 1991. *The Production of Space*. Translated by Donald Nicholson-Smith. Cambridge, MA: Blackwell.

Leonard, Thomas M. 2000. *James K. Polk: A Clear and Unquestionable Destiny*. Vol. 6, *Biographies in American Foreign Policy*. New York: Rowman and Littlefield.

Lessig, Lawrence. 1999. *Code and Other Laws of Cyberspace*. New York: Basic Books.

Lindau, Juan D. 2011. "The Drug War's Impact on Executive Power, Judicial Reform, and Federalism in Mexico." *Political Science Quarterly* 126 (2): 177–200.

Locke, John. (1689) 1764. *The Two Treatises of Civil Government*. Edited by Thomas Hollis. London: A. Millar et al. Digital edition by Online Library of Liberty. Accessed December 3, 2018. http://lf-oll.s3.amazonaws.com/titles/222/Locke _0057_EBk_v6.0.pdf.

Luban, David. 1996. "The Publicity Principle." In *The Theory of Institutional Design*, edited by Robert E. Goodin, 154–98. Cambridge: Cambridge University Press.

Luhnow, David, and Jose de Cordoba. 2009. "The Drug Lord Who Got Away." *Wall Street Journal*, June 13.

Lund, Joshua. 2012. *The Mestizo State: Reading Race in Modern Mexico*. Minneapolis: University of Minnesota Press.

Macpherson, C. B. (1962) 2011. *The Political Theory of Possessive Individualism: Hobbes to Locke*. Oxford: Oxford University Press.

Madrigal, Alejandro. 2011. "Evoluciona narcocorrido en 'movimiento alterado.'" *Milenio*, August 1. http://impreso.milenio.com/node/9001570.

Maier, Charles S. 2006. *Among Empires: American Ascendancy and Its Predecessors*. Cambridge, MA: Harvard University Press.

Maldonado Aranda, Salvador. 2012. "Drogas, violencia y militarización en el México rural. El caso de Michoacán." *Revista Mexicana de Sociología* 74 (1): 5–39.

Manjikian, Mary. 2008. "Diagnosis, Intervention, and Cure: The Illness Narrative in the Discourse of the Failed State." *Alternatives: Global, Local, Political* 33 (3): 335–57.

Marcy, William L. 2010. *The Politics of Cocaine: How US Foreign Policy Has Created a Thriving Drug Industry in Central and South America*. Chicago: Chicago Review Press.

Marey, Macarena. 2017. "A Political Defence of Kant's *Aufklärung*: An Essay." *Critical Horizons* 18 (2): 168–85.

Martin, Christopher. 2013. "'Upscale' News Audiences and the Transformation of Labour News." In *Language and Journalism*, edited by John Richardson, 27–43. New York: Routledge.

Martín-Barbero, Jesús. 1993. *Communication, Culture, and Hegemony: From the Media to Mediations*. Vol. 14, *Communication and Human Values*. Thousand Oaks, CA: Sage.

Martínez, Jorge. 2015. "Consignan a sujeto por hacer apología del delito en redes sociales." *Milenio*, October 6. https://www.milenio.com/policia/consignan-sujeto -apologia-delito-redes-sociales.

Marx, Karl. (1867) 1977. *Capital: A Critique of Political Economy*. Translated by Ben Fowkes. New York: Vintage Books.

McCombs, Maxwell. 2014. *Setting the Agenda: The Mass Media and Public Opinion*. Malden, MA: Polity.

Mei, Todd S. 2011. "An Economic Turn: A Hermeneutical Reinterpretation of Political Economy with Respect to the Question of Land." *Research in Phenomenology* 41 (3): 297–326.

Mercader, Yolanda. 2009. "La censura en el cine mexicano: Una descripción histórica." *Anuario de Investigación*, 191–215.

Miglierini, Julian. 2011. "Mexico 'Twitter Terrorism' Charges Cause Uproar." *BBC News*, September 6. https://www.bbc.com/news/world-latin-america-14800200.

Mill, John Stuart. 1977. *The Collected Works of John Stuart Mill*. Vol. 19, *Essays on Politics and Society Part II*. Edited by John M. Robson. Toronto: University of Toronto Press.

Miller, Robert J. 2006. *Native America, Discovered and Conquered: Thomas Jefferson, Lewis and Clark, and Manifest Destiny*. Native America: Yesterday and Today. Westport, CT: Praeger.

Molzahn, Cory, Octavio Rodriguez Fernandez, and David Shirk. 2013. *Drug Violence in Mexico*. San Diego: Transborder Institute.

Monroy-Hernández, Andrés, and Luis Daniel Palacios. 2014. "Blog del Narco and the Future of Citizen Journalism." *Georgetown Journal of International Affairs* (Summer/Fall): 85–96.

Morrison, Amanda Maria. 2008. "Musical Trafficking: Urban Youth and the Narcocorrido–Hardcore Rap Nexus." *Western Folklore* 67 (4): 379–97.

Morton, Adam David. 2012. "The War on Drugs in Mexico: A Failed State?" *Third World Quarterly* 33 (9): 1631–45.

Mosco, Vincent. 2009. *The Political Economy of Communication*. Thousand Oaks, CA: Sage.

Naone, Erica. 2011. "Anonymous Won't Expose Mexican Cartel's 'Servants.'" Reuters, November 4. www.reuters.com/article/us-mexico-drugs-hackers-idUSTRE7A408C20111105.

Nathan, Deborah. 2002. "Smuggling." In *Mexico and the United States*, edited by Lee Stacy, 761–64. Singapore: Marshall Cavendish.

NBCUniversal. 2015. "Why mun2 Is Now NBC Universo." February 2. www.nbcuniversal.com/article/why-mun2-now-nbc-universo.

Neocleous, Mark. 2006. "The Problem with Normality: Taking Exception to Permanent Emergency." *Alternatives: Global, Local, Political* 31 (2): 191–213.

NHTSA (National Highway Traffic Safety Administration). 2005. "Drugs and Human Performance Fact Sheet." Accessed February 21, 2015. https://one.nhtsa.gov/About-NHTSA/Traffic-Techs/current/Drugs-and-Human-Performance-Fact-Sheets.

O'Connor, Mike. 2010. "Mexican Journalist Said Things 'Very Hard' Just before Murder." Committee to Protect Journalists, February 9. https://cpj.org/blog/2010/02/mexican-journalist-said-situation-very-hard-just-b.php.

Ong, Aihwa. 2006. *Neoliberalism as Exception: Mutations in Citizenship and Sovereignty.* Durham, NC: Duke University Press.

Oswalt, Laura. 2015. "The Structural Semiotics Paradigm for Marketing Research: Theory, Methodology, and Case Analysis." *Semiotica* 205 (June): 1–31.

Pagden, Anthony. 1990. *Spanish Imperialism and the Political Imagination: Studies in European and Spanish-American Social and Political Theory, 1513–1830.* New Haven, CT: Yale University Press.

Pagden, Anthony. 2003. "Human Rights, Natural Rights, and Europe's Imperial Legacy." *Political Theory* 31 (2): 171–99.

Papacharissi, Zizi. 2010. *A Private Sphere: Democracy in a Digital Age.* Digital Media and Society. Cambridge: Polity.

Paredes, Américo. 1958. *"With His Pistol in His Hand": A Border Ballad and Its Hero.* Texas Classics. Austin: University of Texas Press.

Paredes, Américo. 1976. *A Texas-Mexican Cancionero: Folksongs of the Lower Border.* Music in American Life. Urbana: University of Illinois Press.

Peredo Castro, Francisco. 2015. "Catholicism and Mexican Cinema: A Secular State, a Deeply Conservative Society, and a Powerful Catholic Hierarchy." In *Moralizing Cinema: Film, Criticism, and Power*, edited by Daniel Biltereyst and Daniela Treveri Gennari, 66–81. New York: Routledge.

Perlman, Allison. 2016. *Public Interests: Media Advocacy and Struggles over US Television.* New Brunswick, NJ: Rutgers University Press.

Peters, John Durham. 1999. *Speaking into the Air: A History of the Idea of Communication.* Chicago: University of Chicago Press.

Peters, John Durham. 2001. "Witnessing." *Media, Culture, and Society* 23: 707–23.

Petersen, Jennifer. 2017. "Public." In *Keywords for Media Studies*, edited by Laurie Ouellette and Jonathan Gray, 153–56. New York: New York University Press.

Petersilia, Joan. 2001. "Prisoner Reentry: Public Safety and Reintegration Challenges." *Prison Journal* 81 (3): 360–75.

Pettit, Philip. 1999. *Republicanism: A Theory of Freedom and Government.* Vol. 7, *Oxford Political Theory.* Oxford: Clarendon.

Pew Social Trends. 2011. "Wealth Gaps Rise to Record Highs between Whites, Blacks, Hispanics." July 26. https://www.pewsocialtrends.org/2011/07/26/wealth -gaps-rise-to-record-highs-between-whites-blacks-hispanics/.

Pinheiro, John C. 2007. *Manifest Ambition: James K. Polk and Civil-Military Relations during the Mexican War.* In War and in Peace: US Civil-Military Relations. Westport, CT: Praeger.

Pletcher, David M. 1973. *The Diplomacy of Annexation: Texas, Oregon, and the Mexican War.* Columbia: University of Missouri Press.

Polit Dueñas, Gabriela. 2008. "Amidst Weed, Dust, and Lead: A Narcotour through Sinaloa in the Work of Lenin Márquez." *Journal of Latin American Cultural Studies* 17 (2): 203–20.

Polit Dueñas, Gabriela. 2013. *Narrating Narcos: Culiacán and Medellín.* Illuminations: Cultural Formations of the Americas. Pittsburgh: University of Pittsburgh Press.

Porter, Alejandro. 1998. "Social Capital: Its Origins and Applications in Modern Sociology." *Annual Review of Sociology* 24: 1–24.

Porter, Dennis. 1995. *Rousseau's Legacy: Emergence and Eclipse of the Writer in France.* New York: Oxford University Press.

Pratte, Alf. 2013. "USA Today." In *History of Mass Media in the United States: An Encyclopedia,* edited by Margaret Blanchard, 675. New York: Routledge.

Proceso. 2013a. "Antes de cerrar, 'Valor por Tamaulipas' reactiva la página." April 7. https://www.proceso.com.mx/338335/administrador-de-valor-por-tamaulipas -anuncia-cierre-definitivo-de-la-pagina.

Proceso. 2013b. "Gobierno y narco, unidos contra 'Valor por Tamaulipas.'" April 30. https://www.proceso.com.mx/340554/gobierno-y-narco-unidos-contra-valor-por -tamaulipas-2.

Proceso. 2013c. "No todos nos rendiremos ante ustedes, responde 'Valor por Tamau-lipas.'" February 13. www.proceso.com.mx/333505/no-todos-nos-rendiremos-ante -ustedes-responde-valor-por-tamaulipas.

Putnam, Robert. 1995. "Bowling Alone: America's Declining Social Capital." *Journal of Democracy* 6 (1): 65–78.

Quinones, Sam. 2009. "State of War." *Foreign Policy,* September 30. https:// foreignpolicy.com/2009/09/30/state-of-war/.

Quinones, Sam. 2012. "Jenni Rivera's Musical Family Helped Popularize Mexican Narco-Ballads." *Los Angeles Times,* December 10. http://latimesblogs.latimes .com/lanow/2012/12/jenni-riveras-musical-family-helped-popularize-the-narco -ballad.html.

Ragland, Cathy. 2009. *Música norteña: Mexican Migrants Creating a Nation between Nations.* Studies in Latin American and Caribbean Music. Philadelphia: Temple University Press.

Ramírez-Pimienta, Juan Carlos. 2011. *Cantar a los narcos.* Temas de Hoy. Mexico City: Grupo Planeta.

Ravelo, Ricardo. 2011. *El narco en México: Historia e historias de una guerra.* Mexico City: Grijalbo.

Ravelo, Ricardo. 2016. *Ejecuciones de periodistas: Los expedientes.* Mexico City: Grijalbo.

Replogle, Jill. 2011. "Glamorizing Mexico's Drug War for US Profits?" *Fronteras: The Changing America Desk,* October 24. www.fronterasdesk.org/news/2011/oct/24 /corridas-cartel-narcocorrido-violence-music/.

Rios Contreras, Viridiana. 2012. "Why Did Mexico Become So Violent? A Self-Reinforcing Violent Equilibrium Caused by Competition and Enforcement." *Trends in Organized Crime* 16 (2): 138–55.

Rios Contreras, Viridiana. 2013. "Who Started the Mexican Drug War? What Google Taught Us about the 'Narcos.'" *Kennedy School Review* 13: 18–22.

Rios Contreras, Viridiana. 2014. "The Role of Drug-Related Violence and Extortion in Promoting Mexican Migration: Unexpected Consequences of a Drug War." *Latin American Research Review* 49 (3): 199–217.

Rivera, Pedro. N.d. "Quienes Somos." Cintas Acuario Música. Accessed December 6, 2018. www.cintasacuariomusica.com/quienes-somos/.

Roberts, Les. 2014. "The Violence of Non-places." In *Tourism and Violence*, edited by Hazel Andrews, 13–31. Farnham, UK: Ashgate.

Rodríguez Gómez, Guadalupe, ed. 2009. *Diagnóstico sobre la realidad social, económica y cultural de los entornos locales para el diseño de intervenciones en materia de prevención y erradicación de la violencia en la Región Centro: El caso de la zona metropolitana de Guadalajara, Jalisco.* Mexico City: CIESAS-Occidente.

Rosas, Alejandro, and José Manuel Villalpando. 2001. *Los presidentes de México.* Mexico City: Editorial Planeta.

Rose, Carol M. 1994. *Property and Persuasion: Essays on the History, Theory, and Rhetoric of Ownership.* New Perspectives on Law, Culture, and Society. Boulder, CO: Westview.

Rosen, Fred. 2007. "Mexico: Year Zero." *NACLA Report on the Americas* 40 (2): 11–15.

Rosner, Jeremy. 1994. "Is Chaos America's Real Enemy? The Foreign Policy Idea Splitting Clinton's Team." *Washington Post*, August 14, C1.

Rotberg, Robert, ed. 2003. *When States Fail: Causes and Consequences.* Princeton, NJ: Princeton University Press.

Rousseau, Jean-Jacques. (1758) 1889. *Lettre à D'Alembert sur les spectacles.* Paris: Garnier Fréres, Libraries-Éditeurs.

Rubio, Luis. 2009. "Mexico: A Failed State?" *Perspectives on the Americas*, February 12, 1–4.

Salazar, Philippe-Joseph. 2004. "Censorship: A Philological (and Rhetorical) Viewpoint." *Journal of the European Institute for Communication and Culture* 11 (2): 5–18.

Sánchez Barbosa, Luis. 2013. "Derecho, violencia, y narcocorridos." *Nexos*, February 25. https://eljuegodelacorte.nexos.com.mx/?p=2424.

Sánchez Godoy, Jorge A. 2009. "Procesos de institucionalización de la *narcocultura* en Sinaloa." *Frontera Norte* 21 (41): 77–103.

Sanders, James. 2011. "The Vanguard of the Atlantic World: Contesting Modernity in Nineteenth-Century Latin America." *Latin American Research Review* 46 (2): 104–27.

Santa Ana, Otto. 2002. *Brown Tide Rising: Metaphors of Latinos in Contemporary American Public Discourse.* Austin: University of Texas Press.

Sarat, Austin, and Thomas Kearns. 1991. "A Journey through Forgetting: Toward a Jurisprudence of Violence." In *The Fate of Law*, edited by Austin Sarat and Thomas Kearns, 209–73. Ann Arbor: University of Michigan Press.

Sasaki, David. 2010. "Citizen Journalism and Drug Trafficking in Mexico." David Sasaki (website). Accessed October 14, 2015. http://davidsasaki.name/2010/09/citizen-journalism-and-drug-trafficking-inmexico/.

Schaefer, Timo. 2014. "Law of the Land? Hacienda Power and the Challenge of Republicanism in Postindependence Mexico." *Hispanic American Historical Review* 94 (2): 207–36.

Schatz, Sara. 2000. *Elites, Masses, and the Struggle for Democracy in Mexico: A Culturalist Approach.* Westport, CT: Praeger.

Scherer García, Julio. 2008. *La reina del Pacífico: Es la hora de contar.* Mexico City: Grijalbo Mondadori.

Schudson, Michael. 1999. *The Good Citizen: A History of American Civic Life.* Cambridge, MA: Harvard University Press.

Scott, James. 1998. *Seeing Like a State: How Certain Schemes to Improve the Human Condition Have Failed.* New Haven, CT: Yale University Press.

Seligman, Adam B. 1997. *The Problem of Trust.* Princeton, NJ: Princeton University Press.

Shaw, Martin. 2009. "Conceptual and Theoretical Frameworks for Organised Violence." *International Journal of Conflict and Violence* 3 (1): 97–106.

Shelton, Laura. 2010. *For Tranquility and Order: Family and Community on Mexico's Northern Frontier, 1800-1850.* Tucson: University of Arizona Press.

Shirk, David. 2010. "Justice Reform in Mexico: Change and Challenges in the Judicial Sector. Justice in Mexico Project." *Justice in Mexico Project*, May, 1–42.

Shlossberg, Pavel. 2015. *Crafting Identity: Transnational Indian Arts and the Politics of Race in Central Mexico.* Tucson: University of Arizona Press.

Simonett, Helena. 2001a. *Banda: Mexican Musical Life across Borders.* Music/Culture. Middletown, CT: Wesleyan University Press.

Simonett, Helena. 2001b. "Narcocorridos: An Emerging Micromusic in Nuevo L.A." *Society for Ethnomusicology* 45 (2): 315–37.

Sloop, John M. 2008. "Thoughts on Democracy and Mobility." Conference Paper, Rhetoric Society of America, Vanderbilt University, Seattle, WA.

Smith, Rogers M. 2003. *Stories of Peoplehood: The Politics and Morals of Political Membership.* Contemporary Political Theory. Cambridge: Cambridge University Press.

Soberanes, Rodrigo. 2011. "Mexico: Two Accused of 'Terrorism' via Twitter, Facebook." CNN, September 7. https://www.cnn.com/2011/WORLD/americas/09/06/mexico.twitter.terror/index.html.

Soberón Mora, Arturo. 2014. "Los folletos como agentes del debate político: Ciudad de México, 1821-1855." *Historica* 38 (1): 33–59.

Sordo Cedeño, Reynaldo. 2012. "La libertad de prensa en la construcción del estado liberal laico: 1810-1857." In *El estado laico y los derechos humanos en México: 1810-2010*, edited by Margarita Moreno-Bonett and Rosa María Álvarez de Lara, 133–48. Mexico City: Universidad Nacional Autónoma de México.

Squitieri, Tom. 1998. "From a 'New World Order' to 'Age of Chaos,' Conflicts in Africa May Pose the Biggest Threat." *USA Today*, December 31, 12A.

Starr, Paul. 2004. *The Creation of the Media: Political Origins of Modern Communications.* New York: Basic Books.

Stoney, Sierra, and Jeanne Batalova. 2013. "Mexican Immigrants in the United States." Migration Information Source, February 28. www.migrationpolicy.org/article/mexican-immigrants-united-states-3.

Storrs, K. Larry. 1997. "Mexico's Anti-drug Efforts: Effects of Past US Pressures and Sanctions." Published in a CRS Report for Congress, March 13, Washington, DC. https://pdfs.semanticscholar.org/df55/12b3c4afc44e91100e9f70706e6e8f39fdbf.pdf.

Strydom, Piet. 2000. *Discourse and Knowledge: The Making of Enlightenment Sociology.* Studies in Social and Political Thought. Liverpool: Liverpool University Press.

Tait, Sue. 2011. "Consuming Ethics: Conflict Diamonds, the Entertainment Industry, and Celebrity Activism." In *Transnational Celebrity Activism in Global Politics: Changing the World?*, edited by Liza Tsaliki, Christos Frangonikolopoulos, and Asteris Huliaras, 157–74. Bristol, UK: Intellect.

Tirzo, Jorge. 2013. "El plagio, los medios, y El Blog del Narco." *El Toque*, May 27.

Torres, Alejandro, and Fabiola Guarneros. 2001. "Proponen prohibir los narcocorridos." *El Universal*, March 23.

Torres Puga, Gabriel. 2010. *Opinión pública y censura en Nueva España: Indicios de un silencio imposible (1767–1794)*. Mexico City: El Colegio de México.

Tully, James. 1993. "The Possessive Individualism Thesis: A Reconsideration in the Light of Recent Scholarship." In *Democracy and Possessive Individualism: The Intellectual Legacy of C. B. Macpherson*, edited by Joseph H. Carens, 19–45. Albany: State University of New York Press.

UN Office on Drugs and Crime. 2005. *2005 World Drug Report*. Accessed February 12, 2014. www.unodc.org/pdf/WDR_2005/volume_1_web.pdf.

UN Office on Drugs and Crime. 2012. *2012 World Drug Report*. Accessed February 12, 2014. www.unodc.org/documents/data-and-analysis/WDR2012/WDR_2012 _web_small.pdf.

Urry, John. 2000. *Sociology beyond Societies: Mobilities for the Twenty-First Century*. International Library of Sociology. New York: Routledge.

US Joint Forces Command. 2008. *The Joint Operating Environment*. Accessed April 23, 2012. https: //us.jfcom.mil/sites/J5/j59/default.aspx.

Valenzuela Arce, José Manuel. 1992. *Entre la magia y la historia: Tradiciones, mitos, y leyendas de la frontera*. Baja California, Mexico: Programa Cultural de las Fronteras, El Colegio de la Frontera Norte.

Valenzuela Arce, José Manuel. 2010. *Jefe de jefes: Corridos y narcocultura en México*. Mexico City: Colegio de la Frontera.

Van Young, Eric. 2012. *Writing Mexican History*. Stanford, CA: Stanford University Press.

Velázquez Morales, Catalina. 2005. "Diferencias politicas entro los inmigrantes chinos del noroeste de México (1920–1930): El caso de Francisco L. Yuen." *Historia Mexicana* 55 (2): 461–512.

Vogt, Wendy A. 2013. "Crossing Mexico: Structural Violence and the Commodification of Undocumented Central American Migrants." *American Ethnologist* 40 (4): 764–80.

Wald, Elijah. 2001. *Narcocorrido: A Journey into the Music of Drugs, Guns, and Guerrillas*. New York: Rayo.

Wallerstein, Immanuel. 1974. *The Modern World-System*. New York: Academic Press.

Weber, Max. (1919) 2004. "Politics as a Vocation." In *Max Weber: The Vocation Lectures, "Science as a Vocation"; "Politics as a Vocation,"* edited by David Owen and Tracy B. Strong. New York: Hackett.

Weinberg, Bill. 2008. "Guns: The U.S. Threat to Mexican National Security." *NACLA Report on the Americas* 41 (2): 21–26.

Weintraub, Jeff. 1997. "The Theory and Politics of the Public/Private Distinction." In *Public and Private in Thought and Practice: Perspectives on a Grand Economy*, edited by Jeff Weintraub and Krishan Kumar, 1–42. Chicago: University of Chicago Press.

Wilde, Oscar. (1891) 1905. *The Soul of Man under Socialism*. Portland, ME: Thomas B. Mosher.

Wilkinson, Kenton T. 2016. *Spanish-Language Television in the United States: Fifty Years of Development*. Routledge Research in Cultural and Media Studies. New York: Routledge.

Zartman, William. 1995. "Introduction: Posing the Problem of State Collapse." In *Collapsed States: The Disintegration and Restoration of Legitimate Authority*, edited by William Zartman, 1–11. Boulder, CO: Lynne Rienner.

Zermeño Padilla, Guillermo. 1997. "Cine, censura y moralidad en México: En torno al nacionalismo cultural católico, 1929–1960." *Historia y Grafía* 8: 77–102.

Zócalo. 2013. Editorial. March 12. www.zocalo.com.mx/seccion/articulo/editorial -1362992877.

Zolov, Eric. 1999. *Refried Elvis: The Rise of the Mexican Counterculture*. Berkeley: University of California Press.

Index

text for, 20; law-and-order framework for, 12–15, 19; localization of, 47–48; narocorridos' production in presence of, 137–43; politicization of, 226n11

drug wars: between DCOs, 44–48; impact on Latinos of, 154–57; publicity and, 44–54

duty, civic obligation as, 195–98

Dying for the Truth: Undercover inside the Mexican Drug War (Lucy), 197–98, 201

echo-chamber effect, in news media, 206–7

economic crisis of 2008, impact on Latinos of, 154–57

economics: colonialism and, 85–88; media industry in Mexico and, 162–65; publicness and, 216–17

educational institutions, censorship of narcocorridos in, 98–99

Ejecuciones de periodistas (Ravelo), 163

El Blog del Narco (EBDN) (blog), 23, 159, 233n1; anonymity on, 197–98; as citizen journalism, 166–73; civic communication on, 185–90; violent reprisals against, 193–94

El Blog de Lucy, 233n10

El Chapo de Sinaloa (band), 140

"El corrido de Pancho Villa" (song), 150

Eliot, George. *See* Evans, Mary Ann

elites in Mexico, displacement of marginalized groups in, 28

Elizalde, Valentín, 111, 140

El laberinto de la soledad (Páz), 205

El Movimiento Alterado (EMA), 127–28, 140–41, 151, 232n2

El narco en México (Ravelo), 163

ELN guerrillas (Colombia), 68

El Norte newspaper, 66

"El ojo de vidrio" ("The Glass-Eyed Bandit"), 131–32

"El troquero locochón" (song), 149

El Universal newspaper, 38–39, 49–51, 55, 227nn2–3, 233n4

Enfermedad Masiva (Massive Illness) (musical organization and brand), 141

Enlightenment theory: censorship and, 106–13; failed-state discourse and, 69–70; publicness in, 3, 18, 221–22; secret societies and, 181–82; Spanish colonization and, 114–20

Escalante Gonzalbo, Fernando, 230n6

Esperanza por Tamaulipas blog, 166

Espinosa Becerril, Rubén, 163

Essay concerning Human Understanding (Locke), 107–8

Estrada, Luis, 4

European colonialism, property regime and, 83–88

Evans, Mary Ann (George Eliot), 183

experiential simulation, authenticity and, 143–53

exploitive extraction, property regime and, 85–88

Facebook: citizen journalism on, 170–73, 233n8; civic communication on, 188–90

failed state: academic concepts of, 60–61; crisis vs. order in, 70–74; in current political cultures, 75–81; Hobbesian imaginary and, 69–88; Mexico framed as, 21, 57–60; in US discourse, 60–69

Fairclough, Norman, 60

FARC guerrillas (Colombia), 68

Federal Bureau of Narcotics, drug sale statistics, 34

Federalists, 79–81

Federal Law Against Organized Crime, narcocorridos' censorship and, 99

Federal Law on Radio and Television (FLRT), 96–99, 118–19, 121

federal police (*judiciales*), disbanding of, 42–43

"Ferias sinaloenses" ("Sinaloa's State Fairs") (song), 146

Fernández Menéndez, Jorge, 39

feudalism, 70–71, 83–84, 219–20

film: censorship of, 117–19; cocaine trade in, 35–36; drug violence in, 4

Fonseca Carrillo, Ernesto, 31

Forbes magazine, 66

drug narratives and, 2; echo-chamber effect in, 206–7; failed-state discourse and, 62–68; Mexican law and regulation of, 115–20; Mexican state war with DCOs and, 49–54, 227n4; narcocorrido production and, 135–43; publicity theory and, 225n6; publicity violence and, 46–48; research on, 214–17; secrets and publicity in, 173–90; violence against, 6–7, 159–65; visibility and displacement and, 9–11

mediated culture, new technologies and, 9–11

Medina-Mora Icaza, Eduardo, 53

Mendoza Mendoza, Irineo, 105, 111

mercantilism: order as mindset of, 75–81, 89–90; property regime and, 85–88; publicness and, 222–24

metaphor: in digital media, 190; nation-states and importance of, 72–74

Mexican Armed Forces, 8; antidrug programs and, 40; cleanup campaigns in, 42; drug cartels' coexistence with, 39–43; militarization of anti-DCO strategies and, 49–54, 65–68

Mexican Inquisition, 27, 101–2

Mexican League of Decency, 118

Mexican Music Awards, 136

Mexican polka, 132–33

Mexican Production Code, 118

Mexican Revolution, 101–2, 117

Mexican War of Independence, 116, 183

Mexico: campaign against drug violence in, 25–27; Chinese migration to, 28–30; cocaine trafficking in, 37–38; colonialism and property regime in, 83–88; cost of fighting DCOs in, 87; culture of state in, 100–106; democratization and reform in, 38–43; drug wars in, 44–54; failed-state framing of, 21, 57–60; increase of drug crime in, 7; internal colonization in, 84–88; law-and-order framework for drug violence in, 12–15, 20–21; marijuana culture in, 27–30; news censorship in, 159–65; political reform campaigns in,

42–43; post-independence disorder in, 73–74; republicanism in, 113–20; state censorship of narcocorridos in, 96–97; state war with DCOs, 34–38, 48–54; US migration into, 33–34; war with US, 57–58, 84–85

Miami-Dade County, cocaine trafficking in, 36

micropublicity: drug violence in Mexico and, 20; Mexican drug trade and, 54–56; Mexican state war with DCOs and, 48–54; publicity violence and, 46–48

Milenio, 39

militarization of drug conflict, 8; geopolitics and, 54–56; Mexican state war with DCOs and, 49–54

Milken Institute, 67

Mill, John Stuart, 185

Miller, Robert, 83–84

Misanthrope, The (Molière), 109

"Mis dos patrias" ("My Two Nations") (song), 225n4

mobility studies: deterritorialization of popular and, 126; publicness and, 16–18

modernity: deterritorialization of popular and, 126; failed-states discourse, 69–70; mobility studies and globalization and, 17–18; publicness and, 221–24

Molière, 108

Molina Ruiz, Francisco, 40

monarchy: censorship and, 106; colonialism and, 86; order and statehood in, 70–71; property regime and, 83–84

money-laundering operations, 8

Monroy-Hernández, Andrés, 197

Montesquieu (Charles-Louis de Secondat), 181

morality, censorship and, 117–20

"Morir y existir" ("To Die and to Exist") (song), 136, 149

Mosco, Vincent, 230n3

MS-13 gang, 43

Mundo Narco blog, 166

Naranjo, Gerardo, 4

Narcocorrido (Wald), 154

narcocorridos, 4, 22; corridos and, 128–35;
deterritorialization of popular and,
126–35; deterritorialized production
of, 137–43; drug trafficking narrative
in, 132, 144–53, 232n4; early censorship
of, 92–100; experiential simulation
and authenticity in, 143–53; fandom
for, 154–57; legal censorship of, 118–20;
media cultures in production of,
135–43; Mexican Americans' embrace
of, 22–23; Mexican political culture
and suppression of, 100–106; music
videos of, 141–43; narrative modality in, 150–53; political alliances and,
95–97; popularity of, 121–23; republicanism and censorship of, 106, 110–13;
rural, nostalgic, and ethnic identity
in, 134–35; third-person narration in,
150–53; in United States, 22, 124–57

Narco cultura (documentary), 154

narcoculture: censorship of, 91–123; elements of, 226n12; media technologies
and, 10–11; public sphere and, 91–94

narco-mantas signs, publicity violence
and, 46–48, 171

narcoseries (telenovelas), 99

Narcos y perros (film), 4

Narco Violencia blog, 166

National Human Rights Commission
(Comisión Nacional de Derechos
Humanos) (CNDH), 8–9

National Institute to Combat Drugs
(INCD), 39–40

nation-states: citizenship and, 221–22;
cultural environments and, 21–22; DCO
operations and corruption of, 37–38;
definitions of, 69–70; drug violence in
Mexico and, 20–21; foreign pressures
on, 54–56; Hobbes's concept of, 70–74;
jurisdiction and, 229n8; Manifest
Destiny ideology and, 76; Mexican
cultural suspicion of, 58–60; opacity
in, 183–85; order connected to, 75–81;
sovereignty of, 71–72; spatial control

in, 75–81; violence against journalists
by, 161–65

Nation magazine, *The*, 52

natural law, violence and order in,
228n5

Neocleous, Mark, 59

neocolonialism, in US-Mexican relations,
29–30

news coverage: on blogs, 169–73; colonialism and rise of, 115–20; constitutional
boundaries about, 162–65; DCOs' censure of, 230n5; failed-state discourse in,
59–60, 62–68, 228n1; of Mexican state
war with DCOs, 49–54, 227n4; secrecy
and publicity in, 179–90; silencing in
Mexico of, 159–65

New York Times, 59, 62–68

"Ni hoy ni mañana" ("Neither Today nor
Tomorrow") (song), 136

normativity: frameworks of drug violence and, 11–15; publicness of criminal
violence in, 6

norteño music, 132–33, 147–48; rural and
religious life in, 154–55

North American Free Trade Agreement
(NAFTA), 11; drug trade and impact of,
37–38; Mexican drug cartels and, 33

Nueva Generación cartel, 47–48

Obama, Barack, 9

Ochoa Martínez, Jorge, 161

O'Connor, Mike, 161–62, 163

Ong, Aihwa, 215

On Violence (Arendt), 198–99

opacity: anonymity and secrecy and,
175–76; in blogosphere, 158–59, 167–73;
limits of, 191; politics and, 183–84;
publicness and, 176–85, 188–90

OpCartel, 211

openness, blogosphere and, 173–90

Open Veins of Latin America (Galeano), 85

Operation Condor, 34, 36

opiates, effects of, 35

orality: copresence and, 208–9; publicness and, 203–4

Orchard company, The, 142–43

www.ingramcontent.com/pod-product-compliance
Lightning Source LLC
Chambersburg PA
CBHW030349270326
41926CB00009B/1027